IN SEARCH OF STUPIDITY
Over 20 Years of High-Tech Marketing Disasters

IN SEARCH OF STUPIDITY

Over 20 Years of High-Tech Marketing Disasters

Merrill R. Chapman

In Search of Stupidity: Over 20 Years of High-Tech Marketing Disasters
Copyright © 2003 by Merrill R. Chapman

Printed and bound in Canada 10987654321

Trademarked names may appear in this book. Rather than use a trademark symbol with every occurrence of a trademarked name, we use the names only in an editorial fashion and to the benefit of the trademark owner, with no intention of infringement of the trademark.

Editorial Board: Dan Appleman, Craig Berry, Gary Cornell, Tony Davis, Steven Rycroft, Julian Skinner, Martin Streicher, Jim Sumser, Karen Watterson, Gavin Wright, John Zukowski
Assistant Publisher and Project Manager: Grace Wong
Development Editor: Simon Hayes
Copy Editor: Nicole LeClerc
Proofreader: Carol Burbo
Compositor: Diana Van Winkle, Van Winkle Design Group
Interior and Cover Designer: Kurt Krames
Cartoon Artist: Marc F. Richard, www.lartiste.com
Production Manager: Kari Brooks
Manufacturing Manager: Tom Debolski

Library of Congress Cataloging-in-Publication Data

Chapman, Merrill R., 1953-
  In search of stupidity : over 20 years of high-tech marketing disasters / Merrill R. Chapman.
    p. cm.
  ISBN 1-59059-104-6 (hardcover : alk. paper)
  1. Computer software industry--Management--Case studies. 2. Computer industry—Management—Case studies. 3. Business failures--Case studies. I. Title.

HD9696.63.A2C53 2003
338.4'7004--dc21

                                2003009863

Distributed to the book trade in the United States by Springer-Verlag New York, Inc., 175 Fifth Avenue, New York, NY, 10010 and outside the United States by Springer-Verlag GmbH & Co. KG, Tiergartenstr. 17, 69112 Heidelberg, Germany.

In the United States: phone 1-800-SPRINGER, email orders@springer-ny.com, or visit http://www.springer-ny.com. Outside the United States: fax +49 6221 345229, email orders@springer.de, or visit http://www.springer.de.

For information on translations, please contact Apress directly at 2560 Ninth Street, Suite 219, Berkeley, CA 94710. Phone 510-549-5930, fax 510-549-5939, email info@apress.com, or visit http://www.apress.com.

To Ruth, Lili, and, of course, Charlie.

CONTENTS

FOREWORD

IN EVERY HIGH-TECH COMPANY I've known, there's a war going on between the geeks and the suits. Before you start reading a book full of propaganda from software marketing wizard and über-suit Rick Chapman, let me take a moment to tell you what the geeks think.

Play along with me for a minute, will you? Please imagine the most stereotypically pale, Jolt-drinking, Chinese-food-eating, video-game-playing, Slashdot-reading, Linux-command-line-dwelling dork. Because this is just a stereotype, you should be free to imagine either a runt or a kind of chubby fellow, but in either case this isn't the kind of person who plays football with his high-school pals when he visits mom for Thanksgiving. Also, because he's a stereotype, I shouldn't have to make complicated excuses for making him a him.

This is what our stereotypical programmer thinks: "Microsoft makes inferior products, but they have superior marketing, so everybody buys their stuff."

Ask him what he thinks about the marketing people in his own company. "They're really stupid. Yesterday I got into a big argument with this stupid sales drone in the break room, and after ten minutes it was totally clear that she had no clue what the difference between 802.11a and 802.11b is. Duh!"

What do marketing people do, young geek? "I don't know. They play golf with customers or something, when they're not making me correct their idiot spec sheets. If it was up to me I'd fire 'em all."

A nice fellow named Jeffrey Tarter used to publish an annual list, called the Soft_letter 100, of the 100 largest personal computer software publishers. Here's what the top ten looked like in 1984:

Rank	Company	Annual Revenue
1	MicroPro International	$60,000,000
2	Microsoft Corp.	$55,000,000
3	Lotus	$53,000,000
4	Digital Research	$45,000,000
5	VisiCorp	$43,000,000
6	Ashton-Tate	$35,000,000
7	Peachtree	$21,700,000
8	MicroFocus	$15,000,000
9	Software Publishing	$14,000,000
10	Broderbund	$13,000,000

OK, Microsoft is number 2, but it's one of a handful of companies with roughly similar annual revenues. Now let's look at the same list for 2001:

Rank	Company	Annual Revenue
1	Microsoft Corp.	$23,845,000,000
2	Adobe	$1,266,378,000
3	Novell	$1,103,592,000
4	Intuit	$1,076,000,000
5	Autodesk	$926,324,000
6	Symantec	$790,153,000
7	Network Associates	$745,692,000
8	Citrix	$479,446,000
9	Macromedia	$295,997,000
10	Great Plains	$250,231,000

Whoa. Notice, if you will, that every single company except Microsoft has disappeared from the top ten. Also notice, please, that Microsoft is so much larger than the next largest player, it's not even funny. Adobe would double its revenue if it could just get Microsoft's soda pop budget.

The personal computer software market is Microsoft. Microsoft's revenue, it turns out, makes up 69 percent of the total revenue of the top 100 companies combined. This is what we're talking about here.

Is this just superior marketing, as our imaginary geek claims? Or is it the result of an illegal monopoly? (Which begs the question: How did Microsoft get that monopoly? You can't have it both ways.)

According to Rick Chapman, the answer is simpler: Microsoft was the only company on the list that never made a fatal stupid mistake. Whether this was by dint of superior brainpower or just dumb luck, in my opinion the biggest mistake Microsoft made was the talking paperclip. And how bad was that, really? We ridiculed the company, shut off the feature, and went back to using Word, Excel, Outlook, and Internet Explorer every minute of every day.

But for every other software company that once had market leadership and saw it go down the drain, you can point to one or two giant blunders that steered the boat into an iceberg. MicroPro fiddled around rewriting printer architecture instead of upgrading its flagship product, WordStar. Lotus wasted a year and a half shoehorning 1-2-3 to run on 640KB machines, and by the time it was done, Excel was shipping and 640KB machines were a dim memory. Digital Research wildly overcharged for CP/M-86 and lost a chance to be the de-facto standard for PC operating systems. VisiCorp sued itself out of existence. Ashton-Tate never missed an opportunity to piss off dBASE developers, poisoning the fragile ecology that's so vital to a platform vendor's success.

I'm a programmer, of course, so I tend to blame the marketing people for these stupid mistakes. Almost all of them revolve around a failure of nontechnical business people to understand basic technology facts. When Pepsi-pusher John Sculley was developing the Apple Newton, he didn't know something that every computer science major in the country knows: Handwriting recognition isn't possible. This was at the same time that Bill Gates was hauling programmers into meetings, begging them to create a single rich-text edit control that could be reused in all their products. Put Jim Manzi (the suit who let the MBAs take over Lotus) in that meeting and he would be staring blankly and thinking, "What's a rich-text edit control?" It never would have occurred to him to take technological leadership because he didn't grok the technology.

In fact, the very use of the word "grok" in that sentence would probably throw him off.

If you ask me, and I'm biased, no software company can succeed unless there's a programmer at the helm. So far the evidence backs me up. But many of these boneheaded mistakes come from the programmers themselves. Netscape's monumental decision to rewrite its browser instead of improving the old code base cost the company several years of Internet time, during which its market share went from around 90 percent to about 4 percent, and this was the programmers' idea. Of course, the nontechnical and inexperienced management of that company had no idea why this was a bad idea. There are still scads of programmers who defend Netscape's ground-up rewrite: "The old code really sucked, Joel!" Yeah, uh huh. Such programmers should be admired for their love of clean code, but they shouldn't be allowed within 100 feet of any business decisions, because it's obvious that clean code is more important to them than shipping, uh, software.

So I'll concede to Rick a bit and say that if you want to be successful in the software business, you have to have a management team that thoroughly understands and loves programming, but they have to understand and love business, too. Finding a leader with strong aptitude in both dimensions is difficult, but it's the only way to avoid making one of those fatal mistakes that Rick catalogs lovingly in this book. So read the book, chuckle a bit, and if there's a stupid head running your company, get your resume in shape and start looking for a house in Redmond.

—Joel Spolsky
http://www.joelonsoftware.com
http://www.fogcreek.com

ABOUT THE ARTIST

Marc F. Richard was born in France, where he studied at the school of Art Decoratifs in Paris for 4 years. He was commissioned by several companies, including Lufthansa and Monsieur Meuble, to develop artistic design material for advertising and promotion.

Mr. Richard moved to the United States in 1983 and started his own company as a freelance artist specializing in commercial art and cartooning. He has owned and operated his own studio in the Bay Area since 1989, offering clients various forms of artwork, including illustrations, logos, portraits, and caricatures. Some of his clients include Kemper Insurance, Hewlett-Packard, G.T. Global, Novel, Smith Barney, Sun Microsystems, Psychology Today, Goldman Sachs, Kaldair, Compaq, Lehman Brothers, Merrill Lynch, and Viacom. Mr. Richard's cartoons have been published in newspapers and hardback books. He has designed numerous posters for retail companies, including Weatherford BMW and The Stinking Rose A Garlic Restaurant.

ACKNOWLEDGMENTS

JOHN F. KENNEDY ONCE SAID, "Victory has a thousand fathers, but defeat is an orphan." The writing of this book has certainly borne this maxim out: Not only did most of the people I contacted and spoke to during its development not want to be credited, but a few threatened me with dire bodily harm if I did.

Nonetheless, a brave few souls have agreed to allow their contributions to this effort to be recognized, and I'd like to take this opportunity to acknowledge their help and assistance. Those listed in my escutcheon of honor include Ted Finch, Adam Green, Randy Hujar, Maria Johnston, Steve Manes, Mary Marsden, Pete Peterson, Paul Somerson, Joel Spolsky, Jeffrey Tarter, and Alan Zenreich. Those who chose not to be listed also have my deepest thanks and appreciation.

Guy walks into a doctor's office, raises his arm, points to his shoulder, and says, "Doc, it hurts when I do that."

Doctor looks at him and says, "Then don't do that."

—Old vaudeville joke

"Hegel remarks somewhere that all great, world-historical facts and personages occur, as it were, twice. He has forgotten to add: the first time as tragedy, the second as farce."

—Karl Marx

one

INTRODUCTION

IN 1982, HARPER & ROW published *In Search of Excellence: Lessons from America's Best-Run Companies* by Thomas J. Peters and Robert H. Waterman, Jr. *In Search of Excellence* quickly became a seminal work in the category of business management books and made its authors millionaires. Although it's no longer the literary obsession of freshly minted MBAs that it was back in the 1980s, the book's distribution and influence has proved long lasting and pervasive. After its introduction, the book stayed on best-seller lists for almost 4 years and sold over 3 million copies. A survey by WorldCat, an electronic catalog of materials from libraries in the United States and other countries, ranks *In Search of Excellence* as being on more library shelves than any other book in the world. With 3,971 libraries listing it as being in their collections, the book tops the list of 100 books held by libraries. It has held the number one position since 1989.

In Search of Excellence, when it first came out, applied soothing balm to the raw nerves of the American psyche, and this helps account for its tremendous success. The 1970s had been a gloomy time for U.S. businesses. The Japanese had run American companies out of consumer electronics; Japanese cars lasted 100,000 miles, while American cars started breaking down at 20,000; and as the 1980s began, Japanese companies had just started making memory chips more cheaply than their American counterparts. The Japanese even announced they were starting a "Fifth Generation" project to build software that would make computers very very smart indeed, leaving the poor old United States with software systems that would be the technological equivalent of Studebakers. (The project was a complete bust, like all the others emanating from the artificial intelligence hype machine of the 1980s, and it never developed much more than software capable of storing some nice recipes for sushi.) Yes, the United States was doing OK in this new market for little machines called "microcomputers," but the pundits universally agreed that eventually the Japanese were going to move into that industry as well and that would be it for the Americans.[1] Maybe IBM would survive; after all, it did business like the Japanese anyway. For the ambitious young MBA, a start-up position in agribusiness, such as sheep herding, began to look like the fast track to the top.

---

[1] In point of fact, the Japanese did introduce a plethora of CP/M and MS-DOS "clones." Like many other companies, the Japanese firms failed to understand the impact of the IBM standard on the industry and none of the machines made a significant impact on the market. In Japan, NEC and Fujitsu attempted to establish independent hardware standards, but their efforts were eventually overwhelmed by IBM's PC standard. The most important long-term impact the Japanese had on computing technology was Sony's successful introduction of a standard for 3" floppies.

In Search of Excellence helped buck everyone up. All the companies it profiled were **American** firms competing successfully in world markets. It seemed obvious that if you studied the organizations closely, learned the fundamental practices and techniques they used to achieve excellence, and then applied those practices and techniques to your business, it would become excellent too!

The basic thesis of *In Search of Excellence* isn't complex and can be summed up succinctly: Excellent companies create corporate cultures in which success flourishes. (Yes, this is something of a tautology, but it's a nice one and people always like reading it.) An excellent corporate culture is one that loves the customer, loves its employees, loves the company's products, and loves loving the company. Once enough love is flowing through the corporate veins, a company will organically become excellent and in turn create excellent products and services. This will lead to more customer, employee, product, and corporate love, lifting all concerned to even greater heights of selling and purchasing ecstasy. The cycle becomes self-sustaining and a universe of almost sybaritic business success awaits those who master the Zen of Excellence.

Most of *In Search of Excellence* thus functions as the corporate equivalent of the Kama Sutra, profiling different companies as they bend and twist themselves into different postures and techniques designed to build customer desire for the company, increase customer love for the company's products, and provide lasting satisfaction with the company's service. The positions and techniques discussed vary widely and include being reliable, shooting for 100 percent, communicating intensely, being creative, talking about it, talking about it **a lot,** listening a lot, getting on with it, etc. High tech firms are particularly well represented in the book, with IBM, Xerox, DEC, and many others serving as exemplars of how to seize the business world by the tail via the practice of excellence.

For the next several years, copies of *In Search of Excellence* flew off bookstore shelves. Thousands of companies, including most in the high-tech sectors, took its maxims to heart. People walked, talked, and communicated with incredible intensity. Peters became a widely sought-after speaker and business consultant (Waterman dropped out of public sight). He wrote more books, including *A Passion for Excellence* and *The Pursuit of WOW!*, all of which continued the earlier book's quest for that ineffable corporate phlogiston that when ignited leads inexorably to success. America's affair with excellence appeared to be endless.

Unfortunately, while U.S. businesses were vigorously applying excellence to every nook and cranny of their corporate bodies, a few people began to note that many of the firms listed in Peters and Waterman's tome seemed to be, well, less than excellent. As early as 1984, *Business Week* published a cover story entitled "Oops!" that debunked some of the book's claims. Most people dismissed these early criticisms as journalistic carping, but over time it became more difficult to ignore the fact that something was very wrong with the book's concept of business excellence.

Take, for example, its examination of Lanier, a major competitor in what is now a vanished world, that of dedicated word processors. The market for these single-purpose computers had been built and defined by Wang. As the market grew, companies such as Lanier, Xerox, IBM, and almost a hundred others competed fiercely for the privilege of selling $20,000.00 boxes that did what a $99.95 piece of software does today (actually, the software does much more). These dedicated devices were often the only experience many people had with computers throughout much of the 1970s, and to many people word-processing stations epitomized "high tech."

In Search of Excellence thought Lanier was **really** excellent, a company that "lives, sleeps, eats, and breathes customers." The book described how the company's top executives went on sales calls once a month, how the president of the company personally handled service calls (and if you believed **that,** you probably also went out and bought a famous bridge in New York City), how its service was even better than IBM's, and so forth and so on.

And Lanier was a sharp marketing bunch, too! The company knew that the term "word processor" put everybody "off." That's why Lanier called its word processors "No Problem Typewriters." Sheer advertising genius.

The only problem with all of this was that Lanier wasn't an excellent company; it was a dead company, a shot-through-the-head dinosaur whose sluggish nervous system hadn't yet gotten round to telling the rest of its body to lie down and die. In 1981, an Apple II+ running AppleWriter or ScreenWriter[2] did everything a Lanier word processor did, never mind an IBM PC with WordStar. By 1985, the market for dedicated word processing was as extinct as the Tyrannosaurus Rex, but Peters and Waterman seem not to have noticed they were profiling a walking corpse.

---

[2] An early attempt at a true "What You See Is What You Get" (WYSIWYG) word processor. The product displayed your text on a bitmapped screen and could show italicized and underlined text. On a 1MHz Apple II it also ran veery slooowly.

Now, you can argue that market shifts can catch companies unawares and that Lanier was a victim of the unexpected. This, however, can't be true. *In Search of Excellence* was written in 1981 and published in 1982. By 1981, thousands of Apples, Radio Shack Model TRS-80s,[3] Commodore PETs, and a wide variety of CP/M systems were selling monthly. The IBM PC was also launched that year. WordStar, AppleWriter, and Scripsit (popular on the Radio Shack systems) had been available for years. Hundreds of ComputerLand stores, one of the first national franchises dedicated to selling desktop computer systems, were doing business nationwide and dozens more were opening on a monthly basis. Yet somehow Lanier, the company that apparently did everything but have sexual relations with its customers, never found out from a single one of them that they were interested in buying an IBM PC or an Apple with a good word-processing program that did everything a Lanier word processor did at a fraction of the cost and did other things as well, like run a nifty type of new program called a "spreadsheet." You would think an excellent company would have caught on much sooner.

It only became worse as time passed and you kept track of the book's list of "excellent performers," particularly the high-tech ones. For instance, Data General: Gone into oblivion.[4] Wang: Moribund by 1987. DEC: PC roadkill. NCR: A mediocre performer bought up by AT&T was eventually regurgitated by AT&T after proving unpalatable. Texas Instruments: The company that coinvented the microprocessor saw its TI99/4A tossed out of the computer market by 1984. IBM: In 10 years it went from an American icon to an American tragedy.

---

[3] The first computer I ever owned was used Radio Shack TRS-80 Model One, semi-affectionately known by its owners as "Trash Ones." The reliability of early models was less than stellar, and the paint tended to rub off their keyboards, leading older systems to develop a rather decrepit appearance.

[4] Data General made its own contribution to stupidity with the introduction of the Data General One in 1985. This was the first "clamshell" portable and, in terms of weight and functionality, a breakthrough. A fully loaded system cost about $3,000.00, weighed about 12 pounds, supported up to 512KB of RAM, could hold two 3.5" double-sided 700KB floppies, and featured an LCD screen capable of displaying a full 80×25 lines of text, an unusual feature for a portable in that era. It also had enough battery life to allow you to get some work done from your airplane seat. Unfortunately, the LCD screen also sported a surface so shiny and reflective you could literally comb your hair in it, making it almost impossible to view the screen for everyday computing chores. No one could ever quite figure out what had possessed Data General to release a system that basically functioned as a $3,000.00 personal grooming system. I still own one of these systems and once tried to sell it at a garage sale for $25.00. I am happy to discover they're currently worth about $500.00 in the collectibles market.

Xerox, on the ropes by the late 1990s, was on the book's list of hero companies. By the mid-1980s, industry mavens were already puzzling over how a company could develop the graphical user interface (GUI), mouse, object-oriented programming, and Ethernet and fail to make a single successful product from **any** of these groundbreaking innovations. Instead, Xerox made its inaugural debut into the PC market with an obsolete-before-its-release clunker of an 8-bit CP/M machine with the appetizing name of "Worm" that sold just about as well as you would expect.

Atari, for God's sake, even made it to the book's Hall of Excellence. In 1983, the year after *In Search of Excellence*'s publication, the company was close to death after releasing the worst computer game of all time, *E.T.* (based on the movie). Before its product hit the store shelves, an "excellent" company would have used the plastic cartridges that contained this all-time turkey to club to death the parties responsible for producing the game that ruined the Christmas of 1982 for thousands of fresh-faced video game junkies.[5]

It wasn't simply the companies profiled in *In Search of Excellence* that proved to be disappointments. During the 1980s, it was impossible, especially in high tech, to escape the training seminars, book extracts, and corporate programs that sprang up dedicated to ensuring everyone was excellent all the time and every day. Yet, despite all the talking, walking, and communicating, high-tech firms kept doing stupid things. Again and again and again. And every time they did they paid a price. Again and again and again.

One key to the problem may lie in the fact that in 2002, Tom Peters announced the data used to "objectively" measure the performance of the companies profiled in the book was faked. Oops. Well, remember, excellence means never having to say you're sorry.

But despite this little faux pas, a more important answer lies in the types of companies analyzed in *In Search of Excellence*. With only a few exceptions, they were large firms with dominant positions in markets

---

[5] It has been my privilege to meet the person who holds the world record for getting the highest score ever achieved on this game, a young man who worked for me in the late 1990s. (The *E.T.* game and original Atari 2600 game system are somewhat collectible and still used by those interested in retro gaming. If you wish to experience the horror that was *E.T.*, you can download the game and a 2600 emulator for your PC from various Internet sites.) I won't reveal the name of this stalwart gamer because my revelation might permanently damage his career. When I knew him, he suffered from insomnia, and after playing many hours of *E.T.* I can understand why.

that were senescent or static. IBM ruled the world of mainframe computers. DEC and Data General had carved out comfortable fiefdoms in minicomputers. Xerox reigned over copiers. Wang and Lanier both possessed principalities in dedicated word processing.

In these types of business environments, affairs proceed at a measured pace and there's plenty of time available for navel gazing. Their vision clouded by all that lint, companies such as IBM and DEC decided that it was their natural goodness that made them successful and therefore they were successful because they were naturally good. By the time Peters and Waterman got around to interviewing them, most of these firms were ossifying, their internal cultures attempting to cement employee mindsets and processes in place in a futile attempt to freeze the past so as to guarantee the future. These firms weren't excellent, they were arthritic.

For high-tech companies, navel gazing is a particularly inappropriate strategy as markets tend not to stay stable very long. In 1981, for example, distinct markets for spreadsheets, word processors, databases, and business presentation products existed in the software industry. By the late 1980s, word processing alone was a $1 billion category. By 1995, all of these categories had been subsumed by the office suite (particularly Microsoft's).

What, therefore, accounted for the success of companies such as Microsoft, Oracle, and Symantec and the failure of other firms such as Novell, MicroPro, and Ashton-Tate? Was it Microsoft's "respect for the individual," something *In Search of Excellence* told us IBM had in abundance? Well, Bill Gates once stood up at the start of a presentation being given by a new product manager, fixed the unfortunate fellow with a cold stare, and asked, "Where the fuck did we hire you from?"[6] before leaving the room.

Hmm. Perhaps not.

Perhaps it was a "seemingly unjustifiable overcommitment to some form of quality, reliability, or service"? IBM had that in abundance also. Well, Dell Computer is currently the reigning king of PC hardware, not IBM. Although Dell's service is OK, the company isn't "unjustifiable" about it. Oh, Dell pays lip service to the concept of great customer service, and within the constraints of its business model, it does the best it

---

[6] Stephen Manes and Paul Andrews, *Gates: How Microsoft's Mogul Reinvented an Industry—and Made Himself the Richest Man in America* (New York: Simon & Schuster, 1994) p. 378.

can. If you don't like your PC, Dell will probably take it back if you're within the warranty period and you scream loudly enough and pay for the shipping and maybe fork over restocking fee if you're a small business. If your PC breaks, the company will do its best to get **you** to fix the thing. But Michael Dell, unlike the excellent CEO of Lanier, won't be calling your house to handle affairs personally.

That's because Dell has figured out that what people really care about these days in a computer is high performance at a low price. Dell has learned over the years to build such machines. IBM hasn't. Computers are very reliable and on a statistical basis don't break down often. If the ones made by your company do, it **is** possible to sell a great many of them if you price them cheaply enough, as in the case of Packard Bell, a company that briefly became a powerhouse in PC retailing. Alas, the machines were of poor quality, broke often, and few people ever bought a second Packard Bell computer.

On the other hand, Dell computers rarely break. You, the customer, know that. You're willing to buy a Dell PC because you've made a bet in your mind that the risk that the computer you buy won't work isn't worth the extra money it would cost to have your fanny kissed in the event of a breakdown. People who buy desktop PCs aren't a high-roller audience and it makes no sense to treat them like one.

Let's move on.

Or perhaps it was "autonomy and entrepreneurship"? Motorola, a company with a history of allowing different autonomous groups within its phone division to tear at each other's throats while firms like Nokia tore away its market share, surely has **that** in abundance. In the entrepreneurial spirit of "up and at 'em," these groups managed to build what is perhaps the coolest-looking cell phone of all time, the StarTAC. The only problem with the StarTAC was that when it was first introduced it was a very cool analog system when everyone wanted digital phones.

And it was certainly entrepreneurship that led Motorola to launch its Iridium project. Motorola spent $5 billion plus to put 66 low-earth satellites into orbit so that anyone could phone anytime from anywhere with a Motorola phone. Unfortunately, the satellites spend 70 percent of their time over our planet's oceans and aren't usable for much of their life (unless perhaps you're adrift in the middle of the Atlantic); the phones, though they may have worked from the top of Mount Everest, didn't work indoors, in the shadows of buildings, or under trees (early demos of the system enjoined purchasers to "make sure the phone is pointed at the satellite"[7]); the service's monthly cost was high; the phones were huge; and every major metropolitan area already had cheap and reliable cellular systems. In other words, there was no market for Iridium. After the last satellite was launched, the system quickly went bankrupt. Despondent Motorola stockholders, watching the value of their shares plummet as Iridium crashed and burned, suggested sending up the project's marketing and engineering teams in rockets without spacesuits to join their orbiting financial debacle, but current law forbids this. You would think an excellent company with entrepreneurial instincts would notice that 70 percent of the Earth's surface is water.

Uh huh. Maybe that isn't it.

In fact, if you examine high-tech companies, only one factor seems to constantly distinguish the failures from the successes. This factor is stupidity. More successful companies are less stupid than the opposition more of the time. As Forrest Gump astutely noted, "Stupid is as stupid does."

One of stupidity's most endearing traits is its egalitarian nature. Its eternal dull lamp beckons endlessly to those dim bulbs who seek to rip open the hulls of successful companies and ideas on the sharp rocks of bad judgment and ignorance. With stupidity, your reach never exceeds your grasp; any company, no matter how large or small, can aspire to commit acts of skull-numbing idiocy and have a hope of success.

Take, for example, the creation of the worst piece of high-tech marketing collateral ever developed, the brainchild of the founder of a small company, Street Technologies. The front page of Street Technologies' expensive, four-color, 8 1/2 × 11 corporate opus posed the following challenge:

"How to eliminate half your work force."
The inside of the brochure provided the means to rise to the task:

"Get the other half to use your software!"
When it was pointed out to the president of Street Technologies that a marketing campaign designed to create mass unemployment and spark a brutal Darwinian struggle for personal survival in its target audience might not be the most effective of all possible approaches, he airily dismissed the issue with the observation that "the piece was not aimed at the employees but their bosses." He'd apparently not considered the issue of who was going to be opening the mail.

---

[7] I was present at such a demo. I interrupted the demonstrator to inquire "Which one?"

Creating silly collaterals isn't a task reserved only for high tech's small fry. The **second** worst piece of marketing collateral ever created was a noble effort by software giant Computer Associates. This was a brochure designed to be included in a direct marketing campaign for a bundle of OS/2 business software. The piece trumpeted the presence of a free goodie that buyers of the bundle would receive upon purchase—a package of canned sounds you could use to liven up your OS/2 desktop. Sounds highlighted in this amazing bit of literature included "farting," "pissing," and "orgasm." One can only mourn the fact that the package didn't include the noise made when a marketing manager is summarily decapitated for committing an act of boneheaded silliness, such as developing and printing thousands of patently tasteless and offensive four-color brochures.

The reason for the absence of stupidity can vary. In some cases, firms avoid stupidity because the company's culture creates more intelligent behavior. In other cases, it's because a company's personnel are smarter than the competition's and thus avoid making stupid mistakes. In yet others, it's because a business's leadership is smarter than the competition's and thus tends not to behave stupidly. Usually, it's a varying mix of all three. In a sense, the reason for not acting stupidly doesn't matter—the avoidance of it does. By reducing the number of stupid actions you take vis-à-vis your competition, you're more likely to outcompete them over time.

Some may object that stupidity isn't quantifiable but, in point of fact, the opposite is true. Stupid behavior **is** both quantifiable and identifiable. For example, it's stupid to create two products with the same name, price point, functionality, and target audience and attempt to sell them at the same time. This may seem stunningly obvious, but somehow one of the world's largest software companies, MicroPro, publisher of WordStar, a product that once ruled the word-processing market, did exactly that. A few years later, Borland repeated very much the same mistake with very much the same results. Then Novell. After you read Chapter 3 and learn precisely why this is a stupid thing to do and what the likely outcome is, you'll be less likely to make this mistake in your own marketing and sales efforts. That puts you one up on your competition who, unless they've also read this book, are far more likely to repeat MicroPro's fatal blunder.

Nitpickers like to claim that context often changes the nature of what is stupid behavior, but this principle is vastly overstated. For instance, if you spend many millions of dollars successfully creating a consumer brand, and then, when your most important product is revealed to be defective, stupidly attempt to blow off the public (as I describe Intel attempting to do in Chapter 5), you'll suffer. It really doesn't matter what industry you're in or what product you're selling. Expect to be immolated.

Or take the example of Syncronys, publisher of the immortal, never-to-be-forgotten SoftRAM "memory doubling" utility for Windows. Introduced in May 1995 with a list price of $29.95, SoftRAM was designed to "compress" your computer's memory using your computer's memory to give you, effectively, twice the memory you had physically installed (the problem with this concept should be apparent once you think about it). SoftRAM was quite the bestseller upon its release, with the Windows 3.*x* version selling more than 100,000 copies and the Windows 95 version more than *600,000*. The company's president, Rainer Poertner, was dubbed Entrepreneur of the Year by the Software Council of Southern California. Syncronys stock jumped from $.03 per share in March 1995 to a high of $32.00 per share in August 1995.

SoftRAM was a handsome-looking piece of software that after installation presented buyers with a snazzy dashboard that supposedly let them increase their PC's RAM with the touch of a button. Unfortunately for both purchasers of SoftRAM and Syncronys, the software didn't actually *do* that. Actually, it didn't really do *anything* except change a configuration setting in Windows 3.*x* that increased the amount of memory that could be swapped to disk, an operation a Windows user could perform him- or herself in under a minute for free.

It turned out that SoftRAM was an example of what Syncronys coyly called "placeboware," the software equivalent of a deed to the Brooklyn Bridge. The concept annoyed the spoilsports at the Federal Trade Commission (FTC) greatly, who forced the company to stop selling the package and promise to give everyone their money back. (Interestingly enough, no one was prosecuted for fraud in the case, the FTC apparently having bought the argument that the difference between computer sales reps and car salesmen is that car salesmen know when they're lying.) It would seem obvious to anyone with even half an uncompressed brain that no one would ever buy a product from Syncronys again, but in an act of supreme idiocy the *company actually tried to sell other software packages*[8] after the SoftRAM debacle. Sheer imbecility, as Syncronys promptly went out of business.

However, more than just a few trenchant examples of stupidity are needed to support a substantive examination of the subject, which brings me to the point of this book. *In Search of Stupidity* was written to provide you with a more comprehensive look at the topic. Within these pages are documented many of high tech's worst marketing and development programs and strategies, as brought to you by some of its most clueless executives. In my quest to bring you the best of the worst, I made my selections from a wide range of companies, from arrogant smaller hot shots on the path to meltdown to sluggish giants too muscle bound to get out of their own way.

In the interest of fairness, I haven't included hard-luck stories. No natural disasters, plane crashes, or tragic deaths played a part in any of the disasters discussed. All of the blunders, snafus, and screw-ups described in this book's pages were avoidable by the individuals and companies that made them and are avoidable by you and your company. After reading this book, you'll know what they are and you'll be in a position to act less unintelligently. For you, history won't repeat itself.

Of course, it *is* possible that you'll make other stupid mistakes, ones not chronicled in these pages, but not to worry. If your competition is making the mistakes I describe in these pages, as well as all the others, you'll still probably prevail. Remember, the race goes not to the strong, nor swift, nor more intelligent, but to the less stupid.

Besides, I'm planning a sequel.

Best of luck!

---

[8] For instance, another utility called "Big Disk."

two

FIRST MOVERS, FIRST MISTAKES:
IBM, Digital Research, Apple, and Microsoft

The birth of what we now think of as high tech began in 1975 with the introduction of the Altair, the world's first affordable and practical microcomputer, from Micro Instrumentation and Telemetry Systems (MITS) of New Mexico. Units such as the French Micral and the American Scelbi were introduced prior to the Altair, but there wasn't much you could do with them. The brainchild of former U.S. Air Force Engineer Ed Roberts, the Altair was sold in kit form for $397.00, a price that put the unit within reach of a mass audience. Built around a powerful (for its day) 8-bit Intel 8080 processor, an assembled Altair was capable of doing real work, once you added a keyboard, a monitor, memory, storage peripherals (such as a paper-tape reader), and software, none of which were in great supply when the unit was first introduced. However, a generation raised on Isaac Asimov, Robert A. Heinlein, Robby the Robot, and *Star Trek* (particularly *Star Trek*!) wasn't going to let a parts shortage stop them from getting cracking on building the new world. Bliss was it in that dawn to be alive, but to be a young geek was very heaven! (With apologies to Wordsworth.)

~

The Big Bang: The Altair

The Altair exploded upon a universe ready to accept it, but as with the big bang, its time as a force in microcomputing was brief. MITS was mismanaged and destroyed by its own rapid growth, a pattern that would repeat itself many times in the industry. But as the Altair's bright fire burned down and faded away, it left behind a busy new world inhabited by Commodore PETs, Apples, TRS-80s, Cromencos, Osbornes, and a score of other systems now long extinct.

But high tech is a place of fast change, sharp elbows, and ruthless competition. Soon, great powers began to stir, roused by the hum of commerce and rustle of dollars being exchanged in this virgin world of microcomputing. Covetous eyes gazed upon an unconquered landscape and began to plot to make it their own.

A Fistful of Chips

Of all the entities converging on the world of microcomputing during its early formation, none was more dominant than IBM. To many, IBM wasn't simply a high-tech company, IBM *was* high tech, other companies being simply minor stars in an IBM firmament. By 1981, admiration, reverence, and fear of IBM had reached neo-cult status. IBM was "Big Blue," and its chief competitors in the mainframe business were referred to as "The Seven Dwarfs."

Nonetheless, IBM, almost against its will, was increasingly drawn to examine the unknown force that was driving people to go and buy hundreds of millions of dollars worth of "toy" computers. By the early 1980s, IBM had come to the realization it needed to understand this force, participate in its growth, and control it. The IBM PC was IBM's first bid to achieve these ends.

A great deal of mythology surrounds the introduction of this now legendary system. The prevailing belief among many is that microcomputing before IBM's arrival was a rough-and-tumble frontier, full of ornery software and colorful hombres tough enough to buy and tame herds of uncooperative boxes of lowing, obstreperous silicon. But as has so often been the case with historical events, truth and legend are often at odds.

The truth is that the microcomputer industry just before IBM's appearance resembled not so much a rude cow-town but rather a spanking-new steam train, trimmed in polished brass and covered in fresh paint. Most of the passengers boarded the train at Start-up Junction and are looking forward to the ride to Prosperity, the town just up the line. On board and seated in a fancy Pullman car are a diverse set of well-to-do-looking characters, all gussied up in fancy store-bought clothes they've purchased from the proceeds of successful IPOs and healthy sales. These are the hardware dudes, who include Apple, Commodore, and Radio Shack, as well as a score of manufacturers of 8-bit computers running the widely used CP/M operating system. They're a happy-looking lot—they're shipping units to businesses as fast as they can manufacture them.

The home market is equally energetic, though not nearly as profitable, with every general store in town packed at Christmas and every other holiday with parents and their eager-eyed offspring snapping up every VIC-20, Commodore 64, Atari 800, Texas Instruments 94, and Timex Sinclair they can lay their hands on. (In 1982, Macy's,[1] at the time a power in consumer electronics, ran out of *every* home-oriented micro-computer at its flagship Herald Square store in New York City a week before Christmas.)

Riding in the car just in front of the hardware merchants are the software peddlers, and they look almost as content. They're selling copies of VisiCalc, WordStar, and PFS File as fast as they can stuff them into cardboard boxes. In many cases cardboard isn't required; demand is so high that customers are willing to take their software home in plastic baggies. Boom times indeed!

Fabulous Fruit

Of all the characters waiting expectantly for the train to pull out of the station, Apple was probably the best positioned of the early denizens of Microcomputerville to become the town's mayor. Apple's mainstay system, the Apple II, and its immediate successor, the Apple II+, were triumphs of industrial design and utility. Sleek and low slung, the units provided an attractive contrast to the stark industrial designs common to business machines. The Apple was reasonably priced (a fully configured system with a whopping 64KB of RAM, color monitor, and dual floppies cost only about $4,000.00). Its integrated color graphics gave it crossover appeal to the home market, and the system was supported by a wide selection of business and entertainment software. A small company called Corvus had even developed a system for networking Apples together. All in all, it was a compelling, up-to-date package and buyers loved their Apples.

---

[1] At the time I was working at Macy's as a salesman in a fully staffed and stocked high-end retail computer store that was built within the company's flagship Herald Square location on 34th Street. This store was authorized to sell "high-end" systems such as the IBM PC and the Apple II and III, but until it was completed I was put to work in the consumer electronics section of Macy's, which sold "low-end" systems such as the VIC-20 and the Atari 400s and 800s. Several days before Christmas, the only units available for sale to disappointed moms and dads were a few forlorn Sinclairs that were finally scarfed up by desperate shoppers. For a while in 1982, this store became something of a focal point for celebrities and the PC elite because it was one of the few places in the New York area where you could purchase an IBM system without an inordinate wait. Tony Gold, founder of *PC Magazine*, showed up one day at the store to buy systems for himself and several staffers at the magazine. Famous science fiction writer Isaac Asimov showed up one day to learn about microcomputers. I escorted Asimov over to a station where he sat down at an Apple II, typed in a bit of BASIC code, and was promptly stuck because he had no idea how to interrupt the loop he'd just initiated.

Yes, the system did have its idiosyncrasies. You had to buy a hardware upgrade to type in lowercase. Connecting your floppy drive to your Apple incorrectly caused the hapless disk unit to seemingly explode as an internal capacitor[2] blew with a loud pop and a rush of blue smoke out the drive door, but people were willing to overlook these little peccadilloes.

Just as important as its hardware design was the fact that Apple was the first system to run the first spreadsheet, VisiCalc, microcomputing's first killer application. A *killer application* is defined as a product so compelling you'll buy the necessary hardware just to run that particular piece of software. VisiCalc qualified for this rare and honored appellation—once an accountant or CFO saw rows of numbers rippling across a spreadsheet grid as she automatically updated, that person was hooked for life: She *had* to have the product. Management information systems (MIS, later to be called information technology or IT) departments may not have cared for the loss of centralized control that these little boxes represented, but it's a well-known axiom of corporate life that "You don't say no to the CFO." And once the CFO's secretary (now called an administrative assistant) tried out a word-processing program, that was it. Apples, along with any other computer that ran VisiCalc, or some of its early competitors, quickly proliferated across a business frontier that was grateful to get them.

Also contributing to the Apple II's success was its relatively flexible and extensible hardware and software architecture. Unlike most of its competitors, Apple's system was "open." Popping off the cover of an Apple II revealed *slots,* connectors into which it was possible to plug in a host of different accessories and upgrades, including memory extenders, accelerator cards, copy boards (hardware devices you used to help make bitmapped images of software for, er, "archival" purposes), extended graphics cards, CP/M boards that allowed you to run CP/M software on your Apple II, and so on. An extensive industry focused on providing third-party accessories and upgrades quickly coalesced around the Apple II, helping drive sales even further.

In fact, from Apple's point of view, the system was entirely *too* open. By 1980, a burgeoning clone and "gray" market was developing around

---

[2] I observed this happen at a training course for Apple repair certification. I'm an authorized Level I Apple repairman (circa 1982) and an Apple Consumer-Oriented Retailing Education (CORE) graduate. How would you like that Apple III sent to your office?

Apple's flagship as units with names like the Pineapple[3] and the Orange started being shipped into the United States in growing quantities from Taiwan and other points east. Domestically, Apple even had its own Compaq, a New Jersey company called Franklin Computers, which offered a well-made Apple clone that even let you type in lowercase letters right out of the box.

Apple's reaction to this turn of events foreshadowed its future behavior with respect to the Macintosh market. It summoned an army of attorneys who were given the mission of shutting the clone market down. The lawyers accomplished this by convincing the courts that it was illegal for companies to simply copy the Apple *basic input/output system* (BIOS), the built-in set of software instructions that enabled the system to communicate with its internal peripherals. Once this principle was established, the clone market quickly withered because the machines were built by simply replicating the Apple's hardware chassis and equipping it with ROM chips that contained the now "pirated" BIOS code. (Most people obtained the Apple operating system, Apple DOS, by simply copying the floppy on which it came, though Franklin had gone to the trouble of creating its own version of the Apple operating system.) The Taiwanese all sailed back to their island to concentrate on building IBM clones, and the last time Franklin Computer made any noise was at the industry's 1983 COMDEX trade show in Las Vegas. It hired the Beach Boys to regale attendees at a party that turned out to be a musical swan song to the company's imminent wipeout.

At the time, CP/M (short for *Control Program/Monitor* or *Control Program for Microcomputers*) was considered by many to be Apple's great rival (though both Commodore and Tandy systems had their devoted acolytes). Developed in 1974 by Gary Kildall, founder of the whimsically named Intergalactic Digital Research (later just Digital Research), CP/M was designed to run on Intel's widely used 8-bit microprocessor, the 8080, and its several clones, most notably Zilog's Z80 chip. Unlike Apple DOS and its other competitors, CP/M was less closely coupled to a particular microcomputer's underlying hardware. Digital Research capitalized on this trait to build a profitable and growing business licensing CP/M to several dozen companies, such as NCR, Televideo, Sol Processor, Radio Shack (its variant was known as "Pickles and Trout" for some forgotten reason), and one of the industry's earliest

---

[3] I briefly owned a Pineapple and Franklin Apple II clones.

and most spectacular flameouts, Osborne Computing, creator of the first "portable" (at 25 pounds) computer.

CP/M suffered from one tremendous drawback, however. Although it could be easily adopted to run on a wide variety of computers, no de facto hardware standard for CP/M machines existed. Printer ports, monitors, and in particular floppy drives all differed from machine to machine. As a result, a person who purchased MicroPro's WordStar word processor for his Vector system had no assurance the floppy on which the software was stored could be read by a Cromenco computer, despite the fact that both used the CP/M operating system. For a while, resellers such as Lifeboat Systems in New York City did a nice business simply supplying CP/Mers with the software of their choice on floppies their computers could read.

Exploding disk drives and noncompatible floppy formats aside, our train has built up a head of steam and begins to chug forward. But as the engine begins to pull out of the station, a lone rider appears suddenly in the distance, his horse galloping madly in pursuit. Reaching the last car before the train has come up to speed, the outlaw grabs hold of a railing and quickly swings himself up onto the rear platform. As he does, we can see the pursuer is a lean bandito wearing a tattered poncho, his features obscured by a tattered hat pulled low over his face. He enters the train and strides through it toward the special Pullman where our hardware merchants sit unsuspecting. When he reaches their car they turn to face the intruder, trepidation writ large on their faces. There's a long moment of silence. Then the stranger lifts his hat to uncover ice-blue eyes that show no pity and throws back his poncho, revealing a three-piece suit matched with a white shirt and sensible tie. Strapped around the stranger's waist are a pair of 8088s, deadly six-guns with the phrase "16-bit" inscribed on their chromed barrels. Pulling out these engines of destruction by their off-white pearl handles, the stranger mercilessly guns down the hardware dudes one by one. Only a handful escape the initial carnage.

The IBM PC has arrived on the scene.

Building the Perfect Beast

The history of the development and design of the original IBM PC has been told so many times in so many different venues that I need simply cover the basics before examining the system's long-term impact on the industry. Realizing the microcomputer industry was approaching hyper-growth, and worried that IBM might be cut out of the action, a small group of IBM executives decided to act before it was too late. At a meeting of IBM's top management committee in 1980, this group of prescient individuals pitched then IBM President Frank Cary on the necessity of the company building its own PC and doing it quickly. The IBM PC, by the way, was not IBM's first stab at building a microcomputer: An earlier effort in 1975 had produced a management-by-committee machine that was clunky, overengineered, and overpriced. No one wanted it and no one bought it.

To avoid making the same mistake again, IBM agreed to allow an "off-campus" skunkworks to be established to build a new IBM microcomputer, out of the reach of the behemoth's bureaucracy. Heading up the effort were Bill Lowe, Jack Rogers, Jack Sams, Don Estridge, and several others. Estridge, put in charge of the project's day-to-day operations, would one day be known as the "father" of the IBM PC. The location they picked for the project: Bill Lowe's Boca Raton, Florida, lab. Code name for the new computer: Acorn. Time to project completion: 1 year.

In order to meet its self-imposed deadline, the IBM team decided on a radical departure from standard IBM practice. Rather than attempt to build and manufacture the new computer internally, the PC would be built mainly from parts bought from third parties. IBM would assemble, ship, and support the machines, and they would possess the IBM brand identity, but the contractors would supply most of the critical components, including the unit's microprocessor.

Having made this decision, IBM now had to decide on their new machine's fundamental architecture. Would it be a closed box design, or open and accessible like the Apple II series? Apple's success in rapidly building third-party support for their system impressed the PC impresarios of Boca Raton, who regarded Apple as their biggest competitor. After some hesitation and internal debate, the Apple model was chosen. The IBM PC would have slots and an architecture open to third parties.

The chip chosen to be the brains of the PC was Intel's 8088, a less buff version of Intel's new full-fledged 16-bit chip, the 8086. The 8088 was a design compromise, a hybrid chunk of silicon with 16-bit internals and an 8-bit data path for peripherals. IBM liked the 8088's price and 8-bit bus; it brought the cost of the computer down and made it easier for hardware manufacturers to build new accessories to fill the PC's slot.

On the software side of things, IBM purchased the industry's most popular language, BASIC, from Microsoft, the publisher of the industry's most popular variant of that language. For the PC's operating system, IBM, in a contretemps of which the details are still controversial, didn't pick what many regarded as the industry standard, CP/M. The one IBM did pick, MS-DOS, again from Microsoft, very much "resembled" CP/M and like Digital Research's offering was highly transportable to other Intel-based computers.

From a cost standpoint, IBM's use of third-party parts meant a fully loaded IBM PC would only cost you about $4,000.00 to $5,000.00, give or take an accessory or two. This was more than an Apple II but not a huge financial barrier for the small businesses IBM anticipated would be the system's primary customers. To soften any perception that PCs were expensive, IBM even produced a stripped loss-leader model for only $1,265.00 (with 16KB of memory, no monitor, and no floppies). These units turned out to be much prized, as enterprising buyers often bought them[4] and added cheaper, non-IBM parts to make them functional, and in some cases even resold them at a profit to a gray market hungry to get its hands on any unit it could.

In fact, IBM, having made the commitment to an open system, took Apple's original open hardware gambit and surpassed it in several key areas. Unlike Apple, which had used control over its BIOS to shut the cloners down, IBM published its BIOS specifications.[5] It didn't allow you to directly copy the BIOS code, but once everyone understood how it integrated with the PC it was a relatively easy process for smart programmers to reverse engineer its functionality and produce an equivalent BIOS that did everything IBM's did. And IBM also made the PC's hardware interface specifications widely and cheaply available, and made no attempt to enforce patents it held on several aspects of the PC design.

---

[4] Including yours truly. I purchased two of these models while at Macy's and sold one at a nice markup to a friend of mine who worked at a computer store in New York's Greenwich Village. I used my profits to help outfit the other unit.

[5] IBM actually thought this was a clever tactic to prevent cloning, because by publishing its BIOS it thought it would be hard for companies to find programmers to reverse engineer it who could prove they had never read its widely published specifications. But, apparently, IBM was wrong, as several companies successfully built BIOS "clones" within 12 months of the PC's release. It seemed there were plenty of people who had never seen those BIOS specs. At least they said so and IBM's legal department realized it's very very hard to prove someone has read something.

Its path firmly set, IBM moved rapidly and built the IBM PC in a year. Its release in August 1981 was greeted with almost universal huzzahs and overwhelming consumer acclaim. Some of the gearheads of the time argued interminably about whether the computer was really a 16-bit machine, but most sensible people ignored them. The IBM PC was (relatively) inexpensive, was powerful enough for any future anyone could foresee (fully loaded, it supported 640KB of memory, and who would ever need more memory than that?), had a great keyboard, supported color graphics, looked fairly sleek for its day, and came in any color you wanted as long as it was off-white. And, of course, the fact that it was IBM that was selling it sealed the deal. The PC was an instant sales success.

And then, IBM, having introduced a well-designed, highly functional computer with a sterling brand name and an open architecture did the last, most significant thing it would ever do in the microcomputer hardware business. It did nothing. And it did it for 6 crucial years.

With this "action," IBM unleashed the industry's first and to date only "hardware virus." Once introduced into the environment and left to fend for itself, the initially microbial PC hardware standard began to mutate into an enormous Silicon Beast that over the years grew ever larger. Eventually, by dint of its size and influence, the PC standard created a hardware ecosystem around itself that allowed it to continue to grow and flourish without IBM's help or influence. But by the time IBM awoke to the consequences of its historic inaction, it was too late. The Silicon Beast had ambled clear of the ability of any one company to control or manipulate it to its exclusive benefit. A flourishing and open hardware universe had come into being, one that dominates the technology industry to this day.

During this critical period, IBM did introduce new computers, the most notable being its IBM AT in 1984, a system that surpassed the original PC in market acceptance and sales. But the underlying PC platform and architecture remained open and comparatively royalty-free. Anyone could, and many did, jump into the market to make clones of the PC and AT, including firms such as Compaq (maker of the first "luggable" PC), Dell Computer, and for a period of time, literally hundreds of others, most of whom have vanished unremembered into PC history.

To get a sense of how unique this state of affairs is, consider that today, more than 20 years after the release of the original PC, anyone can, if the mood strikes her, assemble a state-of-the-art computer from standardized parts available from hundreds of vendors. Try doing that with a Macintosh or a Sun Microsystems SPARC (or for that matter, your TV, VCR, DVD, or even your toaster). Apple finally took a stab at allowing a clone market to develop around the Macintosh and the Mac operating system (OS) in 1994, but after his reascension to the Apple throne, Steve Jobs promptly squashed the Mac clones. In the late 1980s and early '90s, Sun Microsystems made great noises about how it was going to unleash its SPARC chip and architecture on the industry and create an open, alternate hardware platform. But despite all of Sun Microsystems CEO Scott McNealy's noise and posturing on the issue, the company, via restrictive licensing terms and subtle tweaks to its hardware platform, kept all potential competitors on a tight leash and prevented a free-for-all clone market from ever coalescing around the SPARC.

In 1987, IBM attempted to take it all back and stuff the PC standard back into its cage with the introduction of its PS/2 line. PS/2s sported a completely new hardware architecture and, in contrast to the PC, IBM closely guarded their hardware specifications in the name of "quality control" and demanded comparatively stiff royalties for its use in competing systems. Fierce, drooling patent attorneys with sharp fangs were called out of their legal kennels to stand guard over every chip, connector, and clump of BIOS over which IBM laid exclusive claim. To show it wasn't kidding about its intent to replace the PC with PS/2, IBM announced soon after the introduction of the new machines that it would discontinue selling PC-type computers.

The PS/2 effort was a complete failure. Yes, the new bus was better and faster than the earlier PC standard. But the PC bus was more than good enough for the hardware of the time and remained good enough for several years after the PS/2 introduction. A group of IBM's competitors, led by upstart Compaq, quickly banded together and proclaimed the existence of the royalty-free Extended (no longer IBM) Industry Standard Architecture (EISA) for those who *really* needed more performance. To IBM's chagrin, almost no one came calling with hat in hand to build PS/2 clones, and IBM was forced to retreat from its "only PS/2 for you" stance and continue making good old PCs while the PS/2 began a long and miserable slide into irrelevance. Most manufacturers ignored both new hardware architectures and simply continued pumping out cheaper and cheaper PC clones to a public eager and ready to buy them. Instead of leading the pack, IBM now found itself yoked by the nose to its own creation, forced to drudge along abjectly behind the growing behemoth with the rest of the hoi polloi.

In the meantime, the Silicon Beast slowly and steadily moved into new pastures, wreaking devastation wherever it browsed. First to be driven to extinction were the CP/M machines, comparatively fragile creatures, none of which individually had enough market share to allow it to survive for long. Then the Beast chewed through the Apple II's grazing range, driving it from the business market and into the home and education niches, where it eventually withered and died. The commodity nature of the PC standard made it possible to build ever cheaper PCs, and the Silicon Beast ambled into the home market where it slowly suffocated prosaic creatures such as the Commodore 64 and even more exotic creatures like the Amiga and the Atari ST. All disappeared beneath the Beast's massive bulk, their dying cries scarcely catching the market's attention.

For a brief period, Apple's success with the Macintosh offered the company a chance at battling the Beast by creating one of its own, but as with the II and II+, Apple chose a different path. It created the Macintosh reservation, today a delicate biosphere maintained by Mac fanatics and the print and graphics market. Roped off from the rest of the computing world by fancy industrial designs, Yuppie-pleasing cutting-edge colors, and the forbearance of Bill Gates, who has found Apple's continued existence useful as a means of fending off the Feds, the Macintosh lives a rarefied, hothouse existence. In 2002, Apple possessed a 3 percent to 4 percent market share in hardware and had become the world's largest irrelevant $6 billion company.

Unfortunately for IBM, the Silicon Beast proved to be no respecter of parentage. Almost by accident, the Beast devoured the Peanut, the IBM PC's smaller cousin, in the mid 1980s (an event you'll examine in the next chapter). Next on the menu, as already noted, was the PS/2. The Beast then moved on to cut IBM's mainframe computers off from new pasturage. This market, once the heart of IBM's business model, became first a static and then a slowly shrinking environment. Ditto for the once flourishing Silverlake (the code name for IBM's highly successful AS400 minicomputer line).

Still not sated, the Beast turned its eyes in the 1990s to lucrative UNIX markets and ambled off in search of fresh grazing grounds. Niche UNIX vendors such as SGI found themselves starving for profits as their markets were flooded with high-end PCs stuffed with inexpensive memory and increasingly fast processors. And now even mighty Sun Microsystems sees the possibility of an eclipse as the Beast grows larger, its bulk swollen by huge influxes of cheap PCs running Linux, a free UNIX clone that has begun to compete with Solaris, Sun Microsystems's version of UNIX, in power, performance, and reliability.

The long-term consequences of the choices IBM made in building the PC impacted more than just computer manufacturing. The PC's creation led to the decoupling of software from a reliance on proprietary silicon. Prior to the appearance of the IBM PC standard, firms had rarely purchased computers per se; rather, they bought packaged solutions that combined a company's hardware, software, and services. In this tightly bound environment, IBM had clawed its way to overwhelming dominance by dint of ruthless marketing and good products.

But in IBM's brave new (and unexpected) world, the competitive environment had been recast. For example, prior to the existence of the PC, little attention was paid to the microprocessor, the actual computer that resided at the heart of any system. But as it became obvious to everyone that PCs were simply collections of standardized parts that anyone could assemble, interest grew in the actual distinguishing characteristics of one computer from another. Intel would recognize this opportunity and take advantage of it in the coming years to become the closest thing the industry has to an arbiter of hardware standards, though the company's ability to dictate terms and conditions to the market has never approached IBM's imperial authority.

Even more significant was that the creation and spread of the PC standard meant that software, not hardware, now formed computing's nexus of power. With computers reduced to a growing aggregation of almost identical silicon clones, control over operating systems, data formats, application programming interfaces (APIs), and Web standards would determine market supremacy and company profitability. As IBM slipped from the apex of power, another company would rise to supplant it, a tiny upstart that better understood this new world's new rules and what it would take to master them. Big Blue was fated to be eclipsed by Great Green.

~

Great Green Rising:
Digital Research and Microsoft

In its 2001 rankings of the 100 largest independent PC software companies in the United States, Jeffrey Tarter's *Software Success* newsletter reported that Microsoft represented 69 percent of total revenues. In the categories of operating systems, business applications, development tools, Internet browsers, database management systems, and server software of different types, Microsoft had a monopoly, dominant, or substantial market shares. As the twenty-first century dawned, Microsoft had replaced IBM as the company most people were likely to admire and revere or distrust and hate. And today, no one "ever gets fired for buying Microsoft."

Reluctant Ahab

As with the IBM PC, many myths surround the rise of Microsoft to high tech's position of paramount leader. The seminal myth hearkens back to the company's anointment as the supplier of the OS for the PC, the single greatest coup in the history of business. The popular story (backed up by such sources as *The Pirates of Silicon Valley*, an interesting and well-acted film that does a complete disservice to the cause of truth) is that IBM intended to use Digital Research's buff new 16-bit operating system, CP/M-86, for its new PC.

Kildall, through a series of misunderstandings and miscommunications that to this day are the stuff of legend, refused to talk to IBM's representatives. IBM then turned to Microsoft for its OS. Despite the fact that Microsoft had no such product, the company bamboozled IBM into agreeing to buy a nonexistent product, then turned around and scarfed up Quick and Dirty Operating System (QDOS) from a small computer company, Seattle Computer Products. QDOS was written by Tim Paterson to support an 8086[6] prototyping board that the company was selling to software developers.

---

[6] Ads for this board appeared in *BYTE* magazine.

The reality is a bit different. In 1981, the industry's biggest fish first swam up to Microsoft, not Digital Research, in search of both computer languages and an OS for the PC. At the initial meetings, Gates candidly informed IBM that Microsoft had no OS to sell. At the time, Microsoft made most of its money from the sale of languages, particularly BASIC. Microsoft was overjoyed at the chance to sell its products to IBM, but it suggested that for an OS, IBM representatives should contact Kildall and Digital Research to talk about CP/M-86. Dutifully, the Big Blue Whale traveled south to California to meet with Kildall, who didn't think the initial conference important enough to attend and allowed his wife, a vice president at the firm, to conduct the opening ceremonies. There was an argument about signing a confidentiality letter, neither group found much to like about the other, and IBM left Digital Research without even a preliminary agreement to talk about CP/M-86.

The IBM contingent then asked Gates to talk to Kildall and persuade him to be more receptive to their overtures, but even this led nowhere. IBM was "the establishment" and many programmers brought up in the 1960s and '70s regarded the company with a certain disdain. IBM was big, bureaucratic, and its machines, although beloved by big businesses everywhere, weren't accessible to hackers and hobbyists. Kildall, in tune with the spirit of the Altair and doing a nice business with CP/M, wasn't overly impressed by IBM and saw no need to kowtow. It was only after these initial rebuffs that Microsoft stepped into the OS situation and agreed to provide one for an IBM becoming increasingly nervous about meeting its ship dates for the IBM PC. After all, if IBM couldn't ship its PC, it wouldn't need Microsoft's BASIC. Fortunately for everyone concerned, except Gary Kildall, the serendipitous existence of QDOS made it possible for Microsoft to deliver on its promise.

Over the years, rivers of ink have been spilled bemoaning Gary Kildall's rotten luck and the cruelty of an unfair world, but most of the hand-wringing seems misplaced. Kildall had been placed in the unique position of having had the largest of large blue whales swim up to his door, beach itself in his office, roll over on its belly, and point to the spot where the harpoon should be placed, and he had refused the shot. A fair person can hardly blame Bill Gates for stepping up to the prow for his own throw at the great beast and, unlike Kildall, Gates's aim was true. The contract he negotiated with IBM turned out to be Microsoft's first step on the road to industry supremacy.

Yet, even this happy turn of events for Microsoft was not all it seemed. It would take further blundering on the part of Digital Research before the company was truly and finally fish food.

When the PC first shipped, PC DOS was indeed the operating system of record. But this didn't mean as much as it seems. DOS wasn't pre-loaded on the IBM PC. The unit had no hard disk and DOS wasn't stuffed on a chip in your PC. You booted your OS from a floppy every time you turned on the machine.[7] Nor was DOS bundled into a purchase of a PC. It came in a separate box and you paid for it separately. During the initial rollout, IBM had put no extensive marketing push behind DOS; all of its emphasis was on the PC. But as the system's sales momentum built, IBM did, however, make much of the fact that no less than three OSs were available for the PC: PC DOS; the UCSD p-System, which was really a development system for programmers interested in developing "write once, run anywhere" software (no, Java wasn't the first time someone had that bright idea); and . . . CP/M-86.

CP/M-86? How did that get in there? Hadn't Kildall blown it in those legendary meetings and phone calls?

Well, not completely. As the enormity of what he had done began to sink in, Kildall took a close look at a copy of the forthcoming IBM OS and noticed that, by golly, it sure looked a lot like CP/M. And that didn't seem fair at all. There quickly ensued some legal harpoon rattling, a quick visit to Boca Raton, and voila! CP/M-86 was now an officially supported IBM OS that shipped in an IBM box and was available directly from IBM.

CP/M-86 was late to market, but despite this shortage of software support, it would be no problem for the still feisty DOS competitor. The press and most technical gurus regarded CP/M-86 as superior to DOS, and publishers of older CP/M software hadn't found it hard to port their applications to the new OS. For example, MicroPro, at the time the world's largest microcomputer software company, had ported WordStar, the industry's leading word processor, as well as most of its other business packages, to CP/M-86. Ashton-Tate, publisher of the best-selling dBASE II, had a CP/M-86 version of the program. Other companies produced spreadsheets, games, utilities, and other products in anticipation that CP/M-86 would quickly sweep DOS from the market.

---

[7] As a salesman at Macy's "professional" computer store, I attempted many times to sell prospective customers CP/M-86 instead of IBM DOS. Having worked with CP/M in its 8-bit incarnation, I knew it was a superior choice, but the product's pricing made it almost impossible to sell.

Nothing of the sort happened. Compounding his initial errors, Kildall had made a fundamental pricing mistake with CP/M-86. Upon the introduction of the IBM PC, the cost of PC DOS had been set at $40.00 (when anyone actually paid for it; the product was heavily pirated). This decision by IBM had reset market expectations as to what an OS for a microcomputer should cost (a reality the company would find out 6 years later applied to itself during the introduction of OS/2). CP/M-86 upon its release cost $240.00, a price close to that paid by purchasers of the 8-bit CP/M. The huge disparity in price made it almost impossible to sell CP/M-86 to retail purchasers and the OS began to wither almost immediately.

Years later Kildall would claim that IBM had decided on the price difference between the two operating systems. There is good reason to question this statement. At CP/M East[8] in the autumn of 1983, the last major trade show ever held dedicated to promoting Kildall's brainchild, a group of people[9] from various companies publishing CP/M-86 software cornered Kildall on the busy show floor to discuss pricing and the OS's future. In the impromptu discussion that followed, Kildall was repeatedly implored to adjust CP/M-86's price so that it could compete with PC DOS and warned that failure to do so would kill the product. Kildall was polite, pleasant, and adamant that CP/M-86 was "priced just right." "The market understands the difference between a toy OS and a professional product," he proclaimed before disappearing into the show crowd.

CP/M-86 was effectively defunct by the end of 1984.

A despondent Digital Research would try to make a comeback with GEM, a Macintosh look-alike shell for DOS that enjoyed a brief measure of success before it was crushed by a litigious Apple. In 1987, Digital Research obtained a more solid measure of revenge when it released DR DOS, a "clone" of MS-DOS (though who was the actual clone is a legitimate matter of dispute). Though no major PC vendor ever picked up

---

[8] This show was the first I attended as a MicroPro employee. I spent most of my time demoing InfoStar for CP/M-86 and was one of the people who tracked Gary Kildall down to discuss the pricing issue destroying CP/M-86. This event became legendary among MicroPro employees for what became known inside the company as the "Schmuck 'n' Shark" riot. MicroPro rented out the New England Aquarium for an evening and handed out about 700 tickets for a "Surf 'n' Turf" dinner with an open bar. Approximately 3,000 people crashed the event and a few drunken revelers had to be forcibly restrained from doffing their clothes and diving into the shark tank for a swim. There was a radical contingent from MicroPro in favor of allowing the partygoers to jump in with the sharks and watching what happened, but the more conservative faction prevailed.

[9] I was one of those individuals.

the product, for a couple of years Digital Research did a brisk business selling DR DOS to second- and third-tier manufacturers while simultaneously giving Microsoft and Bill Gates minor fits.

The fun came to an end when Microsoft struck back by placing messages in beta versions of Windows 3.1 that warned users of possible "problems" that might occur if you used DR DOS with Windows.[10] This was all nonsense; DR DOS worked fine with Windows 3.1 and public pressure eventually forced Microsoft to back away from this unsavory tactic, but in the interim a great deal of marketing damage had been done.

More significant were the changes Microsoft made in its licensing agreements that made it difficult to buy MS-DOS without also purchasing Windows, and tied discounts to exclusive purchases of Microsoft products. These were tough tactics and they would come back to haunt Microsoft during its defense against the U.S. government's charges of predatory and monopolistic business practices. But even if Microsoft had been a kinder, gentler opponent, unless a major player such as IBM had intervened, DR DOS could never have amounted to more than a minor presence in a market moving inexorably to a GUI model of computing à la the Macintosh.

Attack of the Clones

The second great myth surrounding Microsoft's rise to power is that the original DOS contract with IBM immediately provided the company with a massive and unfair advantage over its competition. Again, the truth is somewhat different. Over time, Microsoft's DOS contract *did* prove to be a cash cow of legendary proportions, but it took idiocy of monumental proportions on the part of IBM, Apple, and other industry players to transform Microsoft's good deal for its quick-and-dirty DOS into the industry's shiniest gold mine.

From a financial standpoint, the original DOS deal put a nice bit of upfront cash in Microsoft's pocket and provided the company with a lucrative revenue stream from royalties on sales of PC DOS. But far more significant was the fact that the contract gave Microsoft the right

---

[10] Wendy Goldman Rohm, *The Microsoft File: The Secret Case Against Bill Gates* (New York: Times Business Books, 1998). I was a DR DOS user and personally experienced this situation.

to resell DOS to other companies, something the company promptly began to do under the rubric of MS-DOS.

This, however, didn't turn out to be as lucrative a business as Microsoft had initially thought. Many of the first "clones" of the IBM PC weren't true clones; rather, they tried to improve on the PC's design. These machines, from companies such as DEC, Otrona,[11] Radio Shack, Victor, Texas Instruments, Hyperion, and many others that have vanished into obscurity, were collectively known as "MS-DOS clones." Some offered better hard disk support, sported different keyboard layouts, and provided better graphics capabilities, an area in which the original PC was considered weak.

It was the issue of graphics support and compatibility that proved lethal to the MS-DOS machines. Developers for the IBM PC had discovered something about MS-/PC DOS very early on: It displayed graphics slowly. To solve the problem, software developers quickly learned to bypass the OS and directly access IBM's graphics hardware to improve screen performance.

The appearance of the MS-DOS clones presented software developers with a dilemma. Should they build customized versions of their software to support these new computers, most of which didn't possess substantial market share? Or should they hedge their bets and use MS-DOS to handle screen updating? Most hedged, and buyers of MS-DOS clones soon got used to watching their software work veeery slooowly on their systems while IBM PC users enjoyed word processors and spreadsheets that seemed to snap to attention. Interest in the MS-DOS clones, which had been high, was soon replaced by skepticism, and then derision. No one wanted an MS-DOS clone; everyone wanted an IBM PC or a true PC compatible, one able to run IBM PC software out of the box. The MS-DOS clone market quickly collapsed and Microsoft's advantage seemed less significant than it had been.

But fortunately for Bill Gates and company, IBM had unleashed the Silicon Beast. As quickly as the MS-DOS clones withered from the market, they were replaced by hordes of IBM compatibles able to work with PC displays and graphics without any need for machine-specific customization. All the new generation of clones required to go to market was an MS-DOS license. Microsoft's IBM deal started to turn golden indeed.

---

[11] I had use of an Otrona, a "light" portable (around 20 pounds) for about a year in the early 1980s. The unit was retrofitted with a compatibility board that let it run most IBM PC software.

Microsoft's good fortune was compounded by a decade of fumbling stupidity on the part of IBM as it sought a replacement for MS-DOS. First to flop was TopView, a clunky, multitasking, character-based pseudo-OS released in 1985 just as Apple's Macintosh was educating the market on the benefits of a GUI. Next to fail was something called CP-DOS (one of its many names), an abortive attempt to create an OS that took full advantage of the IBM AT's 80286 chip. Along the way, IBM continued to break Gary Kildall's heart with flirtations over different versions of CP/M-86 that never lead to consummation. OS/2 has earned its own inglorious chapter in this book. In the mid-1990s, after its storied divorce from Microsoft, IBM even attempted to sell its own version of DOS in the retail and original equipment manufacturer (OEM) markets and did as well with it as it had with OS/2.

But IBM would never succeed in developing a successor to DOS. Apple would never follow its own early example with the Apple II and liberate the Macintosh OS from its sterile preserve to grow and flourish in an open environment. Digital Research would eventually fade away, unable to ever recover from its early missteps.

Over the next 20 years, Microsoft would make the most of its competitors' mistakes and stupidity as it slowly leveraged its advantage in desktop OSs into absolute control over what would prove to be high tech's most strategic terrain. Using the generically named Windows as its base, it would slowly branch out to take control of the business applications market, and then move from there to a position of preeminence on the Web. Like its competitors, Microsoft wouldn't always be completely ethical or nice in the way it did business. But unlike them, Microsoft would consistently avoid making stupid mistakes again and again and triumph from this ability.

three

A RATHER NUTTY TALE:
IBM and the PC Junior

To fully appreciate the tale you're about to read, we must take a trip back through time. We begin our journey in search of ancient high-tech stupidity by boarding a time machine of the imagination. Step into our conveyance, sit down, hold tight, and let's begin our journey to modern high technology's Paleolithic era. Even the word "microcomputing" gives us a sense of antiquity and great age; these days, we say "desktop computer" or "workstation." Relax as we travel through eons of high-tech time—in fact, all the way back to early 1980s! Enjoy the ride.

As we arrive safely at our destination and fly over the Lost World of Technology, we see it's a strange and archaic place inhabited by even stranger dinosaurs of computing. Let's land, leave our time machine, and explore a bit. It should be fairly safe on the ground—for the most part, the creatures we see are friendly, if a bit hard to use, and won't "byte."

As you step out of the time machine, look over to your left. There you'll see the vanished Elysian Fields of CP/M. Note the wide variety of species. For example, there's a common Blue Case Osborne and its rarer brethren, the earlier brown hide variant. It's a placid beast unless you try to pick it up; then it's liable to dislocate your shoulder. That's because it weighs about 30 pounds. Ouch. Nonetheless, it's the first portable computer! The Osborne came in a sewing machine–style case that included a 5" CRT, dual floppies, and an incredible software bundle consisting of CP/M, WordStar, SuperCalc, BASIC, and later even a database. And all for only $1,795.00! It went extinct when it grew too fast and tried to give birth to a new IBM-compatible offspring before it was ready. You can read more about this fabulous creature in John Dvorak's classic tome, *Hypergrowth: The Rise and Fall of the Osborne Computer Corporation.* Sad.

To the right of those Osbornes, note the Sol Processor unit. It's a handsome beast, with its polished walnut flanks. Lumbering about behind it you can see different varieties of Northstars, Morrows, Kaypros, Cromencos, and similar ungainly looking creatures. We suggest you not get too close—if one of those beasts falls over on your foot, you're liable to break a toe.

Directly ahead you'll see verdant green meadows inhabited by various species of Apple IIs. No shortage of them! Much harder to spot is the rather fragile and delicate Apple III. When it was first introduced, the new system seemed not to work well unless you read an Apple service bulletin advising you to pick the unit up and drop it from a height of several inches to help reseat its memory chips. We believe this species went extinct from sheer embarrassment.

In those woods to your right you'll see many colorful and interesting specimens of the home computer family, including Commodore VIC-20s and 64s, TI99/4As, Atari 800s and 400s, and a bevy of Sinclairs. These species tended to be short lived, with the exception of the Commodore 64, which was prolific. If you look closely you'll see a truly fascinating hybrid, a Coleco Adam. This odd beast was the offspring of Coleco's fabulously successful Cabbage Patch Kids line of amazingly ugly dolls. The company used the profits from the Kids to go high tech, and the Adam was the result. The unit was aimed at the home market but ran the CP/M operating system, which loaded from an integrated tape drive. Historians believe these units were actually designed and built *by* the Cabbage Patch Kids; this would account for the fact that about one-third of the Adams that shipped were DOA and that putting the cassette with your OS on top of an Adam's built-in printer tended to erase it.

If you look directly behind you, you'll notice a giant off-white herd thundering our way. These are IBM PCs, but if you look carefully at the hides of these magnificent beasts, you can see they're undergoing an interesting transformation. The "IBM" is slowly fading from their bodies, and soon the only strong identifying mark on these creatures will be the "PC" mottling. We'll need to move out of the way when the herd gets closer because these voracious beasts devour any other computer in their path.

Now, look closely at the edges of the herd. See those little creatures scuttling out of the way and peering at us from under those rocks? They're rather small and ungainly-looking things: "peanut" sized, in fact. They're IBM PC Juniors and they have an interesting tale to tell.

~

The Gods Themselves,
Coming to Your Home Soon

After the IBM PC's release, the Gods of IBM at Boca Raton were feeling, well, pretty godlike. The PC was selling like gangbusters. IBM's initial projections of 221,000 units over 4 years had been laughably wrong: The company actually shipped 200,000 PCs in its first year on the market and by 1982 couldn't keep up with the demand. The PC's big brother, the PC XT, basically a PC with more memory and a hard drive, proved to be an even stronger seller. IBM's "Little Tramp" advertising campaign, based on the famous character created by silent screen star Charlie Chaplin, was regarded as a triumph of successful product branding. An IBM authorization to sell the PC was a license to become a millionaire. The units were in such demand that gray market purchases of PCs were used as money-laundering vehicles for various enterprises of dubious origin.

The question now arose: What next? IBM had a new rock-em, sock-em box in development, the AT, but it would be a couple of years before it was ready. The Gods at Boca Raton cast their Olympian gaze about the land and it came to fall on the home computer market. It seemed a place ripe for exploitation and conquest.

This is because in 1982 a fairly sharp dividing line separated the world of business and home microcomputing systems. The business market was dominated by the IBM PC, Radio Shack, and a bevy of CP/M systems, all of whom were losing market share to the PC on an almost hourly basis. Apple's III system, intended to replace the Apple II as the company's mainstream business machine, had proved to be an embarrassing flop. The Apple II was still a player in the business market, but it was increasingly seen as a pricey and premium home system.

The market for "computers for the home" was controlled by Apple and a supporting cast of interesting players, including Atari, Commodore, Radio Shack, and Texas Instruments. Aside from Apple, none of these was particularly healthy. Atari, with its 800 computer, should have been in fine shape. This system, the direct ancestor of the even more fabulous Amiga, was almost a decade ahead of its competitors with graphics and sound coprocessors and even a primitive version of today's USB bus. Unfortunately for the company's computer aspirations, by 1982 Atari's core market, gaming consoles, was undergoing a storied meltdown.

The inferno had been lit by the release of the worst game in computing history, an *E.T.* title based on the movie of the same name. Unleashed on an unsuspecting American public just in time for the 1982 Christmas season, *E.T.*'s idiotic story line, ugly graphics, and tedious and illogical game play transformed what was supposed to be a treasured holiday gift into a lump of coal left under the tree. The game was sold in the hundreds of thousands during the holiday season[1] and carted back to stores in almost equal numbers after the season was over, the deluge of returns driven by the screams and wails of America's disappointed tykes. Almost single-handedly, *E.T.* the game destroyed the American video-game industry of the 1980s and transformed Atari's 2600 cash cow game console into cow flop in the living room. The market wouldn't recover from the *E.T.* debacle until Japanese manufacturer Nintendo revived it by ensuring that only games that adhered to basic standards of quality control reached America's TV screens.

Commodore's VIC-20 and C64 units were shipping like crazy and appeared to present a more formidable challenge. Commodore was headed by the semilegendary Jack Tramiel, a Holocaust survivor who had started out in the business as a typewriter repairman in the Bronx. Tramiel, who liked to periodically proclaim that "business is war" followed a "computers for the masses, not the classes" strategy of relentless price cutting. As a result, finances always seemed dicey at Commodore, and although the company shipped lots of units, profits were slim. Quality control was also an issue: When the C64 first shipped, at least 25 percent of the units were DOA.[2] If business was war, no one doubted that IBM would blow Tramiel out of his trenches with a Big Blue cannon.

---

[1] As already noted, I briefly worked in Macy's consumer electronics department. *E.T.* was rolled out in time for the 1982 Christmas season, and I personally sold many copies of this gaming abomination to parents eager to satisfy the consumer longings of their offspring. I must confess I told some people the game was "OK," an act for which, if there is an afterlife, I will undoubtedly pay a suitable penance.

[2] Despite this discouraging start, the unit did go on to have fairly long and successful run, particularly as a gaming machine. Software emulators exist that allow you to experience the joys of early 1980s 8-bit computing with the Commodore 64 on your PC today.

Radio Shack was too busy trying to figure out how to keep its business systems alive in the face of the IBM juggernaut to spend much time worrying about its color computer, though the unit would find a second life overseas in Britain. And speaking of the mother country, British inventor Clive Sinclair's namesake, the black-and-white Sinclair ZX80, was cheap and the computing curious bought quite a few of them, but it was difficult to find someone who actually used the system for much. Industry analysts proclaimed it the first closet computer. You bought it, played with it a bit, and then tossed it in your closet and bought a "real" computer.

Finally, another major contender in the home market, Texas Instruments's TI99/4A, would soon disappear from the market. The TI99/4A was perhaps home computing's most luckless system, the ongoing victim of an incredibly stupid marketing campaign that included the following:

- Shipping the unit with no way for software publishers to write software for it
- Threatening third-party publishers who did figure out how to write software for it
- Hiding the existence of a software language shipped with the machine that made it easier to write software for it
- Providing no storage system for the computer until months after it shipped (not even a cassette player)
- And, finally, initiating a price war with Commodore, the discounting kings of computing, that led to Texas Instruments losing up to $50.00 on every unit shipped

Texas Instruments would withdraw from the home market in 1984 after losing about $500 million on the TI99/4A. This may not have been the last time the industry heard from this system; observers postulate that the TI99/4A returned from the grave in 1998 and possessed the souls of thousands of Internet marketers.

~

The Market Goes Nuts

Thus, with the home front in varying degree of chaos, confusion, and despair, the time seemed right for IBM to step in and bring its brand of peace and order to the market. A new IBM PC for mom, pop, and the kids code named "Peanut" was decreed and announced to a market agog to know more. To heighten industry interest, IBM blanketed the project in tight secrecy and few accurate details about the machine leaked out before its 1983 release. Only a handful of resellers were allowed to see the machine while it was in development, and loose lips were sealed by IBM's threat to relieve blabbermouths of their valuable license-to-print-money IBM authorizations. (IBM wasn't kidding about the Peanut's security—an indiscreet electronics buyer at Macy's who leaked some accurate details about the Peanut to the press lost his job.)

The Peanut's announcement immediately threw the industry into an orgy of feverish speculation. In the months leading up to the system's rollout, an entire mini-industry sprung up dedicated to making pronouncements and prognostications about the Peanut's feature set, its impact on the market, and its effect on the competition. As the Peanut's release date neared, the buzz reached a higher and more frantic pitch. Guesses about the system's configuration and capabilities included statements such as the following:

- The Peanut would have an 8086 processor (the big brother of the PC's 8088).
- The Peanut would have an 80286 processor (the chip that would be the brains of the IBM AT).
- The Peanut would have an 80386 processor (an Intel chip that wasn't built yet).
- The Peanut would have a huge amount of memory, maybe even a whopping 1MB of the stuff (most IBM PCs maxed out at 640KB).
- The Peanut would have a hard drive like the XT, but bigger.
- The Peanut would have multiple coprocessors à la the Atari and Commodores.
- The Peanut would be a supercomputer in a box.

- The Peanut would be a supercomputer in a box and be incredibly inexpensive.

- The Peanut would be a supercomputer in a box and be incredibly inexpensive and look incredibly futuristic and cool.

- The Peanut would help solve world hunger and war. (No, I'm not kidding. You know, because everyone would have a supercomputer on his desktop, he'd be able to communicate with others and thus reach across national/ethnic/religious/political boundaries to create a new world of greater understanding and harmony, etc., etc., kumbayah, kumbayah.)

- The Peanut would have great graphics.

- The Peanut would have *really* great graphics with fabulous symphonic sound.

- The Peanut would have a matter transporter unit that would dematerialize you à la *Star Trek*, and then rematerialize you inside the computer so that you could play games in the first person! (OK, yes, I *am* kidding, but speculation peaked just a bit under these levels.)

But the most interesting bit of prognostication offered about IBM's newest offspring was that the Peanut would be so wonderful, so powerful, and so cheap that everyone would want one instead of an IBM PC. Industry watchers spent much ink and time speculating about how IBM would deal with this new wonder box that would immediately cannibalize the market of its incredibly profitable and fast growing PC franchise. Pity was expressed on behalf of this amazing colossus that didn't even know its own strength.

But whatever the unit did or didn't have, everyone was sure that when it shipped it would be a huge smash. The IBM PC and XT had already proved that IBM could do no wrong. Retailers fought for early allocations of the precious few units that would be available upon the system's official unveiling. Buyers feverishly flooded into stores and laid down their money in advance so that they could be the first on their block to have a precious Peanut. The press drooled. The pundits prayed. The clock slowly ticked. The minutes dragged by. People's hearts felt as if they would seize in their chests. And then . . . in November 1983 . . . the unit . . . shipped.

And the world . . . shrieked.

The Nut Grinder

Not in approval, mind you. With the shell of secrecy surrounding the Peanut finally cracked, it was immediately apparent to observers that something had gone terribly wrong. For starters, the unit was ugly, an ungainly white lump of a system that just seemed to lie there. No swoopy futuristic curves or neat little design fillips. If the PC Junior represented computer designs of the future, the future looked like Mr. Spock's box of Kleenex. And it was an expensive box: A base PC Junior with monitor cost about $1,000. Not that different from a PC.

The PC Junior was also not richly appointed with accessories by any means. It had one measly 5" 360KB floppy drive and no room for another inside the system. And even in 1983, one floppy drive wasn't enough storage to get much done. There was no hard drive and it wasn't easy to add one. There *were* two cartridge slots, which developers had learned to avoid like the plague because shipping software in large bulky plastic chunks drove the cost of goods of your product up by several thousand percent.

There were no slots, either. Instead, you added expansion capabilities to the PC Junior via what were called *slices,* ungainly small white lumps you stuck on to your ungainly large white lump to make a computer that was even lumpier. And they were expensive as well. In fact, all of the PC Junior's accessories were expensive.

A look into the PC Junior's innards was even more disappointing. Not only were there no exotic graphics and display coprocessors, but you also had to buy extra memory to look at an 80-character display instead of the unit's default 40 characters. OK, the unit had 16 colors, and the PC had only 4, but still. You couldn't even add the crummy math coprocessor, used to speed up spreadsheet operations, that you could on the IBM PC. And there was no 8086, 80286, 80386, or any other superchip on Junior's motherboard—just the same stolid 8088 used in the IBM PC running at an unexciting 4.7MHz.

Adding the final insult to injury was the pièce de résistance of the whole ugly, expensive ensemble: the infamous "chiclet" keyboard. This abomination consisted of a plastic slab festooned with small, flat, stiff, rectangular rubbery keys that looked like pieces of chewing gum and provided little feedback when struck. Because these keyboards could be built cheaply, Atari, Texas Instruments, and Commodore had used variants of this design in some of their systems, but users loathed them. Trying to touch type on the PC Junior's unyielding slab was a wearying and frustrating experience; one commentator who received the PC Junior as a Christmas gift described the feeling like that of "having one of Santa's elves continuously whack on your fingertips with his little hammer."

Adding fuel to the fire was the fact that the original IBM PC's keyboard was a storied design loved by many. Many people swore by their IBM boards, which sported a "clicky" and pleasant tactile touch, and vowed they would give them up only when they were pried from their cold, dead fingers. IBM clearly knew how to build something a typist could live with. But this wasn't it.

In short, the PC Junior was obviously a chopped and crippled version of the IBM PC, and after some initial head scratching by the market, people decided they didn't want a second-class computer. Not even promotions like a free replacement keyboard and other goodies could save the PC Junior. Over the next 2 years the system died an ugly and painful death, as did IBM's reputation for marketing invincibility.

What had gone wrong? Well, obviously the Gods of Boca Raton (now reduced in rank to midlevel deities) had been listening very carefully to the words of those who had wondered about the Peanut cannibalizing sales of the PC and had taken very explicit measures to ensure this would never happen. But to achieve its goal, IBM had committed two great marketing sins.

The first, perhaps most forgivable sin was failing to understand the power of the Silicon Beast the company had unleashed on the industry. As early as 1982, the IBM PC's architecture was regarded as the industry standard. Even IBM needed to tread carefully if contemplating changes to it, as the reaction to the PC Junior's slices illustrated.

An alternate strategy did exist to IBM's chop and change approach: "embrace and extend." Although IBM found the market would fiercely resist arbitrary changes to the existing PC hardware standard, the company was, in 1982, still in a position to improve it with proprietary extensions. For example, IBM could have introduced a new graphics coprocessor system (and charged royalties to use it). Or it might have added a new high-speed extension to the PC's underlying bus architecture, perhaps something similar to today's USB technology (and charged royalties to use it). A smarter company than IBM, Microsoft, would learn from these mistakes and years later use the embrace and extend strategy to meet the challenges of "open" standards by converting them to proprietary technologies Microsoft could control and charge for.

~

The Nuttiness of Subtractive Marketing

IBM's second, more serious sin was committing the unholy practice of subtractive marketing. *Subtractive marketing* works by taking a successful product and subtracting key capabilities and features until the product is clearly different from, and inferior to, the original. The subtractive marketer then attempts to pawn off her second-class creation by advertising it as a "value" or a "money saver." It never seems to work. People will, if they have the choice, always refuse to buy something that brands them as not being able to afford anything better. Even people who are thrifty like to go in style; they just don't like paying for it.

Examples of subtractive marketing abound both inside and outside the high technology market. In the auto industry, a classic example is the Ford Falcon. The brainchild of "whiz kid" Robert McNamara, the Falcon was designed from the get-go as a "people's car." In other words, it couldn't go very fast, got good gas mileage, and was economical to run. Extolling these virtues was the car's deliberately plug-ugly design, one that proclaimed the vehicle was in the service of the lumpen proletariat, those who only drive and serve. The lumpen proletariat didn't appreciate the sentiments the Falcon reflected, and although people who couldn't afford anything more bought the Falcon, they drove the car without joy and bought few of the optional accessories that made selling the car profitable.

On the other hand, the Ford Mustang when it was released in 1964 was a phenomenon and Ford couldn't make enough of them to meet demand. Mustangs were fun, sexy, and desirable. Mustang owners were intelligent and cool people with a great sense of value, the type of folks you wished would invite you to a barbecue at their place. Of course, the Mustang also wouldn't go very fast (though it looked like it could), got good gas mileage, and was very economical to run. This is because it was, underneath its alluring sheet metal, nothing more than a reskinned

Ford Falcon. But by dint of good design and the addition of key features that proclaimed the car wasn't for old farts (like a snazzy steering wheel and bucket seats) and sporty options (like high-profit, high-performance engines), the Mustang became a car you could aspire to, whereas the Falcon was just a cheap set of wheels.

The Ford Mustang illustrates the other path IBM could have taken in the design of the PC Junior. Prototypes of other PC Juniors were built and examined before the disastrous "chopped" version was decided on—models that had faster microprocessors than the PC (one promising design incorporated the 80186,[3] a hot little chip for its day), much improved graphics, a hard drive, the PC's bus, and so forth. In point of fact, several of these proposed designs were indeed more powerful and advanced than the IBM PC. Could any of them have been introduced without cannibalizing PC sales?

Easily, by executing a "building toward" marketing strategy. The PC Junior was intended to be a computer for the home, and games and entertainment are an integral part of that environment. To keep the PC Junior out of business, all IBM had to do was

- Integrate a joystick directly into the PC Junior's keyboard.
- Superglue several ROM chips containing the most addictive game titles IBM could find to the PC Junior's motherboard.
- Make the addictive games immediately available to the user at the push of a key (a dedicated "Game" button on a normal keyboard would have been a nice fillip).
- Provide a "one-touch" screen blanker capability.

These features not only would have ensured Junior would not be bought by businesses, but you also would probably have been fired for bringing one into the office. No company would have touched a machine that permitted its employees to play games at their desktop at the touch of a button. Yet no one could have criticized IBM for building a computer that did exactly what it promised to do. And providing the PC Junior with advanced capabilities would have justified its premium pricing.

Subtractive marketing has also proved to be a particular peril for software developers because code bases are so malleable. Again and again companies have taken a popular software product, yanked out

---

[3] In point of fact, Tandy Corporation later introduced a PC based on the 80186, the 2000.

some key features (Whoops! There goes the spelling corrector!), slapped a quick coat of marketing "paint" on the skeletal remains, and voila! A "lite" product is born. Over the years, publishers have created myriad "executive" word processors, "student" spreadsheets, "simple" databases, and so forth, all based on existing and popular products. None has ever been particularly successful.

And, in fact, several software publishers followed the PC Junior down the subtractive path, creating chopped versions of their flagship products. MicroPro, for instance, created a "Junior" version of its market-leading WordStar program.[4] Tens of thousands of copies of the product ended up in the remainder sections of major retailers and in the back pages of *Computer Shopper*. Not having learned its lesson from WordStar Junior, MicroPro made the same mistake with a later "lite" product, Easy.

Amazingly enough, IBM's experience with the PC Junior seemed to teach the company little. With the exception of the IBM AT in 1984, which would be its last unqualified success in the desktop market, IBM continued to release a steady stream of computing clunkers, including the IBM Convertible and the IBM Portable, that missed the mark. IBM's funniest flop was a little-remembered debacle called the XT/286. This was an attempt to shoehorn an AT into an XT case. The XT/286 sported a cacheless microprocessor setup (*cache* is memory dedicated to storing programming instructions for the chip and speeds up operations), thus ensuring the system ran dog-slow, and a case design that prevented buyers from inserting most AT accessory cards into the computer. The XT/286 quickly went to a well-deserved repose in the same landfills holding stacks of unsold PC Juniors and discarded chiclet keyboards.

It all culminated in the disastrous launch of the IBM PS/2 line in 1987, a marketing fiasco that demonstrated to the world that the PC standard now existed independently of IBM's control. Throughout the 1990s, IBM steadily lost ground in a market it had once owned. In 2001, 20 years after the release of the first PC, IBM announced it was exiting the PC desktop market, unable to compete with a company launched by a college kid in his dorm room (Michael Dell), an upstart cloner (Compaq), and a guy who talked to a cow (Gateway).

---

[4] I spent a tedious 3 days in 1984 at a trade show in Boston demoing WordStar for the PC Junior to an audience already cognizant that the system was doomed.

four

POSITIONING PUZZLERS:
MicroPro and Microsoft

In the 1970s, fortunes were once again to be found on the West Coast of the United States, though instead of gold, the new wealth was hacked out of silicon and on computer terminals. As had occurred in the 1840s, hordes of young people from the East Coast headed west seeking fame and fortune and an IPO. One of these hardy pioneers was a fellow by the name of Seymour Rubinstein, a New York transplant who upon his arrival out west soon found work with one of the industry's pioneers, IMSAI, a company building clones of the seminal Altair system. Rubinstein served as the company's marketing director but soon decided the real gold lay in selling software and left to found his own company, MicroPro.

~

Death by Doppelganger: MicroPro

Rubinstein's initial goal in founding MicroPro was to develop and publish a high-end database management system (DBMS) designed to compete with Ashton-Tate's dBASE and similar products, but during his stint at IMSAI, he learned there was a need in the CP/M market for a good programmer's text editor. Because developing one would take less time than a full-blown DBMS system and provide the company with a revenue stream until the database product was ready, Rubinstein hired Rob Barnaby, a top-notch assembly language programmer, to build the product. Barnaby, in an inspired burst of creativity, wrote 137,000 lines of code in 4 months and produced both the editor and a high-speed sorting program intended to be the first component in the forthcoming database program, Supersort.

A Star Is Born

Barnaby's text editor was christened WordMaster and upon its release in 1976 sold so well that Rubinstein made the decision to take the next step and release a full-featured word-processing program based on WordMaster. The new product, named WordStar, hit the market in 1978 and quickly became the dominant product in the CP/M market. The product was so highly regarded that it even became popular on the

Apple II, as people bought CP/M computers on a board and slipped them into their Apples so that they could use WordStar.

There were several reasons for WordStar's early success. The first was power: For its day, the product was feature packed. The second was what came to be known as WordStar's *Control-key interface*. Rubinstein had deliberately designed WordStar to meet the needs of touch typists. To enter commands in the program, you held down the Control key (most CP/M systems of the time had one) and pressed a key. WordStar's layout was not mnemonic; instead, in the interest of fast typing, Rubinstein designed the interface so that all cursor movements were performed with the left hand while less common operations fell to the right hand. WordStar users came to swear by this system, and today diehards still retrofit Microsoft Word and other products with add-ins and utilities that resurrect the WordStar keyboard system.

The third and most important factor was that WordStar was the first "What You See Is What You Get" (WYSIWYG) word processor. Prior to WordStar, formatting text with a software product meant sprinkling formatting commands amongst blocks of text, printing out the document to see the results, and then sprinkling in more commands and reprinting until you were satisfied with the results (a process very similar to working with raw HTML and an editor today). WYSIWYG, a term coined by Rubinstein, meant something far different in 1978 than it means today. WordStar, like all early CP/M and IBM software, ran on character-driven screens that couldn't display different fonts or combine graphics with text à la the Mac or a Windows machine. Nonetheless, the software accurately displayed line length and paragraph breaks (assuming you were willing to concede everything you would print was set in 10 pitch), and allowed you to set margins and tab stops onscreen. Soon most word processors were emulating this new approach to editing.

By 1983, WordStar's success had made MicroPro International the largest microcomputer software company in the world, with sales peaking that year at close to $70 million. During this period, MicroPro attempted to diversify into other markets, publishing InfoStar, Rubinstein's long-dreamed-of database product; ChartStar, a business graphics product; and even an unfortunate spreadsheet called CalcStar. (It was unfortunate because the product was infamous for its bugs. Until the product went to its well-deserved and unheralded demise, an entire row of the CalcStar workspace was nonfunctional, and internally the product was known by such nicknames as "WoofCalc" and "DogSheet.") MicroPro even briefly attempted to manufacture its own CP/M computer, the PBM[1] (supposed to remind you of IBM) until someone came to his senses and shut the project down. However, none of these other software products sold particularly well, and WordStar remained the pillar on which the company's fortunes rested.

Version 3.3 of WordStar for both IBM and CP/M computers was released in 1983, sold briskly, and all seemed right with MicroPro's world. Unfortunately, the situation soon changed. Rubinstein had gotten into a contretemps with his WordStar development team and they, depending on who is telling the story, either A) quit or B) were fired. (The departing programmers promptly set up shop in an office not far from MicroPro headquarters and proceeded to found a new company called NewStar, which published a WordStar clone called NewWord. Their fate and MicroPro's would become closely intertwined.)

In any event, at just about the exact moment MicroPro needed to ship an update to WordStar, it had lost the ability to do so. No update to WordStar would appear in 1984 or even in 1985. A 12- to 18-month upgrade cycle had become the norm in the software industry and competitors were busy building new products that matched, then began to surpass, WordStar's capabilities. Things looked bleak until an unexpected savior appeared on the scene.

This white knight was brought to MicroPro courtesy of AT&T. The phone company was about to begin a disastrous foray into microcomputing by introducing a line of new desktop-based UNIX computers that would fail to sell in any significant quantities. AT&T decreed that some choice software fodder needed to be produced for its forthcoming line of white elephants, and the company proposed that MicroPro port WordStar to its UNIX operating system and the C language in return for some cold, hard cash.

MicroPro actually lacked the capability to do this, but a seeming bit of serendipity intervened. Rubinstein got wind of a new software product developed by a programmer outside the company that was written in

---

[1] These computers were assembled in San Rafael, California, on the checkout counters of a former A&P supermarket. They sported dual Z-80 processors, a 5MB hard drive, a quad density single-sided 5" floppy, and Televideo terminals, and they were preloaded with MicroPro software. Only about 100 were ever built and they were sold off to the company's employees. The units were originally supposed to be called "SyStars" (for Seymour Rubinstein). Rumor had it that the reason MicroPro went briefly into the hardware business was that Seymour was jealous that his friend Adam Osborne had a computer named after him.

C, ran under UNIX, and cloned WordStar's functionality and design. Seymour took a look at the embryonic word processor, bought it, hired the programmer who'd written it, and told him to go hire a small team of coders and port WordStar to UNIX.

Operating outside of MicroPro's normal corporate structure, the team worked busily for several months at their task. When they were done, the results of their work weren't what Seymour had originally envisioned. The new "WordStar port" used a mnemonic set of Control key–based keyboard commands, possessed some features that WordStar lacked, lacked some features that WordStar had, and sported a new file format completely incompatible with the original product. It was written in C, and it did run on PCs and the AT&T UNIX boxes. And it was clearly not WordStar.

But by this time MicroPro was desperate. It was now over a year and a half since the release of WordStar 3.3 and the program was growing very long in the tooth indeed. MicroPro decided to make the new product the focus of its future sales and marketing efforts. The new product was named WordStar 2000 (the idea for the "2000" was lifted from the logo of a local furniture store). WordStar 2000 was priced at $495.00, then the median price for a high-end word processor, and rolled out in 1985. The original WordStar remained on the shelves (it was still selling strongly, though sales were slowly declining) at its suggested retail price (SRP) of $495.00.

All hell promptly broke loose. With its release of WordStar 2000, MicroPro had just committed a fundamental positioning mistake. The company would pay dearly for this mistake, ultimately with its very existence.

The Doctrine of Positioning

Positioning as a marketing concept became all the rage in the 1970s and '80s and a great deal of time and ink has been dedicated to the topic. The Orthodox Creed of Product Positioning, as decreed by one of the Great Cardinals of High Technology Consulting, Regis McKenna, is that positioning is a

> " . . . *psychological location in the consumer's mind, pertaining to the relative qualities a company, product, or service may have with respect to its competition.*"

The "relative" qualities a company, product, or service may aspire to in the buyer's mental geography include the following:

- Low price
- Best quality
- Fastest
- Most popular

And so forth.

The virtual locations most desirable for your product or service depend on its particular characteristics, your market, and your competition. For example, in the case of Joe Whitebox's local computer company, it can't credibly claim that it's the leading manufacturer of desktop computers; Dell, Compaq, Hewlett-Packard, or another company owns that "location" in the market's mind. But Joe Whitebox might seize the "service" terrain because he runs a local business and has a shot at making that claim stick.

The Orthodox Creed has, however, often proved inadequate to the needs of software companies. This is because software, by its nature, is an abstraction. The Reformed Creed of Product Positioning for software states that positioning begins with describing a product in such a way that the purchaser can tie it to a real-world process or object. On the face of it, this seems like an easy, straightforward thing to do, and sometimes it is. For example, when word-processing software for desktop computers was first introduced, most people quickly grasped the idea that these products put "a typewriter in your computer." The benefits of fast revisions, spelling correction, and flexible formatting of documents were immediately apparent.

But for other categories of software, positioning has proved to be far more difficult. One of the most famous examples is Lotus Notes. If you're in the software industry, you've certainly heard of Notes and you may even use it. But when the product was first introduced in 1989, Lotus seemed unable or unwilling to explain what the heck the product did. The Lotus Notes 4.0 documentation, rather pathetically, highlights the problem best:

"What Is Notes Anyway?

People have been asking that question since the beginning of time (or at least since Notes first came onto the market). It has been hard for people to define Notes because you can use it to do so many things."

—FROM THE *Notes 4.0 Beginner's Guide,* PUBLISHED IN 1996

Actually, this documentation never **does** tell you exactly what Notes "is." As you can imagine, the Lotus sales force had a great deal of trouble explaining why someone should buy Notes when the company that published it couldn't explain what it was.

(Oh, what does Notes do? Well, its most popular function is as an e-mail management program, a post-office system for your computer network. The most obvious feature that differentiated the product from its competition was that the electronic letters you sent back and forth could be annotated with notes and comments. Other people could see your comments and add their own "under" yours. Not that hard to explain and tie to the real world, but Lotus somehow could never bring itself to do so.)

Positioning Wars

MicroPro's positioning mistake was of a different nature than Lotus's and far more difficult to manage. The release of WordStar 2000 created an irreconcilable positioning conflict that pitted MicroPro against itself. After the product's release, the WordStar user base took one look at WordStar 2000 and decided no thanks, opting instead to sit on its hands until MicroPro released an upgrade to its favorite product. As a result, MicroPro now found itself selling two high-end word processors called WordStar for $495.00 to people using IBM PCs. Precious marketing resources had to be expended in creating collaterals, ads, and promotions for the two products while attempting to provide a convincing rationale for the existence of both.

It was an impossible task. A day selling WordStar 2000 to the market went something like this:

MicroPro: Hi there! We're here to tell you about WordStar 2000, our new word processor!

The Market: Great to see you! But, we have to tell you that while WordStar is a wonderful product, it's hardly new. You must mean this is the new upgrade. Great! I'm so excited! Let's take a look!

MicroPro: No, no, this is WordStar **2000**! It's really totally new!

The Market: Oh. *(Long pause.)* When are you releasing the upgrade to WordStar? In 2000?

MicroPro: No, no, the upgrade to WordStar will be released real soon now!

The Market: Oh. *(Longer pause.)* Well, why will you release a new product in 2000 when you haven't released the upgrade to WordStar?

MicroPro: No, no, WordStar 2000 is available right now! We just call it "2000" because it's new and powerful and easy to use! But you don't have to wait until 2000 to enjoy all those benefits!

The Market: Oh. *(Dead silence.)* In other words, WordStar, which won't be upgraded until 2000, is old and not powerful and hard to use?

MicroPro: No, no, no. WordStar is a classic and is powerful and has a wonderful interface for touch typists!

The Market: Oh. Does that mean you can't touch type with WordStar 2000?

MicroPro: Don't be silly! Of course you can! It's easy to type with WordStar 2000's new mnemonic commands!

The Market: Then is it hard to type with WordStar's regular commands? And don't call me "silly."

MicroPro: Sorry about that! No, you can type quickly with WordStar!

The Market: Then you have to type slowly with WordStar 2000?

MicroPro: Uh, no. You can type really well with both of them!

The Market: Oh. *(Long, long pause, dead silence.)* Now, what's the difference between WordStar and WordStar 2000 again? And why do I have to wait until 2000 for an upgrade to WordStar?

And so it went. Endlessly. Instead of answering why prospective users should buy WordStar, the MicroPro sales force for years tied itself in knots attempting to explain the difference between two products named WordStar.

The confusion within MicroPro was just as pernicious, as the company began to split internally along WordStar/WordStar 2000 fault lines. Within MicroPro there were WordStar aficionados and WordStar 2000 mavens, and each side wondered what the other saw in its choice of a word processor. At one point, the head of the WordStar product development team forbade team members from talking with WordStar 2000 programmers. (A neat trick, as both programming teams worked in the same building.) By 1987, as MicroPro wrestled itself to the mat, it had ceded its leadership of the word-processing market to Microsoft Word and WordPerfect, at the time an independent company.

Yet when things were darkest, MicroPro seemed to come to its senses. A new president, Leon Williams, and new product management, including myself, were brought in to try to sort out the mess. Two things needed to be done immediately. An upgrade for WordStar had to be released ASAP and something had to be done about the conflict between WordStar and WordStar 2000. The task of figuring out the positioning strategy was given to me.

The first thing Williams did was trot down the street to NewStar software, buy the company, and use its NewWord product as the foundation for an upgrade for the long-suffering WordStar user base. The upgrade, called WordStar version 4.0, sold well into the WordStar installed base, though its feature set wasn't truly competitive with other products of the time. MicroPro even released a new CP/M[2] version, which did surprisingly good business and garnered the company much favorable PR. The gloom surrounding MicroPro started to lift.

Repositioning WordStar 2000 was a more difficult task. The logical thing to do would have been to simply shoot the product. Unfortunately, this wasn't practical. Since WordStar 2000's introduction, a fair number of people had bought the program and its sales represented an important revenue stream. Despite MicroPro's fervent wishes, WordStar 2000 was going to stick around for a while.

---

[2] WordStar 4.0 for CP/M was the last major commercial release of software for this OS. I have a copy on 8" disks.

My short-term answer to the positioning conflict was an approach I came to call "façade." This strategy consists of taking a look at two products in conflict, deciding what key features differentiate them, and repositioning one product "away" from the other. In *The Product Marketing Handbook for Software* I describe the goal of a façade program as an attempt to

". . . Buy time . . . to maneuver yourself out of having to explain the differences between the two products so that you can talk about what the products are and why the buyer wants them."

By its nature, a façade approach to a positioning conflict is a transitional strategy. When done correctly and with finesse, it can provide a company the opportunity to decide if it's possible to kill one of the conflicting products, either via a migration strategy or merger, or perhaps relaunch it into a completely different market.

After a quick analysis of the options, WordStar 2000 was rechristened a "word publisher" (the actual phrase was coined by one of MicroPro's top salesman, Jim Welch, who, along with the rest of the MicroPro sales force, was slowly going insane attempting to explain the differences between the two products). And what, you may ask, is a "word publisher"? Well, a *word publisher* is a word processor with exceptional laser-printing capabilities, a particular strength of WordStar 2000 at that juncture. Of course, this claim couldn't withstand market scrutiny over time; in reality, there was no such thing as a word publisher. The claim to differentiation was credible only as long as WordStar 2000 was superior to its competition in this particular aspect of the product. But in the short term, the campaign worked as intended and bought MicroPro some time and maneuvering room. Sales and market share of both MicroPro word processors increased and the price of MicroPro stock rose.

Stupid Printing Tricks

As a "reward" for my efforts I was "promoted" to group product manager and given responsibility for the product management of the resurgent WordStar. A new version, WordStar 5.0, designed to build upon the momentum built by the successful 4.0 release, was being hurried along to market. If MicroPro could launch it in a timely fashion with a competitive feature set, there was a chance the company could regain its lost market leadership, or at the very least generate enough revenue to branch out to new and more lucrative opportunities in other software categories. The product was slated for release in early 1988.

The first thing a product manager does when he or she is assigned responsibility for a new product is take a look at it, and I was soon handed a fistful of disks on which resided the latest version of WordStar. Like any upgrade, it had a raft of new features and capabilities, but to my annoyance you couldn't print with it. A quick look at the files that made up the program revealed why: The newest version of WordStar lacked a printer database.

Now this was odd, because if there was one thing MicroPro had learned to do over the years it was support printers. In the pre-Windows era it was the responsibility of software developers to obtain, test, and debug printers and their drivers to ensure they worked with their particular products. As of 1987, MicroPro had built a quality database of over 300 printer drivers. The information in this database represented years of careful debugging, testing, and implementation of capabilities specific to each printer. When you installed a printer in WordStar and told the program to print, you could be fairly confident that your text wouldn't appear upside down or in a character set that resembled Sanskrit.

What made the omission of the database even more puzzling was that in 1985 a decision had been made at MicroPro to base all future printing code for other products on the WordStar 2000 printer database. It was tested, debugged, and extensive. A low-end word processor, Easy, had been introduced by MicroPro that utilized the 2000 database. Why wasn't it in WordStar 5.0?

Several inquiries made by me to the development group elicited vague responses about "new support" issues and "implementation ques tions." A sense of dread began to haunt my soul. A heavy weight seemed to descend upon my shoulders. More inquiries elicited even vaguer answers. The weight pressing down on me grew heavier. It was time to find out what was going on.

As a product manager I had developed the habit of periodically stopping by the MicroPro development center to schmooze with the programmers about product features and problems while providing them with feedback on what our customers liked and disliked about our programs. One fateful day I headed to the center and floated by the section occupied by the WordStar programming team. While skulking about, I saw a group of agitated programmers pointing at a screen and arguing heatedly.

Sidling closer, I listened to their conversation with growing horror, and then I heard a word that confirmed the bad news I'd been overhearing. The impact of this word on me was stunningly physical. On hearing it, a bright light burst upon my eyes and filled them with a dazzling clarity, one that let me see the future. Simultaneously, the great weight was lifted from my shoulders. This wasn't because I was feeling better; rather, it was due to the fact that I no longer **had** any shoulders as I underwent a miraculous transformation from product manager to small gray rat desperate to abandon a ship I knew would soon be sinking.

That word was "pointer."

As in a hierarchical pointer. As in a hierarchical database pointer. As in the development group had made the decision to discard the WordStar 2000 database and replace it with a new one based on hierarchical database technology. It was an incredibly foolish thing to do and it sealed MicroPro's fate.

To understand why this was a disastrous course, you need to have an understanding of database technology, something that I, having once worked as DBMS programmer, possessed (and something the previous product manager had not). WordStar 2000's printer database was basically a flat relational table. When you installed, say, an HP LaserJet printer, the WordStar install program looked up the driver information for this unit from a row in the printer database. Specific printer functions, such as boldfacing and italicizing letters, were stored in columns within this row.

The new hierarchical database being built for WordStar discarded this paradigm. Printer information was stored in something that resembled a tree. Pointers were used to locate specific information about printer functions within the tree.

In all fairness, there were some minor technical advantages to this new printer structure. For instance, it would be smaller than the 2000 database. MicroPro might save the cost of a floppy in the WordStar cost of goods. But I also knew that hierarchical systems had fallen into disfavor after the introduction of relational technology. No commercially available programming tools or utilities were available on our desktop development platforms to convert the current flat table structure to a hierarchical one. Porting the printer database to the new model would first require building a series of custom programs to accomplish the task.

This would take months. Then the tools themselves would have to be tested for proper operations, which would take more time. Of course, once the database had been ported to the new structure, all printer operations would have to be retested to ensure the accuracy of the process, which would take even more months. There was no way that WordStar 5.0 was going to meet its projected ship date or even come close to it.

Once I confirmed what was going on,[3] I went squeaking to my boss, the vice president of sales and marketing, and warned him of our impending shipwreck. VP to VP, the head of MicroPro's development assured the head of sales and marketing I was exaggerating the situation. Officially, WordStar 5.0 was still on track in development and would ship on time.

As the weeks went by and WordStar still refused to print, I prepared to move myself and my skinny pink tail to what I hoped would be a more favorable clime (I was wrong, by the way). I accepted a senior product management position at Ashton-Tate (the company had a lousy word processor, but I was pretty sure it would print) and handed in my resignation with a final warning to all that financial projections based upon WordStar 5.0 revenues needed to be revamped. On my last day at MicroPro, as I left corporate headquarters and walked through the parking lot to my car, the company's director of direct promotions bustled over to say good-bye. Before I pulled out of the lot for the last time, he informed me that that morning the vice president of development had finally confessed that WordStar 5.0 wasn't going to meet its ship date. Nor could he provide a firm estimate of when it **would** ship. He quoted my boss as saying, "Rick Chapman told me this was going to happen."

The WordStar development group's decision to discard the company's existing printer technology delayed the critical 5.0 release for over half a year. When the release did ship in late 1988, the new version was widely criticized for having a printer database about one-third the size of that of previous WordStar products. Upgrade sales, as well as sales to first-time buyers, were disappointing. Time spent re-creating the

---

[3] Final confirmation, from my point of view, came during an impromptu basketball game near MicroPro's headquarters. Steve Evangelou, a talented programmer at the company, and I had gotten into the habit of driving over to a nearby court to shoot some hoops and discuss company gossip. During a lull in our game he informed me that the WordStar 5.0 project faced some "issues." Before he went further, I interrupted him and said, "Let me guess. You guys have decided to discard the WordStar 2000 database in favor of some hierarchical system and you have no idea of how to port the data over. And we're not meeting our ship dates." He looked at me and said, "I guess you've got a handle on this after all."

printer database was also time not spent on adding new features to the product that would have made it more competitive. The cumulative effects of three blown financial quarters and disappointing sales led to MicroPro's upper management, including Leon Williams and my former boss, being marched out and treated to a summary executive execution. MicroPro had lost its last chance to regain its footing in the market, though the company staggered on in zombie-like fashion for several more years, living off its steadily decreasing installed base of WordStar users. WordStar finally faded away in the early 1990s, subsumed in a merger with a flock of similarly unsuccessful and second-rate software companies. It was an ignominious end to the career of a great piece of software.

The question that remains, of course, is "Why?" What had possessed the development group to embark down such a destructive path? What were their motivations? The technical case for their actions was never strong. That this was the wrong thing to do from a business standpoint was even clearer.

The answer lay in the positioning conflict unleashed within the company. While MicroPro worked hard to placate a confused market, within the company the WordStar versus WordStar 2000 struggle raged on. The WordStar programming team hated WordStar 2000 with a passion and wanted nothing from that product to pollute "its" WordStar. Its decision to rip out the existing printer technology was based on emotion, not a rational cost-benefit analysis of the consequences of such a course.

Positioning problems constantly plague high-technology companies, particularly software ones, due to the industry's rapid pace of change, the malleable nature of software, and acquisitions. In 1991, Borland International split itself along Paradox versus dBASE lines via its purchase of Ashton-Tate. Novell, like MicroPro, would shoot itself in the foot by creating two competing product lines with its purchase of UNIX from AT&T. And in 1993, Microsoft demonstrated with the release of Windows NT that previous success doesn't necessarily provide protection against future stupidity.

∼

Two Software Nags:
Windows 95 vs. Windows NT

The buildup to NT began after the incredibly successful launch of Windows 3.0 in 1990. For the next 3 years, Microsoft spent considerable time proclaiming that this new version of the product, once known as OS/2 3.0, would be the 32-bit successor to the 16-bit Windows 3.*x* product line. But as NT neared completion, complaints began to surface that the product was too big and resource-hungry to fit the existing desktop profile. Microsoft had heard these complaints before with other products, but Moore's Law which, roughly paraphrased, states that computing capacity doubles every 18 months, had always bailed out the company in the past. In a rare case of Microsoft losing its nerve, NT was quickly hustled offstage and repositioned as a local area network (LAN) alternative to Novell's NetWare where, with Novell's unwitting assistance, it enjoyed tremendous success.

Microsoft then cobbled together a DOS-based 32-bit hybrid that would eventually be known as Windows 95 and switched promotional gears, telling everyone that **this** product was in fact the desktop upgrade Microsoft had been promising. Windows 3.*x*'s huge installed base, IBM's ineptitude in marketing the competing OS/2, and a massive promotional campaign all contributed to Windows 95's tremendous sales success. But over time, the positioning problem grew in the critical desktop arena. Windows NT, then 2000 (the more things change . . .), had always been available in a "workstation" version that directly competed with the Windows 9*x* family. After all, both product lines were called Windows. They were both 32-bit operating systems. The desktop versions were comparably priced. They even looked alike. So, which to buy?

Microsoft tried to help customers make the decision via a classically bad 1996 ad campaign many referred to as "Two Nags Racing." A two-page spread, it featured a picture of two horses running neck-and-neck with the caption "You See a Horse Race. We See Two Thoroughbreds." Apparently no one at Microsoft had realized that, well, yes, but the horses **are** racing. And as we all know, only one horse can win. So, which customer is going to ride the losing steed? Faced with such a choice, corporate America paused (and the ad was quickly yanked). Two years after the release of Windows 95, over 60 percent of the U.S. corporate market was still using Windows 3.*x*. This didn't seem to particularly bother Microsoft; after all, businesses would have to upgrade sooner or later and they had only one choice. A Microsoft choice. Right? Right.

~

Some New Nags

A nd then Java appeared. With its siren call of "Write Once, Run Anywhere," corporate America, frozen in place by indecision, decided to give the newcomer a close look. Perhaps this was a safer choice than attempting to pick the right pony in the Microsoft OS sweepstakes. Microsoft, taken by surprise, was forced to "embrace" Java via a humiliating agreement to license it from archrival Sun Microsystems. That done, Microsoft spent enormous amounts of time, effort, and money trying to convert the supposedly platform-independent Java into a proprietary extension of Windows (whichever Windows) **and** introducing a new programming language, C#, to compete with it.

To complicate matters further, Linux, an open-source OS based on UNIX that came with its source code, began making a considerable splash in the market. Bundled with the freeware Apache Web server application by such firms as Red Hat , Linux has made significant inroads into the server marketplace and has relieved Microsoft's NT, Sun Microsystems's Solaris, and Novell's NetWare of significant market share.

Java's future and Linux's ultimate success in loosening Microsoft's iron grip on the OS market are unclear. Microsoft finally learned its lesson and announced that in the future there would be only one Windows product line, XP, with different versions aimed at different users and platforms. But it's also unclear how long and how successful Microsoft's plans to migrate users from all the various other Windows variants will be. As of this writing, Windows 98, really no more than an upgrade of Windows 95, is still the most popular operating system in the world. What's clear is that Microsoft's situation would have been very different if the market had been focused on how to upgrade from Windows 3.*x* and not what to upgrade to. When you give customers a reason to shop, you can be sure they will. The ghosts of WordStar and WordStar 2000, still locked in eternal combat, gibber from high tech's graveyard, a warning to all of the grim fate that awaits those who dare to repeat MicroPro's positioning sin.

five

WE HATE YOU,
WE REALLY HATE YOU:
Ed Esber and Ashton-Tate

In 1987, while working at MicroPro as WordStar product manager, I was assigned to participate in one of high tech's hoariest rituals: a press tour. A press tour consists of arranging for members of your senior management team to meet with key members of the fourth estate and analysts who write about and cover your market. The hope is that once you've established a backslapping, hail-fellow-well-met relationship with an editor from *PC Magazine* or a guru from Gartner they'll be more inclined to write nice things about your company and its products. Sometimes it works out that way. The quid pro quo driving the tour is that in return for putting up with you disturbing their day, you'll provide fresh news for the press and buy research from the analysts. Sometimes it works out that way as well.

Tour personnel usually consist of at least one member of upper management, one member of middle management capable of giving a comprehensive product demonstration (informally, this person is referred to as "the demo dolly"), and a PR person. For this tour, upper management was represented by Leon Williams, then president of MicroPro, I appeared in the role of the demo dolly, and rounding out the group was a sad little PR type who confessed at the end of our trip that she really didn't like working with members of the press. Once you've been on one or two press tours, most people regard them with the same affection as a root canal. Most tours consist of a trip to New York, Boston, and San Francisco, the three major hubs for high-tech media and analysis.

Our itinerary included a side trip to Austin, Texas, to meet Jim Seymour, long-time editor and columnist for the Ziff publishing empire. On the day of our appointed meeting, we trekked out to Seymour's house in the Austin hills, where I dutifully demonstrated the latest, greatest version of WordStar 5.0, the one that couldn't print. Luckily for me, Seymour, engrossed by the Macintosh (as were most members of the press at the time), paid only cursory attention to the demo, and instead insisted on demoing his latest Mac toys for us. Once everyone was done showing off, we settled down for the obligatory period of chitchat before we headed off to the airport and our next stop in the never-ending tour.

~

Heart of Darkness

For no particular reason that I can remember, the topic turned to Ashton-Tate, publisher of the widely popular dBASE database program. Seymour started talking about a meeting he'd attended with other members of the press where Ed Esber, CEO of the database giant, addressed the group. As he began talking about Esber, his face suddenly developed an expression of contempt. He told us how during the speech Esber had stated at one point that he wasn't necessarily the smartest guy in software. Seymour paused, then looked at our group and said, "We were all thinking, boy, you've got that right, Ed." The venom in his voice was surprising.

I didn't pay much attention to the exchange at the time, but after leaving MicroPro to become a product manager at Ashton-Tate, I later realized I'd had my first glimpse into the dark heart of one of software's biggest and most unexpected meltdowns. As events progressed in the industry, it became clear that as far as the PC press was concerned, it was "Ed Esber. He dead." They wanted his head on a stake.

Ashton-Tate at its height in the 1980s was one of software's "Big Three," the other members of the triumvirate being Microsoft and Lotus. Microsoft had DOS, Lotus ruled spreadsheets, and Ashton-Tate was the database king. The lucrative word-processing franchise was being fought over by MicroPro, WordPerfect, MultiMate, Microsoft with its Word product, and a host of smaller players.

dBASE was originally designed to help place winning bets in football pools and was the creation of Wayne Ratliff, a contract programmer at the U.S. Jet Propulsion Laboratory. Although Ratliff didn't get rich on sports betting, he did decide his new software program had commercial potential. Named "Vulcan" in honor of the home planet of *Star Trek*'s Mr. Spock, Ratliff placed his first ad for the product in the October 1979 issue of *BYTE* magazine. At its release, Vulcan was priced at $50.00, and though there was flurry of initial interest,[1] the stress of trying to

---

[1] I was one of the initial purchasers. After purchasing my copy of Vulcan, I taught myself how to program in it and began developing applications that ran on CP/M and MP/M, the multiuser version of CP/M. My specialty was in building inventory tracking and control programs for beer and soda distributors in New York City.

ship, support, and manage a one-man company was overwhelming. Ratliff was on the verge of ceasing operations when software reseller George Tate contacted him.

Tate and his partner, Hal Lashlee, took a look at Vulcan, quickly realized its potential, and bought exclusive distribution rights. At the time of the deal they were running a not-very-successful mail-order software company called Software Plus. Believing that Vulcan would turn things around for their company, they renamed the company Ashton-Tate to give it a more "upscale" image. (A great deal of speculation has centered over where Tate came up with "Ashton"—no one who worked at the company had that name. The general belief is it was picked because Ashton sounded "British." It should be noted, however, that Tate had a pet parrot named Ashton.)

After a quick trademark search uncovered potential problems with the name Vulcan, the product was rechristened dBASE II. There was no dBASE I, but even in the early 1980s people were reluctant to buy 1.0 releases of software products. The company upped the cost of dBASE II to $695.00, a very competitive price for a product in its class and with its capabilities, and placed full-page magazine ads featuring a picture of a sump pump and the proclamation that while the pump might suck, dBASE didn't (or words to that effect). Sales took off and by 1985 Ashton-Tate's revenues were over $100 million a year and climbing, mostly from sales of dBASE II and it successors, dBASE III and III+. The company also enjoyed modest sales success with its Framework integrated product. *Integrated* products attempted to combine word processing, database management, a spreadsheet, and graphics all within a single program. Framework was considered the best of breed in this market segment, but the integrateds, which included titles such as Lotus Symphony and Ability,[2] never sold in the numbers projected, and the category largely disappeared in the early 1990s.

In addition to ads featuring plumbing, another reason for dBASE's quick rise to prominence was that the company made much of the fact

---

[2] The success of Lotus 1-2-3 convinced the industry that if adding rudimentary graphics and some simple sorting capabilities to a spreadsheet was good, then adding the kitchen sink had to be better. Integrated products usually added word processing, more graphics, better database capabilities, and communications to the mix. Some of the integrateds simply extended an existing product further; Lotus Symphony, for instance, allowed you to create documents in one big cell in a spreadsheet. Ashton-Tate's Framework operated on an outline paradigm. Integrated products tended to be big and cumbersome wads of code that lacked robust capabilities, the worst of both worlds.

that dBASE was a *relational database management system* (RDBMS). The relational model was first introduced in a paper published in 1969 by an English computer scientist, Dr. E. F. Codd, who worked for IBM. More flexible and expandable than competing technologies, relational products over time were adopted by most DBMS developers and users.

In addition to a table-oriented paradigm, Codd's definition of a RDBMS also incorporated several key capabilities and functions a product needed to possess before it could be called a "truly" relational system. None of the early RDMBS systems for the PC incorporated all of Codd's requirements, and religious arguments raged constantly over which product was "more" or "less" relational than another. dBASE II was probably "less" relational than some of its competitors, but that also meant it could run on systems with less memory and reach a broader audience. Despite the pooh-poohing of purists, for several years dBASE became almost synonymous with the relational concept.

In 1985, George Tate died unexpectedly of a heart attack at the age of 40 and Ed Esber, his second in command, took over the leadership of Ashton-Tate. Esber was a Harvard-trained MBA and a former product manager at VisiCorp, the company that had seen its VisiCalc spreadsheet eclipsed by Lotus 1-2-3. Esber announced he was going to bring a more professional management style to Ashton-Tate, replacing George Tate's more hands-on and emotional approach. Despite having a bachelor's degree in computer engineering, Esber didn't have a reputation of being technically astute.

Esber did fancy himself something of a business guru, and one of his favorite quotes was "A computer will not make a good manager out of a bad manager. It makes a good manager better faster and a bad manager worse faster." He had something there. It had taken George Tate about 5 years to build Ashton-Tate to software giant status; it would take Ed Esber only 2 1/2 years to put the company on the road to ruin. And Esber had a PC on his desk the entire time.

The key to Ashton-Tate's downfall lay in Esber's idiotic mishandling of the dBASE development community and the impact his actions had on the public's perception of the company. Developers were key to dBASE's early success. This is because in addition to its relational status, dBASE II was one of desktop software's first major "shelfware" products. Despite the inevitable claims that dBASE II was "easy to use," thousands of people who bought it and tried to use it quickly put the product away on a shelf or gave it to a programmer friend. The next database they bought was usually a dirt-simple "Rolodex-in-a-box" bit of software such as PFS File or even Ashton-Tate's own Friday product.

The reason for this was simple and remains true to this day: Powerful database programs are intrinsically hard to learn and use. Properly organizing and structuring data for a task of any size and complexity requires a great deal of thought, planning, and design. As a result, DBMS products are primarily bought by people who write programs for other people.

With dBASE's head start in the market, relational capabilities, and reasonable pricing, a massive aftermarket quickly sprang up around Wayne Ratliff's creation. There were programming utilities that extended the product and made up for its deficiencies, books that taught you how to program in dBASE, training programs that provided hands-on instruction in the product, and thousands of programmers and consultants dedicated to building products and services around dBASE. This third-party market was an invaluable asset to Ashton-Tate because it served as an unpaid sales force of influencers and recommenders that helped push dBASE into new accounts and markets.

Over time, however, Esber came to resent this third-party market and relationships began to sour between the company and the developers. One area of friction lay in the delicate balance the company had to maintain between publishers of third-party utilities for dBASE and Ashton-Tate's natural desire to enhance its product. Ashton-Tate began to develop a reputation among the development community for spotting a profitable opportunity in the dBASE utilities market and then prematurely announcing it was going to release an addition to dBASE that would incorporate the third-party product's functionality in the soon-to-be-released update. The inevitable result of these announcements was that sales of the third-party product would immediately come to a screeching halt as the market waited for the real thing to be released from Ashton-Tate. Unfortunately for several of these companies, many of Ashton-Tate's announcements proved to be hype and vaporware. These antics succeeded in destroying several third-party firms, most notably Fox & Geller, pioneers in providing add-ons for dBASE II and III. The development community began to bubble with resentment toward what it perceived as Ashton-Tate's highhanded and misleading tactics.

An even greater area of friction lay in the nature of dBASE itself. At heart, the product was simply a language and not much more. Products such as dBASE III and III+ provided a simple code-generating shell that allowed neophytes to build very basic programs, but experienced developers used the language and a variety of third-party tools to build more advanced applications. Once an application was complete, it would be distributed with a "runtime" module, a piece of the dBASE code that could run programs but didn't allow you to modify them. Ashton-Tate charged hefty fees for its runtime product. To avoid these fees, developers started building *compilers,* programs that would take dBASE instructions and transform them into *machine code,* .exe files that ran completely independent of any Ashton-Tate product. Sales of the dBASE runtime quickly disappeared, a development Esber didn't appreciate. Worse, he realized that the logical next step was the development of third-party products that combined the dBASE language and a compiler. These programs would compete directly with the company's flagship.

In an attempt to forestall the competition, Esber began to rattle legal sabers, threatening lawsuits against people who he thought were poaching the dBASE franchise. At the beginning, Esber was a bit vague about exactly what the dBASE franchise consisted of, but nonetheless his threats went over very poorly with the dBASE community, who felt it "owned" a piece of the product as well. After all, it was the community's utilities, evangelizing, and development efforts that had helped make Ed Esber a rich man and Ashton-Tate a market leader. Just who was Ed Esber, a man who'd probably never written a line of dBASE code in his miserable MBA existence, to threaten them?

While preparing to unleash the legal dogs of war, Esber simultaneously embarked on an ill-thought-out plan of diversification. In 1985, Ashton-Tate purchased MultiMate, then a leader in the word-processing market, and in 1986, Ashton-Tate bought Decision Resources, publisher of a leading line of business graphics. Although on the face of it the acquisitions made sense, both proved to be big mistakes.

Hartford, Connecticut–based MultiMate got its start in the early 1980s when an insurance firm hired a small group of contract programmers to write a clone of the Wang word-processing system to run on their PCs. Once the project was complete, the group founded a software company to market their new Wang work-alike. For a few years the MultiMate word processor enjoyed brisk sales, particularly in corporations that already had Wang systems installed.

By the mid-1980s, however, MultiMate was already running out of steam. The company wasn't particularly well managed and some of its marketing and advertising programs were amateurish and misfired. One of the company's funniest blunders was its "All He Could Do" ad series. Seeking to capitalize on the fact that the company sold only word-processing products, MultiMate ran a full-page four-color ad that featured Babe Ruth with the caption "All He Could Do Was Hit." Apparently no one at MultiMate realized that when the Bambino was traded from the Boston Red Sox in 1918 he was an all-star pitcher **and** outfielder. (Ruth's lifetime record as a pitcher: 94 wins, 46 losses, .671 pct., 2.28 ERA. After his trade to New York, he pitched infrequently.)

Of more concern was the fact that MultiMate was a nasty and recalcitrant piece of code. From a performance standpoint, the product emulated a 1970s-era Wang word processor all too well; for example, it allowed you to see only one page of a document onscreen at a time, a holdover from an era when memory requirements imposed that limitation. The product's underlying architecture consisted of a poorly documented mass of assembly language spaghetti that over time proved increasingly difficult to extend and improve.

By 1987, MultiMate was consistently placing near the bottom in press reviews and competitive rankings, and sales began to run out of steam. After the best programming minds at Ashton-Tate spent months reviewing the situation,[3] the decision was made that the only way to solve the problem was to rewrite MultiMate from the ground up (or buy a new product and call it MultiMate). Of course, the company was planning to release a new OS/2-specific word processor and that would probably be the final answer to all the problems. In the meantime, Ashton-Tate began resorting to "stuffing the channel" to keep sales of MultiMate moving.

Channel stuffing is a time-honored tactic used by high-tech firms to mask slowing sales. It works by inducing distributors and resellers to accept large amounts of inventory in their warehouses, shipments the company then books as revenue. Incentives include crazy low prices, generous payment terms and, most important of all, agreeing to take all the inventory back if it can't be moved. At one point, inventory

---

[3] I attended some of the meetings in order to provide marketing input into the deliberations. I spent a great deal of time saying "You really really need to ship an update to the product soon" but was ignored for the most part.

representing about 2 years of sales of MultiMate lay moldering in warehouses all about the country.

Decision Resources proved to be a similar headache. The ChartMaster family of products were poorly architected masses of BASIC language spaghetti that over time proved increasingly difficult to extend and improve. By 1987, the ChartMaster product line, like MultiMate, was consistently placing near the bottom in press reviews and competitive rankings. The company did have an "ace in the hole," a minicomputer graphics program that had been ported to the PC that Decision Resources extolled during its negotiations with Ashton-Tate as "state-of-the-art." After the purchase, a closer examination of this graphics gobbler, later released in a fit of desperation as "Draw Applause," revealed a program with an interface so obtuse and illogical that an internal marketing team evaluating the product was reduced to giggling hysterics[4] as they attempted to use it.

As with MultiMate, sales began to rapidly run out of steam. After the best programming minds at Ashton-Tate spent months reviewing the situation, the decision was made that the only way to solve the problem was to rewrite ChartMaster from the ground up (or buy a new product and call it ChartMaster). Of course, the company was planning to release a new OS/2-specific business graphics product and that would probably be the final answer to all the problems. In the meantime, Ashton-Tate began resorting to stuffing the channel to keep sales of the product moving. Soon, inventory representing about 1 year of sales of ChartMaster lay moldering in warehouses all about the country.

The Decision Resources purchase also proved to be an open morale sore within Ashton-Tate. Many of the employees of what was now the company's new East Coast graphics and word-processing division soon realized that Ashton-Tate had bought their companies based strictly on an analysis of their cash flow contribution. It became clear to them that Ashton-Tate had little interest in investing in the MultiMate and ChartMaster products, and resentment in the company's "orphan" division flared. One expression of the bad feelings was the release of Ashton-Tate's very own underground comic entitled "Graphic Violence."[5] Different strips included depictions of company employees shooting down upper management, Ashton-Tate's development group as

---

[4] I was a member of the evaluation team.

[5] I still have a complete set of the series.

a bunch of stoned druggies, and Draw Applause as an overweight superhero munching on memory. New releases of Graphic Violence became much prized within Ashton-Tate.

~

Making Ed's Day

The year 1987 also proved to be a time of decision in another way, as Esber formally declared war on major segments of the dBASE community. An independent committee of third parties who had started an effort to create a "standard dBASE" specification was threatened with a lawsuit if it continued its work.[6] The committee promptly stopped work on the dBASE standard and began work on efforts to create what was now a "standard **xBase**" specification.

Fresh from this triumph, Esber struck harder and deeper. The company announced that the dBASE language was "proprietary"[7] and couldn't be used without permission[8] from Ashton-Tate. He was quoted in the press as calling the third-party companies "parasites." Ashton-Tate mailed out legal cease-and-desist letters to consultants such as Adam Green, one of the industry's most noted dBASE gurus, to stop using the name "dBASE" on many of their training and teaching materials. At a Software Publishing Association conference, Esber got up before a crowd of developers and bellowed "Make my day!"[9] while threatening to sue anybody who dared build a dBASE-compatible product.

Nor did Esber restrict use of his honeyed tongue to people outside Ashton-Tate. Once at a company party he took the occasion to tell Wayne Ratliff, a figure much revered in and out of Ashton-Tate, that he was just as valuable to the company as its janitors.[10] Observers believe that Esber was probably just trying to advance the theory that everyone at

---

[6] *PC World* magazine, April 1989.

[7] The company made the announcement by way of a lawsuit filed in federal court against The Santa Cruz Corporation and Fox Software in 1989.

[8] See http://www.lgu.com/publications/softcopy/14.shtml.

[9] Several members of Ashton-Tate's management were in the audience when Esber made his threat, including Product Manager Randy Hujar, who remembers cringing as Esber spoke.

[10] This story was mentioned in an article on Ashton-Tate that appeared in the *The Wall Street Journal* after Esber's departure from the company.

Ashton-Tate was a cog in one big happy marketing machine, but Ratliff apparently missed this subtle point and soon after left the company.

One of the potential targets of Ashton-Tate's legal jihad included a company called Fox Software, publisher of a dBASE "clone" that was increasingly well thought of by the dBASE community. Interestingly enough, Ashton-Tate made an attempt to buy the product with the idea of using it as the next major upgrade to dBASE III+, but the negotiations fell through. Soon after the release of dBASE IV, Ashton-Tate did indeed sue Fox.

As the development community became steadily more roiled and resentful, word began to circulate that Ed Esber was "ashamed" of dBASE because he thought it wasn't "relational" enough. Because most people felt that Esber wasn't technically astute enough to distinguish between a relational database and a close relation, this observation simply exasperated everyone further. Esber then made a puzzling deal with Microsoft to jointly market a SQL server product from Sybase. SQL applications are designed to store actual application data on remote computers called servers while a desktop PC (the client) processes the code that deals with screen displays and data entry, and then transmits records to and from the servers.

The new partnership had many in the industry scratching their heads. It was no secret that Microsoft was looking longingly at the database market and seeking entry. Ashton-Tate was still the unchallenged PC database leader and possessed the resources and clout to buy or partner with a major SQL provider on its own. To many the deal seemed a public confirmation that Esber lacked confidence in dBASE and its capability to adapt to the future, a viewpoint not appreciated by a development community that depended on dBASE for its livelihood. (Ashton-Tate eventually did purchase its own SQL product, but by that time the company was so badly damaged it was unable to do much with the product.)

The legal push finally culminated in Ashton-Tate filing papers in court attempting to declare the dBASE language the property of the company.[11] The move was seen by many as an attempt by Ashton-Tate to lock them out of the market and take the bread off their table. By this time Esber was thoroughly loathed by the dBASE community with a passion never before seen in the software industry.

---

[11] *PC World* magazine, April 1989.

Esber apparently didn't realize that as he was making himself public enemy number one with every dBASE developer and programmer on earth, he was also making himself radioactive from the press's viewpoint. In high tech, as in many other industries, writers and editors rely on a stable of gurus and notables to provide them with quotes and background information on the companies they cover. Beginning in 1987, when members of the press called up their favorite dBASE experts to ask them their opinions about the latest developments and news from Ashton-Tate, they were often treated to observations such as "Ed Esber is a diseased amoeboid life form with the intelligence of a sick protozoa" (actual quote[12]).

This type of thing takes its toll, and as 1988 rolled by and the industry waited for the release of Ashton-Tate's next big product, dBASE IV, Ed Esber fell about even in popularity with Satan in the eyes of the developer and press communities. Not helping things was the fact that as dBASE IV kept slipping its release date, promised features whose announcements had helped kill and wound several third-party products and companies began to drop out of the final version. Third-party market resentment swelled to a crescendo.

Also not helping the situation was the fact that Ashton-Tate's dBASE IV development effort was seriously broken, but no one seemed to know it. An important reason for this lay in the fact that, lulled by Ashton-Tate's mid-1980s success, Esber had hired a new company president, Luther Nussbaum, to run the company's day-to-day operations. Esber remained in overall charge as CEO and spent his days thinking deep strategic thoughts while simultaneously pursuing his campaign of becoming the most hated man in software.

Nussbaum's hiring was a mistake. Less technically astute than even Esber (he'd previously worked at a company that built diesel engines), he quickly developed a reputation within Ashton-Tate for preferring to rule by bullying and intimidation. Management by fear can be an effective tactic (at least in the short term), but it doesn't work well if you're not sure what you're threatening people about. In his new role of supreme corporate-strategy guru, Esber had stopped coming to critical meetings that tracked the development and release date of dBASE IV, and he was out of touch with the technical difficulties surrounding the development effort. The result was that upper management was unaware of the true nature of the product they finally released in October 1988.

---

[12] As relayed to me by an enraged dBASE developer while I was working in product management for Ashton-Tate.

~

The Horror, the Horror

The dBASE IV launch was a disaster. The product had serious memory management issues, contained plenty of bugs, and lacked promised capabilities such as an integrated compiler. In the words of dBASE maven Adam Green, it "didn't work." The reviews were devastating and the development community howled loudly in disdain at a product one developer publicly stated was "an abortion in a box."[13]

Now, there's no question that dBASE IV had serious deficiencies, and Ashton-Tate should have expected to take its well-deserved lumps. Nonetheless, the reaction to dBASE IV was out of line with normal industry scenarios. Database products are some of the most complex pieces of software to develop, and the industry is rife with examples of full-point releases (i.e., 3.0 to 4.0) that "don't work" (just ask any long-time Oracle user). When faced with this situation, an astute company positions the new upgrade as an "opportunity to learn" about the release, "test" its features, and build "prototypes." In the meantime, the publisher works frantically to fix bugs and push out the "4.1" and the "4.2" releases, the ones that actually *do* work. If the company is in good odor with the press and its developers, this approach can often help finesse a new release flop. The press will spank the publisher, but developers and third parties will tend to rally round the product because their self-interest is involved. They'll begin developing programming workarounds, exchange tips on dealing with problems, and assure the press that once the bugs are all worked out the new release is eventually going to be mondo boffo.

This dynamic was absent at Ashton-Tate Sensing blood in the water, the dBASE community had no intention of letting up until it had Ed Esber's testicles in hand. It had all become personal. When the press called up a dBASE developer the first time for quotes and comments, they received an earful about the horrors of dBASE IV and the awfulness of Ed Esber. The ensuing bad reviews and karma upset all the other

---

[13] I was present in 1990 at a New York special interest group (SIG) meeting devoted to dBASE when a developer stood up and made this comment, but I can no longer remember his name.

developers, who saw their investment in dBASE training and development threatened, thus ensuring that the *next* time the press called they received an even louder earful about the incredible evil that was dBASE IV and the intergalactic menace to humanity represented by Ed Esber.

None of this was helped by the fact that Ashton-Tate, instead of quickly acknowledging dBASE IV's problems and embarking on a crash course to fix them, spent 6 months denying the problems existed and then told everyone that it was planning an OS/2 version of dBASE that would make everything better. At this juncture, the press began hearing from the development community that dBASE IV was a genocidal plot against all sentient life in the universe and that Ed Esber wasn't simply as bad as Satan but was Satan himself. This unvirtuous marketing cycle unleashed a mob mentality whose goal was Ed Esber's destruction. The corresponding devastation of Ashton-Tate was simply collateral damage.

Revenue growth at the company came to a screeching halt in 1989 as sales of dBASE IV stopped. Spooked by the turmoil surrounding the company, the distributors and resellers decided that this might also be a good time to return all those copies of MultiMate and ChartMaster gathering dust in their warehouses. Ashton-Tate, whose size had peaked at about $350 million, lost more than $60 million over the next several quarters. In 1990, its legal case against Fox Software was tossed out of court when it ruled that because Ashton-Tate had failed to disclose that dBASE was based on the JPLDIS language, the company had no proprietary rights to the dBASE "dialect." Shortly thereafter the board of directors tossed out Ed Esber and brought in an innocuous fellow by the name of Bill Lyons to head the now barely twitching company. Lyons astounded everyone by convincing Philippe Kahn of Borland in 1991 to pay $440 million (in stock) for Ashton-Tate. There's speculation that Philippe, a French immigrant, thought he was counting in francs instead of dollars.

six

THE IDIOT PIPER:
OS/2 and IBM

Almost from the moment IBM signed its first contract to use MS-DOS with the original IBM PC, the company began planning to replace the Microsoft OS with something else. Even by the standards of the time, DOS was regarded by many as a "toy" OS. It was a given that IBM would replace it with a more serious system as the PC market grew and developed. The question everyone was asking was "With what?"

After several fits and starts, it turned out that "what" was something eventually christened "OS/2," the real OS that Big Blue intended to follow in the footsteps of other classic IBM OSs such as VM and MVS. Once IBM had made up its mind about what it wanted to do, no one doubted that OS/2 was destined to be the next chapter in IBM's unmatched record of sales triumphs. Sure, the company made occasional missteps such as its Stretch computer of the 1950s and more recently its bungled development of the PC Junior, but to many these were mere sideshows. IBM had designated its next-generation OS for its PCs as "strategic," and when IBM made a proclamation like that the die was cast. OS/2 was destined for greatness.

It didn't turn out that way. Instead of being a new chapter in "success," OS/2 turned out to be a tragicomedy that played out for over a decade and ended in disaster for IBM. Before OS/2, IBM was a company apart from all others that people viewed with a sense of awe that bordered on reverence. The company was famous for its no-layoff policy, feared for its power, and worshipped for its profitability. To be an IBM employee meant one was automatically a member of America's working elite. IBM CEOs were always promoted from within, their ascension to the Big Blue Throne treated by the American business press as mini-coronations.

After OS/2's collapse, IBM's iconic status in the eyes of America was lost. Upstarts such as Compaq, Dell, and Gateway decimated IBM's PC business. Microsoft and a handful of others carted away the desktop software riches IBM had assumed it would one day inherit. As its mainframe and minicomputer businesses shrank, IBM lost billions in the 1990s, almost $5 billion alone in 1992, which proved to be a mere warm-up for 1993's $8 billion shortfall.[1] The no-layoff policy was scrapped and 200,000 people eventually lost their jobs. IBM CEO John Akers was summarily tossed off the Big Blue Throne and cigarette salesman Lou Gerstner was installed in his place. And while Gerstner

---

[1] Gary Rivlin, *The Plot to Get Bill Gates* (New York: Times Books/Random House, 1999).

stopped the flow of red ink and made the company mildly profitable again, IBM's growth during the 1990s was lackluster: a 3 percent compound annual rate. Not very impressive when compared with the company's 10.6 percent annual rate in the 1980s. To the world at large, IBM had become just another company: still big and powerful, but also often sluggish and stupid.

The fallout from OS/2's failure also had a serious and, in some cases, fatal impact on many of the companies that had followed IBM's lead. Before OS/2, IBM had played the role of Pied Piper to the industry's software publishers. Whenever Big Blue's dulcet tones sounded, companies dutifully lined up to follow. After OS/2, IBM's flute was broken. In the words of the founder of a small utilities company that bet big on OS/2 and lost, "OS/2 took a lot of us over the cliff. The product was IBM's Idiot Piper."

But in 1985, the Piper's tones were still clear and seductive. That year, as a member of MicroPro International's far-flung sales force (I'd been flung to Secaucus, New Jersey, microwave antenna capital of the United States, in the role of support engineer attached to the local office), I was summoned to Marin County, California, to attend the company's national sales meeting. This event consisted of 3 days of sales briefings, gossip, and some serious wining and dining, and it was normally the highlight of the company's year. I, however, showed up in a cranky mood and nothing about the next few days of frivolity changed it.

I maintained my despondent demeanor throughout the meeting's gala finale, a dinner at which special achievement awards were handed out. By the end of the meal my bad humor should have disappeared. I'd won an award for field sales engineer of the year and had been told informally by the powers that were that I had a shot at moving into product management, something I badly wanted.

Unfortunately for my peace of mind, a couple of weeks before the national sales meeting I had attended a regional IBM trade show in New York City,[2] where I'd spent an excruciating day demonstrating MicroPro's latest word processor, Easy. Easy was the brainchild of then MicroPro President Glen Haney, a nice but fairly clueless fellow. For some reason,

---

[2] The ostensible highlight of this show was supposed to be the IBM Convertible, yet another hardware gobbler that continued the process begun with the PC Junior of puncturing IBM's image of marketing acumen and invincibility. The unit lacked a serial and parallel port, meaning you couldn't use a modem or print with the computer unless you bought a pricey option.

Haney had gotten it into his head that the most important thing MicroPro could do was compete with PFS Write from Software Publishing Corporation (SPC). Founded by Fred Gibbons, SPC had made its mark in the industry with PFS File, an easy-to-use database program for the Apple II, then the PC. The company had subsequently spun off several new PFS-brand products, including Write, and had done fairly well with them. Haney was sure MicroPro was losing future market share to Fred Gibbons and was determined to do something about it. Hence Easy.

When it was introduced, Easy had two main claims to fame. One was that it was, er, easy to use, at least by the standards of the time. As with all such products, much of this ease of use was achieved by stripping out a good portion of WordStar's feature set. The product thus had no appeal to WordStar or WordStar 2000 users, who were used to paying more for a WordStar upgrade than the full retail price of Easy. Like all the other "lite" word processors, Easy never amounted to much and eventually faded away.[3]

~

A Dog's View

Easy's other mark of distinction was its much-heralded TopView compatibility. TopView was IBM's first attempt to steer an independent course from Microsoft, and its introduction in 1985 had given Bill Gates a severe case of heartburn. TopView was a "shell" that added rudimentary cut-and-paste capabilities between programs as well as multitasking to DOS. Multitasking would allow a user to, for instance, call up WordStar while recalculating a spreadsheet in Lotus. Unfortunately, this capability was somewhat theoretical. TopView sucked up most of the resources of any PC it ran on, making multitasking any but the smallest applications difficult, if not impossible. TopView was also character

---

[3] An attempt was made by MicroPro to use Easy as the foundation of a new version of WordStar, and several members of the press were invited to view the work in progress. Invitees included Paul Somerson and Steve Manes, journalists for *PC Magazine*, coauthors of *Underground WordStar,* and publishers of StarFixer, a WordStar "tune-up" utility. After sitting through a demo of the prospective new WordStar, they and several other members of the contingent warned members of the MicroPro staff that if MicroPro released the new WordStar in the form they had just seen it, the company would undoubtedly be very unhappy with the press reaction. The Easy-to-WordStar project was quickly discontinued.

based, unlike the Mac OS and Windows. It was therefore unable to integrate graphics and text within a document or display different fonts and type sizes.

For products written specifically to the TopView API, the integration between products became more robust and memory management somewhat more effective. MicroPro had spent a considerable amount of time and internal development resources learning how to integrate TopView into their software. The company expected this investment would pay off in big dividends in increased functionality in future MicroPro products and stronger sales.

Despite these expectations, TopView compatibility hadn't gone over well at the conference. For one thing, a bunch of Macophiles from the press had for some reason shown up and taken a great deal of pleasure in torturing me during demos of Easy. "Show us again how you cut and paste text," they'd say. "You call **that** easy?! Bwwwaaaaahhhhhaaaahhhhhaaaa!" they brayed as I banged on a keyboard instead of brandishing a mouse. "Now, how do you display a font onscreen? You **can't**?! Wow! We can see why TopView is so fabulous!" they howled as they held their sides and laughed hysterically.

By the end of the show I hated Mac users and Macs.

On the other hand, PC types had hardly been more complimentary. At one point, John Dvorak, the long-time columnist at *InfoWorld* who was now working at *PC Magazine,* strolled by.

"Hi, John!" I called out brightly. "Care to see a demonstration of Easy, the TopView-compatible word processor, in action?"

He stared at me with distaste. "I have no desire to see, hear, or do anything that has anything to do with TopDog," he stated with emphasis. "When is the next update of WordStar shipping?"

"Uh, real soon now! In the meantime, would you care to see a demonstration of WordStar 2000?"

He walked away without saying a word. Great.

A few minutes later, up walked a pleasant-looking gentleman whose show badge indicated he worked for the IT department of a major New York bank.

"Hi! Care to see a demonstration of Easy, the TopView-compatible word processor from MicroPro, publisher of WordStar?" I chirped.

He looked sad. "I don't think so. We're a major IBM customer, but when we brought in some copies of TopView and showed them to our

PCs, they began to whine and howl and tried to crawl off their desks and hide under the chairs. By the way, could you let me know when the next version of WordStar is shipping?" He gave me his card and walked away.

Another fellow stepped up briskly to my demo station, stopped abruptly, and peered intently at the monitor. His greasy hair and slight but redolent tang of BO told me before I glanced at his badge that he was programmer.

"Hello!" I caroled. "Care to see a demonstration of Easy, the TopView-com—"

"TopView? **TopView**?!" he interrupted hoarsely. "I want to know when the next version of WordStar is shipping!" Gobbling sounds began to issue from the back of his throat. He made the sign of the cross at me and hurried away.

It was a long, long day.

The memory of my humiliation fresh in mind, I decided to do something about it. After all, I was the field sales engineer of the year, damn it. I stalked over to the table where MicroPro's vice president of development was peaceably minding his own business, sat down, and announced in what I hoped were my richest, most persuasive tones that "We need to forget about TopView and support Windows."

He blinked at me. "Rick, we're talking about IBM. TopView is endorsed by IBM. Bill Lowe has personally told me that TopView is the future of IBM operating systems on the PC. And IBM is the company that sets the standards."

"No," I countered. "The wisdom of the field says that TopView is doomed. Customers don't like it. They've seen the Mac; that's what they want on their PCs. The press hates TopView; they think the Mac is where it's at. Developers hate TopView; they want to make cool Mac-like things for PCs. Everyone hates TopView! On the PC side of things, the only viable thing close to the Mac is Windows. If we write for Windows, we can do a cool Mac-like word processor for the PC and be the only one! By default, we'll lead the PC market in our ability to do things like display graphics and text within a document."

"Besides," I said, my enthusiasm reaching a fevered pitch, "Why spend so much time supporting IBM? They're notorious for working with companies, then stealing their good ideas and driving them out of business. We need to work with Microsoft! They're much smaller and will be far easier to deal with!"

Rarely is one privileged to be so right for so wrong a reason.

As I'd predicted, the market, enthralled by the Mac and discouraged by TopView's sluggish performance, rejected IBM's first attempt at breaking free from Microsoft's yoke. TopView was out of sight by the end of 1985; the company literally could not give the thing away.

Chastened by its failure, IBM paused to consider its options. It had two basics tracks down which it could go. It could simply cut the cord with Microsoft at some point and develop its own desktop OSs. Or it could decide to remain in partnership with Microsoft and ship new versions of DOS on its PC and eventually Windows, the GUI extension to DOS that Gates had been pushing since 1983 and had finally shipped in 1985.

After pondering the situation a bit, IBM decided to do both. It would stay in partnership with Gates but make the little geek jump through hoops building a new OS that did all the things IBM thought it needed to do, up to and including supporting old TopView applications, all two or three of them, despite the fact that no one cared about this. Oh, and IBM programmers would develop significant parts of the new OS. Oh, and the new OS would come in two versions, one that Microsoft could license to third parties à la DOS and another, higher-end version that would have additional capabilities and only run on IBM PCs (in theory—this turned out not to be true). And oh, by the way, everyone agreed that Windows could stick around for a while. The first edition had gotten bad reviews and the product was clearly harmless.[4]

Gates, in a display of manly fortitude (well, perhaps not that manly. Gates would have supported Commodore DOS if that's what it took to keep IBM's business) that paid off handsomely, agreed to everything IBM wanted. Work on the next generation of PC OSs commenced.

---

[4] Windows was formally introduced to the world at large at the 1983 Las Vegas COMDEX trade show, which I attended with MicroPro. It was impossible to walk around the show floor and not see demo screens of an evergreen viewed through a window (get it?). Windows wouldn't actually ship until late in 1985, and when it did, it was viewed with contempt by GUI gurus enamored of Apple's far more polished system.

~

An OS Is Born

While IBM and Microsoft were involved in their negotiations, rumors of the new PC OS began to float throughout the industry. For a while it was called CP/DOS, or DOS 286, or DOS 5.0, and then finally Presentation Manager. It would have multitasking and multi-threading (whatever that was) and semaphores and all manner of good stuff, but most important, it would have a GUI, just like the Mac! This interface would be based on Windows, only much better, obviously, and Windows and the new interface would be so similar that anyone who developed a Windows product could port it to Presentation Manager when it was ready to ship with a snap of the fingers and a twinkle of a compiler. Write two products for the price of one. And boy, that sounded really good to all the developers!

And though no one would actually confirm the date on which the new wonder OS would ship, everyone assumed it would be sometime in 1986 or at the very least 1987. And that sounded good, too, because by 1986, Atari ST[5] owners had a pretty sophisticated GUI for their machines, for God's sake, whereas PC types still had to clunk along in character-based DOS. And PC owners were sure getting tired of all those Mac snobs laughing at them and twirling those damned mice under their noses and getting all the girls because Macs were so cool. In fact, a fair number of them started buying up Macs so they could twirl mice and be cool, too. But most were still content to wait for IBM to ship a cool Mac-like OS so that they could twirl their mice while avoiding paying Apple those 50 percent profit margins it got on its systems. But they were sure eager to get their hands on that new OS and those mice.

Then IBM threw SAA into the mix and everything changed.

---

[5] The Atari ST OS TOS (Tramiel Operating System) was based on Digital Research's GEM. The ST was the brainchild of Jack Tramiel of Commodore fame. After losing control of Commodore, Tramiel and his sons took control over Atari's nearly defunct computer business and had some short-term success in reviving it. The ST series launched Atari's rebirth under its new management, and for a while the system enjoyed some success in the market, particularly as an inexpensive music synthesizer (the ST included a MIDI port). I purchased an Atari 520 ST running TOS in 1985 (and I still have the unit). Tramiel, as always, relied on a low price strategy, but over time Atari was driven out of the market by the inevitable depredations of the Silicon Beast.

SAA, which stood for Systems Application Architecture, was an attempt by IBM to develop a cross-platform OS (or something close to it) that would run on all IBM mainframes, minicomputers, and PCs. (An inadvertently hilarious book about this heroic effort was written several years ago. It was referred to by industry wags as "The Soul of a Giant Three-Ring Binder.") This initiative had been sparked by IBM's annoyance at having to listen to its archrival in the lucrative minicomputer market, DEC, trumpet that it, DEC, "had it now."

What DEC[6] had "now" was a unified OS and application environment for its entire product line. In theory, no matter what size computer you bought from DEC, they all used the same OS and ran the same software. (This wasn't entirely true in practice, but DEC certainly was way ahead of IBM in this regard.) By contrast, IBM supported over a dozen incompatible hardware and OS platforms. Moving an accounting package from, for example, an IBM minicomputer system to a mainframe required an extensive rewrite of the software.

SAA was designed to close this perceived competitive gap, but IBM was targeting a chimera. True, in the late 1980s, DEC's profits and revenue presented the picture of a company in the pink, but this was an illusion. In reality, DEC's appearance was more akin to the hectic flush a consumptive develops before death. DEC's business model consisted of selling minicomputers and small mainframes to companies at the departmental and divisional level. This was precisely the market companies such as Novell and 3Com were targeting with their networking OSs. Herds of Silicon Beasts yoked together with NetWare were a fraction of the cost of DEC's expensive and overengineered hardware products and required less support. LAN systems were also starting to offer a broader

---

[6] DEC had taken a stab at the market for small systems in the early 1980s with the simultaneous introduction of no less than three incompatible microcomputers. The most widely publicized and purchased system was the Rainbow, an MS-DOS–compatible machine that also sported a Z-80 processor for running 8-bit software. The machine quickly met the fate of all the other MS-DOS clones. The computer is best remembered for DEC's obnoxious practice of shipping the machine without a format program for its unusual nonstandard floppy drives, ostensibly forcing users to purchase amazingly expensive preformatted floppies directly from DEC. (Enterprising programmers soon developed several freeware formatting programs for the Rainbow and the ploy failed.) DEC also developed a hilarious series of ads that depicted style-conscious yuppies drooling over the Rainbow's sleek keyboard and monitor, with the big bulky computer itself absent from the picture. Urban professionals nationwide were treated to a nasty surprise when they bit on the ads, bought a Rainbow, and developed hernias lugging their I-got-far-more-than-I-expected PC out of the store.

and cheaper selection of software to compete with the minicomputer market's offerings.

Some ominous reports from the field began to filter into DEC headquarters over defections in the company's customer base, but these were ignored until it was far too late. Over time, the concept of much cheaper and more choices beat "has it now" hands-down and DEC, along with most of the minicomputer market, disappeared in the late 1990s. For good measure, SAA proved to be a massive waste of IBM's time and money and eventually sank without a trace as well.

Nonetheless, what IBM said still went, and work on integrating SAA technology into Presentation Manager moved forward. Much of this work involved building support for a whole host of IBM mainframe terminals into the new OS. This all took much time and effort, and it was soon apparent there would be no wonder OS in 1986. In fact, the new OS with the cool graphical interface would not be ready until 1988. Oh, and you know all that stuff about a simple recompile being all you needed to do to port your Windows product to Presentation Manager? Forget it. You were going to have to do a major code rewrite to get your product to run under the new OS after all. Which, by the way, was going to be called OS/2. A nice fit, IBM thought, with its new PS/2 line of microcomputers.

Then, in an act of supreme stupidity that would characterize IBM's marketing of OS/2 for the rest of the product's ill-starred existence, the company announced it would indeed ship the first version of OS/2 in 1987. Only it wouldn't have a cool Mac-like GUI—just the same DOS-like character interface everyone was heartily sick of. Few cared that underneath the hood of the new OS was a quantum-leap improvement over DOS in functionality. With this single stroke, IBM had created TopView II.

IBM's motive for this act wasn't hard to discern. OS/2 had become a draftee in the company's war on the hardware cloners, and it had been assigned to ride shotgun alongside its new computers into battle. By 1987, the company had woken up to the consequences of unleashing the Silicon Beast on the market and was looking to take it all back. The PS/2 line would ship with a new bus, the Micro Channel, that had more patents stuck to it than bugs on a fly strip hanging from the ceiling of a Texas gas station. The new BIOS chip, called Advanced BIOS or ABIOS, reared up and bit you on the finger if you tried to reverse engineer it. The units shipped in April 1987 with plain old DOS, and IBM badly wanted something that could better showcase their new darlings. OS/2 1.0 was it.

While this was all well and good for IBM, software publishers were less than thrilled. Companies were being asked to throw a considerable amount of time and money into supporting an OS version whose sales prospects were dubious. Making everyone feel worse was IBM's pricing of OS/2 1.0: $340.00 for a retail copy, a price that generated sticker shock. IBM had established a low price point for desktop OSs with the introduction in 1981 of DOS 1.0 for $40.00, and no one thought the OS/2 pricing strategy was a smart move. Once a market's pricing structure is established, it takes time and effort (and perhaps a helpful monopoly) to change it, if you ever do. Yes, many people would eventually obtain the product via bundling, but strong retail sales would help kick start acceptance of OS/2 and generate sales of OS/2-specific products. And that was unlikely to happen with a $340.00 desktop OS that lacked a GUI.

And speaking of pricing, IBM and Microsoft had placed a $3,000.00 price tag on the OS/2 software development kit (SDK). That was no problem for larger software companies, but smaller firms complained bitterly. Microsoft practically gave away its Windows development tools. Even Apple set more reasonable prices for its SDKs.

IBM also seemed oblivious to the need to provide marketing assistance to independent software vendors (ISVs) building OS/2 applications. The company had no direct mail programs a third party could access that would help promote new OS/2 products. IBM had no expertise or influence in software distribution channels and seemed uninterested in developing any. IBM made no attempt to garner critical "shelf space" in major resellers. There were no co-op advertising programs. There were only a few scattered attempts to build a supporting infrastructure of books, publications, shows, and events that would stimulate interest in buying OS/2 and OS/2-related products. IBM's attitude was that what had worked for the company since the Great Depression would work today. And, to an extent, it did. Several major publishers, including Ashton-Tate, Lotus, SPC, and MicroPro, as well as a few daring start-ups, committed themselves heart and soul to OS/2.

Exacerbating all the aforementioned issues was an event beyond IBM's control: a rapid spike in memory prices during the OS/2 introduction. This was a big problem as OS/2 required a "whopping" 4MB of memory to be useful, 8MB to step along smartly, and 16MB to really hum. A 1MB memory stick that was projected to sell for about $100.00 shot up to almost $400.00 before the bubble burst.

What wasn't beyond IBM's control was the fact that the company was one of the largest producers of memory in the world at the time and in a position to take advantage of a rare opportunity to use hardware to drive software sales. As a glum product manager from DeScribe, a start-up that was introducing an OS/2-specific word processor, pointed out, "OS/2 without memory was a $1,000.00 upgrade. Bundled with a handsomely discounted 4MB memory stick, it was a million-copy seller." But IBM was unresponsive to that idea.

The name "OS/2" also proved to be a problem. Many people assumed the new OS ran only on IBM's PS/2 computers, a misperception IBM did little to dispel. Nor did the existence of two versions of the product, the "standard" and "extended" editions, help matters.

All these factors combined to ensure the introduction of OS/2 1.0 was an unmitigated flop. No one bought the package and no one made any money developing software for it. The desktop market as a whole was becoming restive and showed signs of slipping from IBM's control. Its PS/2 line met stiff resistance from competitors such as Compaq, which spearheaded an effort to develop an independent hardware platform, EISA. After examining IBM's stiff licensing and royalty demands, most potential OEMs decided to stay with the existing PC architecture and refused to build PS/2 clones.

Still, this was IBM after all. It set the standards. The software industry turned its impatient eyes toward OS/2 1.1, the "real" OS/2, the one that would finally ship with that cool Mac-like interface. After due deliberation, IBM announced it would ship OS/2 1.1 in October 1988. Considering that by then Mac users would have been using a modern GUI for 4 years while PC users labored in computing's version of the Stone Age, this seemed rather tardy, but OK. Most people were still ready to wait, though sales of Macs continued to grow briskly.

And while you were biding your time there **was** this increasingly interesting Windows alternative. Windows 2.0 had shipped in April 1987, and though the critics still mocked it, 2.0 was clearly an improvement over the last version. There was even a special version, Windows 386, that took advantage of some of that chip's special features. You could do some real work with Windows, especially the 386 version, and now there were even some good software packages for it. Desktop publisher PageMaker, for one. And Microsoft's new spreadsheet, Excel, which had received glowing reviews upon release. When you bought the package, which came in well under $100.00, it said it had Presentation Manager. In other words, you were sort of getting a sneak preview of IBM's new wonder OS. That was a nice little bonus, when you stopped to think about it.

Microsoft had also done something really quite clever. It had released a runtime version of Windows[7] to developers, ensuring that if you didn't have Windows, you could still buy a Windows application you could run on your system. If you were a PC user with a 386 and Windows, you might not be ready to twirl that mouse, but you were certainly entitled to swing it a bit. Windows 2.0 sales started to become quite robust, hitting about 10,000 units a month through the retail channels. But no one got carried away. OS/2 1.1 was on the way.

IBM kept its promise. OS/2 1.1 with the Presentation Manager GUI was officially released in October 1988, on Halloween. It had a cool Mac-like GUI, though by now GUIs weren't really that cool anymore, just necessary if you wanted to be competitive. The market sighed in relief. There was a flurry of initial purchases. OS/2 appeared ready to take off!

And then everyone found out you... couldn't... print... with OS/2 1.1.

This was because in addition to providing no support for third-party software developers, IBM had also made no attempt to garner support for manufacturers of non-IBM hardware.[8] And although IBM made some very nice printers, most people hadn't bought them. They'd bought a wide variety of different printers from different manufacturers, most notably HP LaserJets, and OS/2 1.1 had no idea of what to do with them.

And, unfortunately for IBM, memory prices had remained high as well. Because OS/2 1.1 needed even more memory than OS/2 1.0, upgrade costs were around $2,000.00 per PC. And no, IBM hadn't changed its mind about a hardware/software bundle of memory and OS/2.

---

[7] The runtime version of Windows was discontinued with the introduction of version 3.0 despite the dismayed screams of many software publishers.

[8] IBM did take some stabs at addressing the situation. For example, at a seminar held for the press extolling the virtues of OS/2, several attendees pointed out that the difficulty of obtaining drivers for printers and other types of hardware was hurting OS/2 in the market. An IBM employee held up a disk he claimed had several hundred drivers and announced IBM was prepared to sell the collection to all comers for $300.00. Many members of the press were utterly dazzled by this display of silliness on the part of IBM and promptly went out and bought Windows.

The company then proceeded to make the day of OS/2 developers everywhere by announcing that it had licensed the NeXTStep interface from Steve Jobs's NeXT Software. Rumors immediately began to spread that NeXTStep would become a part of OS/2.

NeXTStep ran on the NeXT computer, Steve Jobs's incredibly cool black cube desktop PC that cost $10,000.00 per unit. At that price, no one actually intended to **buy** a NeXT box themselves, but everyone hoped someone would buy one for them so that they could put it on their desk and look as cool as Steve Jobs. The NeXTStep interface was certainly state-of-the-art, with chiseled icons and slick graphics—no one had ever doubted Steve Jobs's ability to create great-looking icons. But if it were true that it was going to eventually replace Presentation Manager, why write applications for OS/2 now? Everything would have to be extensively rewritten once NeXTStep was integrated into OS/2. Better to wait. On the other hand, everyone was just sick to death of character-based interfaces. (IBM never did anything with NeXTStep.)

The market lowed and shifted about restlessly. More people went out and bought Macs. Had Apple not been in its way every bit as stupid as IBM, the company was in a position to become the Microsoft of OSs. But we all know how that turned out.

Sales of Windows 2.0 hit 50,000 units per month.

OS/2 1.2 shipped a few months later. Most people still couldn't print with it. IBM announced it was now talking to a company called Metaphor about **its** really cool OS and interface. (IBM never did anything with Metaphor.)

The lows and the bleatings became louder. The tension rose higher. It was now 1990.

Microsoft announced Windows 3.0. It looked pretty good. It was inexpensive. It supported 16MB of memory but ran OK in 4MB. The memory bubble had burst. Windows really needed a mouse. There were several good programs available for it, including spreadsheets and word processors, the most popular applications. You could print with it. It was 6 damn years after the Mac had first shipped.

The market bellowed loudly and stampeded toward Windows 3.0.

IBM shipped OS/2 1.3. It could—usually—print. It was highly functional. IBM's Desktop Software division even had a lineup of nice OS/2-specific applications available for it. When did it ship? It doesn't matter. No one cared.

Before the herd broke, IBM had one last chance to stop the stampede. In 1988, the company had formed its Desktop Software division in Milford, Connecticut. The group was deliberately staffed with young honchos from outside the company who were supposed to show IBM how to succeed in the rough-and-tumble world of PC software. In short order, Desktop Software built a fairly polished stable of OS/2 applications, including word processing, business presentation, and desktop publishing products. All the programs were scheduled to be available in Windows versions, though these were going to ship well after their OS/2 counterparts were out the door.

Alarmed at the growing presence of Windows, and aware that OS/2 needed more time to build momentum in the marketplace, the Desktop Software group petitioned to meet with no less an august personage than IBM President John Akers himself to explain the situation. They had taken a close look at Windows and, despite Microsoft's soothing words, realized it presented a serious competitive challenge to OS/2. They were also aware that the development market was on the cusp; if events broke the wrong way, software publishers might be forced to abandon OS/2 if they felt Windows would allow them to meet the pent-up demand for GUI-type products on the PC. After submitting their request, they were duly granted an audience before the Big Blue Throne.

At this point, IBM still had the ability to checkmate Microsoft's plans for Windows. One way was to buy a new OS from a company called GeoWorks. The company had developed a highly optimized product with a slick GUI that could run in a small hardware footprint; GeoWorks ran with amazing alacrity even on the original IBM PC. This was the path favored by the Desktop Software division.

Another option, one widely discussed within IBM and Microsoft, was to release a version of DOS with the Presentation Manager interface. And, as it had been since 1981, Digital Research was still sniffing about forlornly while proffering GEM and DR DOS. If all else failed, IBM's final option was to simply threaten Microsoft with termination of the joint development agreement between the two companies and strike out on its own. At this point, IBM still held the upper hand in the relationship and in the marketplace, and Microsoft would have had to back down.

The day of the meeting arrived and the Desktop Software contingent, led by Product Marketing Manager for IBM Corporation, Randy Hujar,[9] was escorted before IBM's reigning monarch and given the chance to make their case. Akers received a detailed briefing on the situation, as well as a series of recommendations. When the team was done, he called them "a group of good kids" and proceeded to explain the facts of life to the naïfs before him. IBM, he told them, controlled these markets and set the standards, and it always would. Bill Gates "was a nice boy," and IBM fully understood how to position OS/2 vis-à-vis Windows. It was all well taken care of. They could go back to their cubicles and not worry their precious little heads about the problem.

The Desktop Software group was then escorted out of the august presence and reoccupied their cubicles. IBM proceeded to develop a ludicrous agreement with Microsoft that said that Windows was just great for "low-end machines" (i.e., the ones that most people had) and that OS/2 was great for "high-end machines" (i.e., the ones they would one day own). Windows 3.0 shipped as planned.

IBM shut down its Desktop Software group in 1992, just in time to ensure that the division's applications wouldn't be available to support the rollout of OS/2 2.0. That same year John Akers was kicked out of the CEO position at IBM. Microsoft was estimated to have shipped approximately 30 million Windows 3.0 and 3.1 licenses by that time.

~

Who Killed OS/2?

Yet, despite IBM's record of stunning marketing and sales incompetence, OS/2 refused to die. Work continued on the product despite the Microsoft tsunami, and in 1992 IBM released OS/2 2.0. This version of the product was years ahead of Windows in terms of raw functionality, and only until the release of Windows 2000 did a comparable product exist. Unlike the 16-bit Windows and OS/2 1.x, 2.0 was a 32-bit OS that could take full advantage of the 386, 486, and Pentium processors. It sported a powerful new "object-oriented" interface that, though initially confusing to many, made older approaches to GUIs seem toy-like in

---

[9] I first met Randy when we were both product managers at Ashton-Tate.

comparison. It even had decent hardware support and could print, most of the time.

IBM had also made a few improvements in its attempts to sell OS/2. It had consolidated all marketing and development efforts in its Austin, Texas, facilities; this helped provide some focus to the OS/2 effort. The new Austin unit founded the IBM Independent Vendor League (IVL), a business group chartered to help encourage the development of OS/2 books, courseware, certification exams, and similar aftermarket materials. IVL also helped launch two magazines dedicated to OS/2: *OS/2 Professional* and *OS/2 World*. In addition, several prominent online forums were founded to extol the virtues of OS/2 and encourage its use, foremost among them Will Zachman's Canopus forum on CompuServe.

Helping the situation along was the fact that the industry was learning that Microsoft could be every bit as tough and brutal a competitor as IBM in its heyday. As the company tightened its grip on the desktop OS environment, it used its cash and brilliant marketing to drive toward dominance of the lucrative desktop applications markets. IBM's competitors were increasingly in a panic. OS/2 offered, perhaps, an opportunity to regroup and regain lost market share and revenue on a more level playing field.

Unfortunately for these hopes, although IBM had learned a few lessons it hadn't learned enough. The aforementioned shutdown of IBM's Desktop Software group robbed OS/2 of critical application support when it needed it most. In addition, IBM had entered into yet **another** OS deal, this one with Apple. This was Taligent, a joint development effort between IBM and Apple that burned up about half a billion dollars before collapsing of its own weight.

Taligent started out as an attempt to build yet another next-generation OS, which then morphed into a half-witted effort to build an OS that would run other OSs. When this proved unfeasible, Taligent decided to waste more time and money creating a series of middleware tools that no one understood or bought before someone woke up and pulled the plug on the entire fiasco. But in the meantime, the industry was abuzz with rumors that OS/2 was simply an intermediate step on the way to this newest wonder OS. Then rumors began to spread that IBM and Apple would merge and that OS/2 would soon adopt the **Macintosh** interface. OS/2 developers had heard all this before and fortunately for IBM, many chose to ignore the idiot mutterings from Big Blue and focus on trying to sell their software.

Which wasn't easy, because another lesson IBM still hadn't learned, despite the success of IVL, was the need to help ISVs sell their products in order to ensure OS/2's success. The company still had no direct marketing and distribution channel programs in place to help get OS/2 applications seen and bought. Several attempts were made to convince the powers that were to create software promotional bundles with OS/2, or at the very least include trialware versions of applications in retail units of the product. All such attempts foundered.

The problem of developer support was compounded by yet another IBM mistake: the decision to incorporate Windows 3.0 and 3.1 into different versions of OS/2 2.0 and 2.1, respectively. IBM positioned OS/2 2.0 as a one-size-fits-all OS capable of running DOS, OS/2 and Windows applications. In fact, IBM regularly claimed in its marketing literature that OS/2 ran Windows better than, well, Windows. This immediately raised the question of why anyone should buy an OS/2-specific application if her Windows solutions ran so much better in OS/2. It also raised a credibility issue, as it seemed unlikely to many that IBM would be able or inclined to provide increased functionality and support for what was now OS/2's bitter rival. And the existence of Windows within OS/2 allowed developers who were under pressure to develop OS/2 applications to fudge the issue by claiming that "Yes, indeedy, our applications run under OS/2 (Windows) just fine."

In adopting this strategy, IBM was ignoring the lessons of history. Other attempts had been made in the past to create one-size-fits-all computers and OSs. In the early 1980s there was the Dimension computer[10], a system that ran Apple DOS, TRS-DOS (for the Radio Shack line), and CP/M via plug-in boards. What all the makers of these products soon found out was most people didn't want a one-size-fits-all product; they wanted a single product that did what they wanted and did it quickly and well. Mastering the complexities of multiple OSs within a single desktop environment was something that was of interest only to a small group of hobbyists and IT experimenters.

And even though IBM's other marketing processes had improved, the company's marketing groups still managed to provide some inadvertently hilarious lessons in how not to execute the basics. For example,

---

[10] I first saw this system in action at the first PC Expo, held in 1983 in New York City's now defunct Coliseum. For years PC Expo was considered the industry's second most important trade show after COMDEX.

IBM printed an infamous OS/2 brochure whose front piece showed a yuppie type flinging open a window to explore the wonderful new world of OS/2. Behind the window was a viscous green mass in which the yuppie had immersed his face. It looked a lot like what happens when the Blob ingests its victims.

Then there was IBM's sponsorship of college football's Fiesta Bowl (soon known internally as "The Fiasco Bowl"). To many observers, it was unclear what benefit IBM derived from slapping the name "OS/2" on a second-tier sporting event. No demographic information seemed to exist that indicated that people who watched the Fiesta Bowl were also highly interested in 32-bit OSs, nor was there much proof that watching a college football game would make people more inclined to rush home and demand computer resellers stock up on OS/2.

Regardless, after buying the sponsorship, the Fiesta Bowl was duly renamed the IBM OS/2 Fiesta Bowl, and the organizers of the event asked IBM for their line-up of sponsors. "Uh, what sponsors?" the IBMers replied. At this point, IBM learned that along with the right to advertise its own products during the football game, it had **also** bought a series of time slots it was supposed to allot to the third-party vendors of its choice. IBM's Austin group had no experience with this sort of activity, and the news sparked a series of frantic phone calls out to local Austin businesses[11]—barbecue restaurants, transmission shops, auto dealerships, and so forth—asking if they'd like to advertise their wares during the IBM OS/2 Fiesta Bowl. (Eventually a professional was brought in to manage the process.)

But despite IBM's best efforts, OS/2 proved to be a survivor and soldiered on. The technical excellence of the product was hard to ignore. Windows, still a 16-bit application with firm DOS roots, was looking increasingly antique and out-of-date in contrast with OS/2 and its sleek, object-oriented interface. The release of Windows NT, the 32-bit OS originally intended to be the successor to Windows 3.*x*, and the announcement by Microsoft that it was developing yet another 32-bit OS for the "home" and the "desktop," a product that would eventually be known as Windows 95, was generating intense confusion in the market. And developer antagonism toward Microsoft was rising steadily. But

---

[11] I was consulting for IBM's PSP group at this time. This organization had responsibility for all OS/2 marketing and promotion programs, and I learned about IBM's Fiesta Bowl woes firsthand from the people responsible for these programs.

IBM was up to the challenge. With the introduction of OS/2 3.0, the company finally managed to put a stake through OS/2's tough little heart.

The 3.0 release of OS/2 in early 1995 was accompanied by a name change. Henceforth, OS/2 was to be called OS/2 "Warp." The genesis of this truly unfortunate moniker began with IBM's habit of using code names lifted from the popular and seemingly eternal TV and movie series, *Star Trek*. Previous beta versions of OS/2 were named "Borg," "Ferengi," and "Klingon" (all alien races on the show), and the 3.0 beta version was called Warp (as in "warp speed," as in really really fast). But as Warp neared its release date, IBM puzzled over what to call the released product, until Chairman Lou Gerstner decreed that the product should be known as . . . Warp.

It seemed an excellent idea! Earlier versions of OS/2 had been criticized by some as being slow, though this was more a function of memory requirements and setup than a technical deficiency. *Star Trek* was cool, futuristic, and familiar, a seemingly perfect match of product image to functionality. IBM moved ahead and designed a marketing campaign around a *Star Trek* theme. They rented a hall in New York City and invited hundreds to see Patrick Stewart, the then current captain of the *Starship Enterprise* to help roll out the product in a gala event. (Stewart was a no-show.)

The only problem was that no one at IBM had bothered to check with Paramount, owner and guardian of the *Star Trek* franchise and all related trademarks and marketing rights, about what it thought of this idea. Now, Paramount had no right to trademark the name "Warp"— science-fiction writers had been using the word since the 1930s. But IBM's public use of "Klingon" and "Ferengi" had annoyed Paramount, and the company wasn't about to let IBM appropriate *Star Trek* for its own marketing purposes. Sharp letters were sent to IBM and threats were voiced. As a result, IBM decided to drop any *Star Trek* marketing concepts for Warp.

This was a problem. Without a cool futuristic concept tied to the word and the product, IBM had to rely on the traditional meanings of the word. Like "bent." "Twisted." "Warped" out of shape. And other, less conventional meanings. For instance, if you were alive during the 1960s (if you **remember** the 1960s), "warped" was something you became after ingesting certain substances that time and experience have shown to be bad for memory recall and possibly your genetic heritage.

The result was that IBM ended up creating a very odd advertising and marketing campaign redolent of hash brownies and magic mushrooms. Twisty "Age of Aquarius" type was splashed across ad posters all over the land, proclaiming that people were "Warping" their computers. Edwin Black, publisher of *OS/2 Professional* magazine, described in an editorial of nearly having an apoplectic fit[12] as he gazed upon one such IBM ad plastered up on the walls of Chicago's O'Hare Airport. It featured Phil Jackson, former coach of the mighty Michael Jordan–led Chicago Bulls and the flower child of NBA basketball with the New York Knicks in the 1970s, smiling through his bushy mustache at the prospect of "warping" **his** computer. Everyone, of course, was thrilled at the prospect of running a psychedelic, warping OS that smoked dope and had flashbacks when you asked it to retrieve a file.

But despite even this, OS/2 continued to squirm and twist toward survival. Microsoft's increasingly public woes with the U.S. Department of Justice seemed about to slow the Windows juggernaut down a bit. The slow trickle of OS/2-specific applications coming to market began to swell. Sales of OS/2 through the retail channel became brisk. At IBM's 1994 Technical Interchange trade show, many vendors offering OS/2 applications had sold out by the event's end.[13] Although OS/2 was far from reaching parity with Windows, it was close to achieving the status of a strong second-place contender with significant market share.

Then IBM rolled out the big guns. IBM PR and Lou Gerstner himself.

---

[12] Edwin had many such moments in his dealings with IBM's marketing and sales system. He later wrote a scathing article in *OS/2 Professional* about IBM's marketing and sales mishandling of an excellent search utility for OS/2, SearchManager, called "DOA." This was an editorial act of some courage, as IBM accounted for a large percentage of *OS/2 Professional*'s advertising budget. Edwin took over the product, renamed it "Bloodhound," and had some sales success with it before OS/2 died.

[13] I was present at this event and gave a series of presentations to OS/2 software publishers on effective high-tech marketing practices.

~

Coup de Grace

In the pre-PC era, IBM's PR strategy was a conventional but effective "big company" approach that garnered IBM a great deal of public respect. The company invested in public charities, sponsorships of select TV and theater programs, advertising, and the usual editorial placements in a wide variety of publications to build and maintain its public image. Its approach was held up as a model of effective PR and marketing communications.

However, as was true of most IBM marketing programs, its PR program was highly centralized, not designed to communicate with its product marketing groups, and technically ignorant. This didn't work well in the new era of press reviews and analysis that sprang up in the 1980s. Powerful columnists and influencers such as John Dvorak (an OS/2 fan) and Jerry Pournelle had little interest in IBM's sponsorship of Hallmark's annual showing of *A Christmas Carol* or its contributions to the United Way. But they were very interested in discussing the newest and hottest technology, playing with the latest technical toys, and having their egos stroked by people who were knowledgeable about the industry.

Over time, IBM developed an involuntary two-track approach to PC press relations. The first track consisted of IBM's conventional PR program, which clanked along, oblivious to its increasing irrelevance in the new world.

The second track was an unruly back channel of former and current IBM employees who talked to the press on an ad-hoc basis, churning out gossip and fueling speculation. A mini-industry of "IBM watchers" sprang up, who were dedicated to deciphering the various statements and pronouncements of the different officers, divisions, and spokespeople.

Even worse was the fact that IBM had no formalized approach to managing its products' review cycles, a problem that has plagued IBM since the release of the IBM PC and that continues to this day. Once an IBM software product is released, the product is on its own. Not surprisingly, very few IBM software products ever receive stellar reviews.

The first body blow to long-suffering OS/2 occurred when, in a major speech to business analysts, IBM CEO Lou Gerstner was quoted in August 1995 by the *New York Times* as saying that worrying about

OSs was fighting the "last war."[14] Later in the speech, he added that it was too late for IBM to "go after the desktop." Several newspapers immediately reported this speech as an admission by IBM that OS/2 was a failure. The *New York Times* article was headlined "IBM Chief Concedes OS/2 Has Lost Desktop War."

The fallout was immediate and wide-ranging. OS/2 software vendors began to publicly question whether it made any sense to further invest in the OS. Many large corporate accounts that had committed to installing OS/2 on an enterprise level announced they were reconsidering their positions. Key advocates and columnists such as Will Zachman began to publicly question their support of OS/2.[15]

The next, and even more devastating, blow came from a completely unexpected source. In his August 6, 1995, in the *New York Times* "Technology Column," Peter Lewis ran a story called "OS/2 No Longer at Home at Home." It was full of juicy quotes from an IBM spokesman. Among them: "OS/2 is a great operating system" but "Sony's Betamax was a better system than VHS . . ." and "I'm going to put Windows 95 on the machines in my house."

What made these quotes truly memorable was that the source was David Barnes, IBM's Mr. OS/2 himself. Highly photogenic and comfortable in front of a crowd, Barnes had traveled thousands of miles over the previous 3 years conducting competitive demonstrations of OS/2 and Windows, had been a keynote speaker at trade shows, and had appeared on radio and TV extolling OS/2's virtues. It was as if Bill Gates had been quoted as saying that Windows was really an inferior product to OS/2 and he wouldn't be caught dead using the thing himself.

Reaction in the OS/2 community made the Gerstner faux pas seem insignificant. Online OS/2-friendly forums exploded. Tens of thousands of messages were posted electronically over the next several weeks, most asking for an explanation of Barnes's remarks. Famous long-time OS/2 aficionado James Fallows, columnist for *The Atlantic Monthly*, former editor of *U.S. News & World Report*, and a noted writer, posted several public messages[16] asking what on earth IBM was doing.

---

[14] "IBM Chief Concedes OS/2 Has Lost Desktop War." *New York Times*, August 1, 1995.

[15] On Zachman's OS/2 advocacy forum, Canopus.

[16] Including on Zachman's Canopus forum.

After the Barnes story broke, IBM did nothing for several weeks. Corrections weren't published; Barnes didn't write a letter of clarification to the editor of the *New York Times*; no IBM spokesperson appeared on any online services, Usenet forums, or SIGs to correct or explain Barnes's statements.

Finally, after more OS/2 customers announced their defection from the product, IBM reacted. Barnes published a statement claiming that Lewis had taken his statements out of context. IBM assured everyone it was still committed to OS/2. Various IBM spokespeople made comforting noises. No one read any of these statements, and before Microsoft had even released Windows 95, its desktop OS, OS/2 was truly dead.

Cynics have pointed out that perhaps IBM was attempting to signal to the marketplace that it was discontinuing its support for OS/2. If this is true, it's hard to imagine a more self-defeating strategy. At the very least, IBM could have waited until after Windows 95 had shipped to judge market response. But after the Gerstner/Barnes remarks, Microsoft could have waited another year to release Windows 95. It wouldn't have mattered.

As already noted, OS/2's failure not only had a profound impact on IBM, but it also altered the fate of many companies in the industry. Perhaps the saddest case was that of SPC, the firm that through no fault of its own had years ago inadvertently yoked me to TopView for that one miserable day. SPC had divested itself of its PFS line by the late 1980s and, via its purchase of Harvard Graphics, was for a brief period the leader in the PC presentation graphics market. SPC made a "bet-the-company" wager on IBM and OS/2 and developed InfoAlliance, a high-end OS/2 database product. Such was SPC's confidence in OS/2's future that it literally ordered its sales force to cease selling its market-leading Harvard Graphics package and concentrate on InfoAlliance. Whoops. When it became clear this bet wasn't going to pay off, SPC turned around and spent 2 years rewriting the package for Windows, but by the time the project was done, the company was out of cash and market share.

Even those companies who avoided being sucked into OS/2 development efforts ended up paying the price. Many mistook the market's failure to adopt OS/2 as a repudiation of GUIs. They had several clues this wasn't true—the enthusiastic reaction to Microsoft Excel and Word for Windows being but two examples. Apple's Macintosh success, despite the fact the company was held in distaste by much of corporate IT,[17] was another. But such was IBM's hold on the market's perception that many believed that DOS would remain supreme on PCs for several more years.

Had companies such as Borland, Lotus, and WordPerfect committed to Windows development efforts in 1988 or 1989, they would have been in a position to compete with Microsoft on a fairly level playing field when Windows 3.0 took the market by storm in 1990 and 1991. The opportunity was certainly there; during this time period Microsoft was desperate to garner ISV support and went to great lengths to court potential developers.[18]

Much ink would be spilled in the mid-1990s over Microsoft's creation of "secret" API calls that supposedly gave it an unfair advantage over its rivals. Most of this was nonsense. What hurt these companies was not code but time—the time they had to take to play catch-up with Microsoft, which was ready to release what the market wanted: robust, GUI-based Windows products.

Even more ink has been spilled in bemoaning Microsoft's supposed perfidy in taking advantage of poor old trusting IBM in their joint venture to bring OS/2 to market. Such sympathy is wasted. IBM bears almost complete and direct responsibility for the failure of OS/2. From advertising and pricing through to positioning and naming, it's difficult to find a marketing mistake IBM **didn't** make. The truth is that by 1990, the PC market was ready to accept almost any GUI-based system that worked, and Microsoft simply provided what everyone wanted. Bill

---

[17] Especially after Apple's "Lemmings" ad, which ran during the Super Bowl the year after its famous "1984" ad. The "Lemmings" ad featured a group of IBM-crazed corporate IT types marching to their demise over the edge of cliff while maniacally chanting "Hi ho, hi ho, it's off to work we go." IT managers worldwide developed an instant dislike of Apple, and the ad was being thrown back in the company's face years after its first and only airing. IBM would later fulfill Apple's apocalyptic vision with OS/2 and the software publishing community.

[18] From 1983 through 1989, Microsoft sent "evangelists" out to other software publishers at every opportunity, especially during trade shows. Prior to the widespread adoption of e-mail and the Internet, these events were considered prime opportunities to beg and cajole other companies to support Windows. During this time frame, the company was ready and eager to share technical specifications for Windows, do joint marketing, and make wide-ranging concessions in return for developer support. Most companies, with the exception of a handful such as Micrografix, a Texas-based publisher of graphics and drawing programs, rejected Microsoft in favor of IBM's strategic OS for the desktop, OS/2.

Gates is undoubtedly a very smart guy, but someone with half his brains could have whipped IBM.

What ailed IBM then and what ails it today is that the company is simply too big. Although no one has ever been able to identify exactly when a company becomes so huge it can no longer effectively compete, by the early 1990s IBM had clearly reached that point. With 400,000+ employees, and products that competed in every segment of the market in almost every country of any note, IBM of necessity had to manage and assign priorities to a welter of competing interests and initiatives. It was a task of dizzying complexity and perhaps a business genius could have managed it. Large organizations, however, tend not to promote geniuses to top managerial positions. Geniuses tend to be monomaniacal in their focus, less than solicitous of other people's feelings, and often make those around them uneasy (a description that reminds many of Bill Gates). Smart politicians are the types who usually climb to the pinnacle of corporate success in large companies, but a company of IBM's size needs more than an affable organization man to kick it in a desired direction. Though during his tenure at IBM, Lou Gerstner was lauded by the press for the company's modest turnaround, his financial accomplishments came more from cost cutting and retrenchment than renewed business growth. And shortly after Gerstner's departure, his successor announced that, yes, things were still rather slow at IBM and more layoffs would be coming.

The answer to IBM's problem, ironically, was discovered by the U.S. government in the 1970s when it attempted to break IBM up. IBM fought the government tooth and nail and eventually prevailed, allowing the company to remain an increasingly unresponsive muscle-bound giant unable to get out of its own way. By the early 1990s, John Akers decided the government had been right after all and developed a plan to split the company into several autonomous divisions. Akers was shown the door before he could put his plan in motion and IBM remained intact, but these were Pyrrhic victories. Voluntarily, of its own accord, IBM should break itself up into different companies and allow each to pursue its own destiny. Some will fail, but the units that succeed will restore growth and vitality to individual businesses that now, collectively, have very little.

seven

FRENCHMAN EATS FROG, CHOKES TO DEATH:
Borland and Philippe Kahn

FROM ITS INCEPTION, Borland International was the *Animal House* of high tech, a group of self-proclaimed software barbarians who broke all the rules and had all the fun. Led by its wide-girthed founder, Philippe Kahn, a Frenchman who started the company with no green card and very little cash, Borland seemed to lead a charmed life for the first few years of its existence. But the trouble with barbarians is their appetite. They tend to like to sit down at the table, rip off a big slab of meat from a half-cooked haunch, and eat rapidly without properly chewing their food. Combine this unfortunate habit with Kahn's Gallic background and the stage was set for tragedy. Confronted with software's biggest frog, the Frenchman's savage nature got the best of him and he choked to death attempting to swallow what any civilized person would have realized was a very unpalatable amphibian indeed.

Borland made its debut in the industry in a big way with the release of Turbo Pascal in November 1983. Turbo Pascal was a port to DOS and CP/M of Anders Hejlsberg's COMPAS Pascal, and it was rereleased by Borland at a price that seemed amazing at the time: $49.95, about one-tenth the price of comparable products. With a single stroke, Kahn had upset the price structure of a market category, a tactic he would employ again and again in the future. Even better for buyers was the product's capabilities: Turbo Pascal[1] integrated an editor, debugger, and compiler in what would later become known as an *integrated development environment* (IDE). The product was a runaway smash and to this day Borland dominates the market in Pascal-based development tools.

Turbo Pascal was a breakthrough in another way. It was the first product of its type to bypass the software distribution channel and be sold directly to customers. Readers of *BYTE* magazine who bit on Borland's full-page ads for Turbo Pascal sent their 50 bucks straight to the company. Borland's marketing coup heralded the beginning of a struggle that high tech wrestles with each day: the desire of companies to bypass the intermediary and sell directly to their customers versus the power of distribution systems to "break bulk" and reach a wide audience of potential buyers quickly.

As befits its *Animal House* antecedents, Borland pulled off a frat house–style prank to get its advertising placed that has entered the annals of industry legend. As Turbo Pascal neared completion, the company

---

[1] Those interested in exploring a piece of software history can download Turbo Pascal version 1.0 for free from the Borland Web site (http://www.borland.com).

found itself long on chutzpah but short of the cash needed to place its ad in *BYTE*. Borland dealt with the problem by inviting a *BYTE* ad salesperson to visit Borland and meet Kahn to discuss ad placement. While this individual waited outside Kahn's office, the *BYTE* ad salesperson managed to "overhear" a conversation between the company president and a company employee masquerading as a salesperson from a rival magazine discussing Borland's advertising plans with that publication. Ad salespeople having the morals of, well, software barbarians, the *BYTE* representative agreed to cut a deal that allowed Borland to place its ad in *BYTE*[2] without an upfront payment if Borland would agree to change its placement strategy and "emphasis." Borland was glad to agree and history was made.

After Turbo Pascal's introduction, the company continued to release a steady stream of successful utilities and programs, including a keyboard macro product, a low-end database, more languages, and most famously Sidekick, the first of a short-lived class of *terminate and stay resident* (TSR) products. TSRs took advantage of an oddity in DOS that allowed them to stick around in memory after they'd been shut down. A keystroke combination recalled the product, which popped up in a window over your current application. Sidekick integrated an editor, a calculator, a phone dialer, and some other goodies in a neat little package that gave buyers an early taste of the joys of a multitasking software environment.[3]

Borland was aided in its growth by Kahn's astute handling of the media. In addition to his ability to sweet-talk the publishing side of the PC press, Kahn was also a favorite of the editors and writers. Kahn played saxophone, was a karate black belt, gave good quote, and always seemed to be involved in some newsworthy antic, such as Borland's wild toga party at the 1984 COMDEX trade show. He also possessed a talent for getting under Bill Gates's skin, and the press always appreciates a good gladiatorial contest.

An example of Kahn's persuasiveness was demonstrated when he convinced *PC Magazine* to give Borland's minor-league TSR spelling and

---

[2] *BYTE* magazine, perhaps the microcomputer industry's most respected publication for much of the 1970s and '80s, ceased print publication in 1998, though an online version of the magazine still exists (http://www.byte.com).

[3] The age of the TSR would prove to be short. This class of software had sharp little virtual elbows and different programs didn't play together well. Loading more than one TSR into your system frequently led to system lockups and crashes.

thesaurus utility, Turbo Lightning (for a while practically every product in Borland was "turboized"), front cover status. The accompanying article was a breathless piece that discussed how Turbo Lightning was going to revolutionize . . . uh . . . spelling. (The author of the article, pundit Paul Somerson, was still living that one down years later.)

Kahn was also quick to promise end users that they too would share in the booty when Borland's conquest of the software universe was complete. He became famous in the mid-1980s for decrying the high price of software, proclaiming that it should be priced like a "book," and pointing to the pricing of Turbo Pascal as the wave of the future. The crowds, as could be expected, roared their approval and for a while Philippe Kahn was the most popular man in software.

~

Barbarian Conquests

Borland made its first play for big-league status with its 1987 purchase of Ansa and its Paradox database. Now buried in the Corel Office suite, Paradox, first released in 1985, has never received the credit it deserves for its innovative design and breakthrough performance. The product's initial claim to fame was its introduction of *query by example* (QBE) capabilities to PC relational databases. Instead of typing in long lines of obscure queries, a Paradox user could quickly recall records by simply checking off boxes from an onscreen image of the database, and then save these visual queries for future use. This capability, combined with powerful form creation and scripting features, made the product a viable competitor to Ashton-Tate's dBASE and the various Xbase clones. The product often, if not always, came in first in reviews and competitive analyses, and by the 3.0 release Paradox was widely considered to be the "best of breed" in the DBMS desktop market.

Even better from Borland's standpoint was the fact that the product couldn't be easily cloned. The Paradox scripting language manipulated "objects" such as queries, reports, and forms within the Paradox environment and resisted compilation technology. On the other hand, Paradox was accessible enough to allow third parties to develop utilities for and extensions to the product. The combination of power, price, and third-party push helped Paradox begin to make major inroads into a market formerly dominated by Ashton-Tate and the Xbase alternatives. By the time of Borland's takeover of Ashton-Tate in 1991, Paradox owned about one-third of the market for PC desktop databases. Interestingly enough, Borland kept the price of Paradox at $695.00, then the median price for high-end database products. It seemed the software barbarian was willing to ape the ways of civilization when they suited his purposes.

After Ansa and Paradox, Borland purchased the Surpass spreadsheet from Seymour Rubinstein of WordStar fame,[4] renamed it Quattro, and entered the spreadsheet market with barbarian zest. As part of his slash-and-burn tactics, Kahn launched what became known as a *competitive upgrade* promotion against Lotus, which had lagged in releasing its new 3.0 version of 1-2-3. The competitive upgrade works by offering the user of another product your product at a reduced price in return for the user ostensibly "turning in" her current product—a desirable marketing "twofer" because the upgrade increases your installed base while simultaneously decreasing your competition's. Quattro's pricing was initially lower than the $495.00 median for spreadsheets but, as with Paradox, by 1990 it was repriced to match industry standards. The competitive upgrade was kept sharp and at hand in Borland's promotional arsenal, and periodically the company launched one when it spotted an opportunity. Wielded in the hands of barbarians, cutthroat pricing and competitive upgrades were fearsome weapons, but they were ones that more civilized warriors could also employ, as Borland would one day discover.

In 1991, Borland reached over $200 million in annual revenue, mainly on the strength of growing Paradox sales. Kahn was now at the height of his ambitions and looking for new conquests. Casting his fierce gaze about, it came to rest on Ashton-Tate, a wounded company that seemed ripe for the picking. Negotiations commenced between the barbarian and his intended prey. Alas, a group of smooth-talking and decadent civilized men seem to have seen the savage coming and talked him into forking over the princely sum of $440 million in Borland stock for the privilege of raising the Borland tribal standard over once mighty Ashton-Tate.

---

[4] Seymour Rubinstein decided to sell Surpass after determining he didn't have the resources to compete with Lotus and its market-leading 1-2-3 spreadsheet. As you would expect, Rubinstein first offered the product to MicroPro. Leon Williams, the then president of the company, asked my opinion about the purchase. I advised against it, as I felt MicroPro was having enough trouble selling word processors and was in no position to compete with Lotus. Another case of being right for the wrong reason.

Ashton-Tate upon its purchase proved to be a pretty warty property and by no means worth what Kahn shelled out. (A sum in the neighborhood of $200 million would have been more realistic. Maybe.) The company's "crown jewel," dBASE IV, was an ugly frog that showed no inclination to turn into a prince anytime soon, and the rest of Ashton-Tate's software portfolio was pretty toad-like as well. Its MultiMate word processor was obsolete and sales were dying. Ditto for its ChartMaster family of products. There was also an unsellable desktop-publishing program, Byline. Framework was a fine little bit of code, but the brief day of the integrateds was almost over. Ashton-Tate's Mac products weren't bad, but by 1991 it was becoming clear that Windows was going to reduce Macintosh software to a niche market, and Kahn wasn't interested in investing in it. Reduced to its essence, what Borland had bought for its $440 million was a mailing list of dBASE customers and an installed base that was quickly rotting away as developers fled dBASE into the arms of the Xbase alternatives or Borland's own Paradox.

Making matters even more problematic was Microsoft's purchase of Fox Software and its FoxPro product line for $173 million. FoxPro was considered to be the best of the Xbase clones, and many people thought that if Kahn wanted to compete in the dBASE market, this was the product he should have bought. Fox's programs were fast, stable, state-of-the-art, and could have been bought for much less than what Borland paid for Ashton-Tate. Large portions of the dBASE market had already defected to FoxPro, and Borland would need to provide a compelling reason for the migration to stop.

From an employee morale and company-building perspective, the purchase was a fairly savage affair. On the day of the Borland takeover of Ashton-Tate, Kahn, with that unique blend of tact and subtle understanding of the sensibilities of others for which the French are so famous, flew down to Ashton-Tate's Torrance, California, headquarters so that he could watch the company logo taken from the building and dumped in the office parking lot the minute the deal was official. Borland's internal company briefings on the reorganization made it clear that the Ashton-Tate employees were second-class citizens in the Borland empire. Barbarians, after all, don't pussyfoot around when they swagger into conquered territory.

The conquered population demonstrated their appreciation for the barbarian point of view by carrying out numerous acts of petty vandalism, destroying customer databases, and leaving the merged firm as rapidly as they could find jobs elsewhere. On the way out, many took time to call key dBASE gurus and influencers to commiserate on how it had all turned out. The whole process ended up rubbing raw nerves even rawer within what was a rapidly shrinking dBASE community.

The purchase of dBASE also unleashed a positioning conflict within Borland similar to the one that had bedeviled MicroPro years ago with its WordStar versus WordStar 2000 battle. There was no natural technical synergy between the two products; they approached the task of creating applications so differently that there was no hope of ever "merging" them into one product. The Paradox development community thus paid no attention to dBASE and continued to focus on its side of things. From an emotional standpoint, Borland personnel had been taught to regard dBASE as the database product from hell. The company had even once started to build a dBASE clone (yes, Turbo Base) but had canceled it because, in the words of Kahn, "dBASE is a dirty language."[5]

From the Ashton-Tate side of things, many of the surviving employees had little incentive to care about dirty old dBASE and were uncertain about the product's future. A new version, 1.1, released before the takeover, had fixed some of 1.0's many bugs, but dBASE was no longer competitive with the clones and didn't include the long-promised compiler. It seemed clear to many that if you wanted to survive and prosper as an employee at Borland, Paradox marketing and development was the place to be. Complicating matters was the fact that customer and developer interest was turning increasingly toward the release of Windows-based databases.

Borland only made the situation worse with the positioning strategy it finally did hammer out. In this scheme, dBASE was to be the "high-end" product, whereas Paradox was repositioned to be the "end-user" database. Borland, however, didn't reprice Paradox to reflect its new end-user status, and the Paradox development community[6] never considered throwing away the time it had invested in mastering the product

---

[5] *BYTE* magazine, October 1987.

[6] Some of the main social events of the Paradox community were the yearly parties held at the New Jersey home of Paradox guru Alan Zenreich, author of *Paradox Programmer's Guide* and a personal friend of mine. These parties were 2-day affairs attended by leading Paradox developers from across the nation and were much anticipated by all attendees. I attended several of these gatherings, and even after the Borland purchase of Ashton-Tate, dBASE was never discussed during the festivities.

in order to learn a language it had already decided it didn't care for. Instead, the community just politely asked Borland when the next version of Paradox would ship, mailed in its wish lists, and continued about its business.

The dBASE community appreciated Borland's nice sentiments but was more interested in action. If Borland was going to hold onto the dBASE market, it would have to initiate a crash program of releasing high quality, competitive products as quickly as possible. This didn't and wouldn't ever happen during Borland's stewardship of dBASE. Despite public pronouncements to the contrary, it soon became clear that Paradox remained Borland's fair-haired darling. Paradox was assigned the bulk of Borland's advertising and marketing budget for its database products. New releases of Paradox were consistently released earlier and with greater fanfare than new dBASE versions. dBASE would always be treated by Borland as the company's ugly stepchild.

By 1992, the dBASE development community, fearful that the product on which it relied for its livelihood was doomed to become a dead end, was in an irascible mood. Borland found out just how irascible at its 1992 annual developer's conference, when the dBASE attendees began shouting at the dBASE IV 1.5 product manager during a product demo. The 1.5 version would have been a smash hit in 1988, but by 1992 it was another me-too product and there was **still** no compiler. Previous experiences with Ed Esber had taught the developers that the best way to get a company's attention was to throw a miniriot, and though Borland was a much nicer company than Ashton-Tate, people tend to revert back to type under stress. Bullhorns had to be brought in to quiet the crowd down, and everyone from the dBASE side of things went home in a cranky mood. Upgrade sales of dBASE IV 1.5 were very disappointing, and the migration to Microsoft's FoxPro and the other Xbase products accelerated.

~

The Object of It All

In the meantime, Philippe Kahn underwent an experience common to barbarians and pagans throughout the centuries: He had, like Constantine, a religious epiphany. In his case, revealed truth came in the guise of object-oriented programming (OOP). Having been struck down by the light, Kahn arose a changed soul determined to bring his new truth to all of Borland's products. In the future, all of them would have big heaping dollops of objects integrated into their very beings.

The result of Kahn's conversion was a promotional strategy in 1992 and 1993 that centered around telling Borland's resellers and customers about the wonders of objects and the amazing benefits their presence in your software brought to humanity. Bemused resellers nationwide packed into crowded seminar rooms throughout the United States[7] to learn about the hottest new features in the latest releases of Paradox and Quattro were instead first treated to exciting lessons on encapsulation, polymorphism, and inheritance, key elements of object-oriented code. The launch was a less-than-stellar success, as the loud sounds made by stultified attendees slipping to the floor in a deep state of unconsciousness tended to be a distraction to those who successfully remained awake.

And speaking of OOP, what exactly is it? This excerpt from "What is Object-Oriented Software?" by Terry Montlick of Software Design Consultants (http://www.softwaredesign.com) should explain it all to you:

"An object is a 'black box' which receives and sends messages. *A black box actually contains* code *(sequences of computer instructions) and* data *(information which the instruction operates on). Traditionally, code and data have been kept apart. For example, in the C language, units of code are called* functions, *while units of data are called* structures. *Functions and structures are not formally connected in C. A C function can operate on more than one type of structure and more than one function can operate on the same structure.*

---

[7] I attended one such seminar and still have my free copies of Paradox for Windows and DOS that were handed out at the end of the session.

"Not so for object-oriented software! In o-o (object-oriented) pro-gramming, code and data are merged into a single indivisible thing—an object. This has some big advantages, as you'll see in a moment. But first, here is why SDC developed the 'black box' metaphor for an object. A primary rule of object-oriented pro-gramming is this: as the user of an object, you should never need to peek inside the box!"

From this, many potential buyers of Borland software derived the idea that a) Borland software came in black boxes, and b) it was potentially dangerous to open those boxes.

All humor aside, building a promotional campaign for business soft-ware around a technology that was incomprehensible to anyone but pro-grammers was obviously a ridiculous thing to do, but preaching religious moderation to the newly enlightened is often difficult. Kahn didn't stop with Borland's promotions, however. He began to closely supervise the development process of Borland's products, particularly that of the in-the-lab Windows version of Paradox, in order to ensure it adhered to proscribed orthodoxy. Kahn became personally involved in making sure the product had enough object-oriented capabilities, possessed the right "methods" and, of course, as a newly civilized man, was garbed in an appropriate color scheme. The scheduled release date predictably slipped under these ministrations, and the introduction of Paradox for Windows scheduled for early 1992 drifted into 1993.

It's a common reaction for the newly converted to build a monument to mark the occasion of their exaltation into the faith, and Kahn decided to build his. This was a brand-new $120 million Scotts Valley, California, office complex (observers noted the design looked suspiciously like the Microsoft campus in Redmond, Washington) that company humorists designated "Versailles." The need for this expenditure was questioned by many, because as sales of dBASE IV continued to deteriorate the company wasn't exactly rolling in profits.

Music is also part of the ritual of worship, and Kahn, an enthusiastic amateur saxophonist and jazz aficionado, began releasing CDs featuring him and other jazz enthusiasts playing their little hearts out. The cost of producing these CDs was about $300,000.00 a pop, and they didn't turn out to be profit centers. The need for these expenditures was also ques-tioned by many, as Borland stock slid from a high of $86.00 per share to about $5.00 per share. (Those who listened to the CDs proclaimed the music to be "pleasant.")

~

Gates at the Barbarian

While Philippe Kahn was being ravished by the object-oriented light, Microsoft released its Office suite in 1991 for a retail price of around $495.00 and immediately began to do serious damage to its competitors in the business applications market. Microsoft Office was not so much a well-thought-out strategy as it was an attempt by Microsoft to punish Borland for all those competitive upgrade promotions the company was constantly launching at its software rivals. When the suite was first introduced, firms such as Borland, Lotus, and WordPerfect proclaimed their confidence in the best-of-breed theory of software purchasing. Customers, they said, would reject a cobbled-together bundle of inferior software in favor of buying the best product from the best company and rely on Windows and their own ingenuity to achieve whatever integration between applications they felt was needed.

The only problem with this theory was that the competition didn't have the best-of-breed products; Microsoft did. Though Quattro was always well rated by the press and usually beat Lotus 1-2-3 in head-to-head competitions, it almost invariably was an also-ran to the top-ranked product, Microsoft Excel. WordPerfect's botched release of its first Windows-based word processor had landed the one-time ruler of the category in third place. First and second places were usually fought over by Microsoft Word and Lotus's AmiPro. Microsoft PowerPoint and Lotus Freelance usually struggled for the business presentation graphics crown, but the spreadsheet and word-processing elements were the most important factors in a buyer's decision. Advantage: Microsoft.

Both Borland and WordPerfect attempted to fight back with competing office suites assembled from each other's respective products (with SPC's faded Harvard Graphics thrown into the mix), but they were unsuccessful. Not surprisingly, the new suites lacked the integration of Microsoft Office, but more important, they were bundles of second- and third-class programs competing against top-ranked contenders. Lotus SmartSuite faced a similar problem. Lotus 1-2-3 for Windows never placed higher than second in competitive face-offs and usually came in third place (a shocking comedown for the one-time category leader). AmiPro sometimes outplaced Microsoft Word, but Lotus was, after all, the **spreadsheet** company. Freelance usually placed second to PowerPoint in reviews, and the suite's database, Approach, although a decent product, wasn't well known and brought little extra credibility to the package.

~

The Fall of the Barbarian Empire

Faced with both pricing and feature disadvantages, sales of Quattro, as well as WordPerfect, 1-2-3, and others, began to sag. Shocked out of his civilized demeanor, Kahn fell back on barbarian tactics. Borland launched an inept series of promotions designed to stop erosion in Quattro sales. The company accomplished the exact opposite instead, destroying the product's credibility.

The first disaster was the Quattro "WinDOS" bundle. The promotion was Kahn's idea, and he insisted on its execution over the strenuous objections of his marketing staff, who feared the promotion would puzzle the market. WinDOS included both the DOS and Windows versions of Quattro in the same box. Once launched, it quickly became clear that Borland's Cassandras were correct: WinDOS wreaked total confusion amongst prospective buyers. Some people thought that the WinDOS "product" was a hybrid of Windows and DOS. Some thought it was a DOS product that looked like Windows. Some thought it was a special Windows version of Quattro that ran under DOS. Some figured out the box contained the complete versions of both products.

In addition to being confusing, the promotion proved to be a sales killer. It turned out that someone who wanted the Windows version of the product had little interest in the DOS version and vice versa. Many people took advantage of Borland's generosity to help friends and neighbors handle their spreadsheet needs with a leftover Quattro for Windows or DOS. As one observer noted, "WinDOS worked like a competitive upgrade's evil twin." The promotion was hastily canceled, and Kahn, in the spirit of "Le Roi can do no wrong," fired a few of the marketing personnel who had advised against the whole fiasco.[8]

WinDOS was followed by a series of price-slashing campaigns that finished what the earlier promotion had started. Although some of the

---

[8] In all fairness, Philippe Kahn apparently did have some second thoughts about the promotion before its launch. At the rollout of the WinDOS promotion, which took place in England at a swanky London hotel and featured large, billowing clouds of dry ice–generated fog, a giant stage-mounted vinyl WinDOS box that inflated on cue, enough flashing lights to restore the age of disco, and similar items of bad taste, a crowd of about 1,000 people consisting of key customers and journalists was kept waiting for over an hour while Kahn and several Borland vice presidents considered revamping or canceling the whole idea. They didn't, and thus was born one of high tech's most boneheaded marketing campaigns.

early price cuts temporarily boosted sales, this soon stopped as the market wised up and tried to calculate just how low Borland would go. The answer turned out to be $29.95 for a product that a few months earlier had an SRP of $495.00. The pricing strategy reached its nadir when Borland actually ran full-page color ads announcing "Quattro Pro—That's like being offered a Mercedes for the price of a Hyundai."[9] (Apparently Borland didn't realize that the type of people who actually offer you a Lexus for the price of a Hyundai are often named "Vinnie" and have five Rolexes wrapped around their arms and a car trunk full of TVs they'll sell to you cheap.) Interest in buying Quattro turned to skepticism as people wondered why Borland had to sell it at a bargain-basement price or speculated that the company was looking to dump inventory before unloading the product.

Complicating things further was that as its woes with Quattro grew, Borland saw its clout with the U.S. channel sharply diminish. Quattro had often functioned as a loss leader for Borland, a lever it used to ensure distributors and resellers also carried generous quantities of the company's more profitable but lower selling databases. As the spreadsheet's sales and profitability collapsed, distributors and resellers decided they needed to carry fewer Borland database products and wanted better terms on those they did stock, putting increasing pressure on Borland's bottom line.

In the meantime, Microsoft announced it was going to be shipping its long-awaited Windows database, Access, in November 1992, beating Borland's Paradox for Windows to market by 3 months. This was surprising, as Microsoft had pulled the plug on an earlier effort to develop a Windows-specific product and had started again from scratch. Borland, however, in the grip of its object-oriented fervor, had decided it wasn't going to ship Paradox for Windows until it was "right," and it wasn't right enough in 1992.

Microsoft also informed everyone that the new database would have a $99.95 introductory price and would be a part of the Microsoft Office suite. Borland immediately cried foul, but it was hard to feel much sympathy for the company. After all, wasn't Paradox supposed to be an

---

[9] In my work as a marketing consultant I had used the Lexus/Hyundai comparison for years as an example of the value of credibility in positioning a product, and I was very excited to find out a major software company had actually been stupid enough to create an ad of this sort.

"end-user" product? That's how Microsoft was positioning Access, with the Fox line serving as its high-end "developer" product, and $695.00 for a starter DBMS seemed a bit dear.

People also remembered that before Borland purchased Ashton-Tate it had launched a competitive upgrade program against its former rival, offering dBASE users a "lite" version of Paradox for $149.95. It seemed only fair that if the software barbarians were willing to swing the price sword, they should be prepared to defend against it.

Access 1.0 met its November ship date and was greeted with generally decent reviews. The product lacked certain features prized by developers, but it was surprisingly stable for a first release, intelligently copied many of the ease-of-use features of Paradox, and the price was certainly right. It also incorporated a specialized version of Microsoft's Visual Basic, allowing developers to leverage their existing skills when developing applications with the new product.

The release of Access could have triggered a positioning war within Microsoft à la what was happening at Borland, but Microsoft was able to finesse the situation. The acquisition of FoxPro had been very friendly, and former Fox employees, flush with Microsoft stock options and cash, were treated well and, in the main, were happy to cooperate with their Microsoft colleagues and their new database. For example, they helped integrate Fox's heralded "Rushmore" technology, a system of binary indexing that speeded up data querying and data retrieval, into Access, a move that helped make the product more competitive with Paradox. And though over the years Access received the lion's share of Microsoft's marketing and PR attention, a situation that engendered some resentment amongst Fox acolytes, FoxPro **was** regularly updated and improved. This helped soothe wounded feelings and, just as important, kept the dBASE community (or at least Fox's portion of it) from looking for other alternatives to buy and recommend.

January 1993 saw the long-awaited arrival of Paradox for Windows 1.0 at an introductory price of $129.95, Borland's counter to Microsoft's pricing gambit. Unlike with Access, initial reactions were decidedly mixed. Paradox for Windows had serious memory management issues and many bugs (if you've read Chapter 5, this should sound familiar). Features that the developers had requested and hoped would be in the product, such as macros, referential integrity checking, and a data dictionary, were missing. Reviews of the product were polite (Philippe Kahn wasn't Ed Esber) but not enthusiastic, and many urged buyers to wait until the next release. Sales of the product were disappointing.

From the standpoint of Paradox developers, there was a bigger problem. Paradox for Windows was indeed very object oriented. In fact, it was **so** object oriented that it was a completely new system. Developing applications in it meant learning a new scripting language and starting from scratch. Existing applications couldn't be ported to the Windows version but had to be totally rewritten. Borland now had three mutually incompatible development platforms: dBASE, Paradox for DOS, and Paradox for Windows. Only Paradox for DOS had any claim to the title "best of breed," but the DOS market was rapidly shrinking.

Speaking of DOS, although it was shipping Paradox for Windows, Borland also released a new version of Paradox for DOS. It was a solid improvement over the previous product in many ways, but it still lacked many key features that had been long requested. It did have Turbo Vision, though, an object-oriented new interface that required you rewrite a great deal of your previous applications. And it had a new object-oriented version of the old script language. Then Borland introduced ObjectVision, which was sort of a database but really wasn't. Some developers began to think that all this object stuff was getting out of hand.

Faced with this dilemma, the development community hesitated. If you were going to have to rewrite and relearn everything anyway, perhaps it made sense to take a closer look at Access and even FoxPro. Microsoft was certainly selling a great many units of both and, unlike Borland, seemed to be in good financial shape. This is an important consideration to developers, who don't want to see the companies that provide their development tools go out of business and leave them and their applications stranded. Many did take a look and some decided that Microsoft was the place to be.

Later that year, Borland shipped a new release of Paradox for Windows that fixed the bugs, but the learning curve and rewrite issues remained. The financial news at Borland had only gotten worse in the meantime. More developers left the Borland fold.

In the meantime, Microsoft released its first version of FoxPro for Windows in January 1993 to excellent reviews. The migration from dBASE to FoxPro and other clones accelerated. In March 1993, Borland released dBASE IV 2.0. It didn't include the complier, but you could buy it separately. It was a decent product, but DOS was becoming increasingly irrelevant. No one appreciated that little game with the compiler, either. And where was dBASE for Windows? More dBASE developers slipped away from Borland's embrace. They were joined by yet more Paradox developers who were convinced it was time to leave a sinking ship.

In 1994, Borland finally shipped its first version of dBASE for Windows. Demonstrating that the company could be every bit as obtuse as Ashton-Tate at its finest, the product lacked a compiler. It was also difficult to use and master. Sales of Paradox, dBASE, and Quattro continued to collapse. By this time, the trickle of dBASE and Paradox developers leaving Borland had become a hemorrhage.

Desperate to regain its footing, Borland bought a Windows dBASE clone from a small company called Arago and released it not long after as dBASE for Windows. Unlike its first dBASE for Windows, this was a solid, high-performance piece of code with all the features the developers wanted. Incredibly enough, it even included a compiler. At this point, Borland had two incompatible versions of dBASE for Windows, dBASE for DOS, Paradox for DOS, and Paradox for Windows to market and support. Those who weren't confused were indifferent, as fewer and fewer people were buying any Borland database. The company was on the brink of extinction and few people wanted to invest in development tools from a firm in this condition.

By this time the Borland barbarians were restive, and in 1995 a tribal revolt led to Philippe Kahn being kicked out of the company he had founded and of which he remained chief stockholder. Borland exited the business applications market as quickly as it could, selling off Quattro and Paradox to Novell. Corel then proceeded to buy WordPerfect and PresentationPerfect from Novell, combined them with its Borland acquisitions in its own office bundle, and then demonstrated how to lose millions of dollars by attempting to sell a suite of second-tier products directly against Microsoft.

Borland then decided to change its name to Inprise. Half the market thought the company was called Imprise, and when they found out they were wrong, people often looked quite comical as they attempted to reprogram their vocal cords to say the word correctly. After some time had passed, everyone got tired of a name that made you simulate a speech impediment and Inprise went back to being Borland.

The company also decided to return to its development and language roots. Despite being given up for dead, Borland successfully morphed hoary Turbo Pascal into a spiffy new development application called Delphi and crawled back from the edge of the abyss. In 2001, Borland's revenue rose 16 percent to $221 million and profits climbed 11 percent over the prior year to $23 million. Borland ended 2001 with nearly $300 million in cash.

Philippe the Barbarian was dead, but Philippe Kahn survived and went off to found Starfish Software, a company that combined the long-forgotten Sidekick program with wireless technology. The company was purchased by Motorola in 1998 for $400 million. Kahn then went off and founded a new start-up called LightSurf Technologies. Reportedly, his table manners these days are impeccable.

MANAGEMENT

THE REAL CONFESSIONS OF TOM PETERS

Did In Search of Excellence fake data? A magazine suggests it did

Oops! Again. Nearly two decades ago, the top-selling management book of all time made its debut. *In Search of Excellence*, by McKinsey & Co. consultants Tom Peters and Robert Waterman, immediately vaulted onto the best-seller list and ushered in an era of management gurus, management fads, and popular business books that endures to this day.

But now, the outspoken and flamboyant Peters, 59, shockingly admits that he and his co-author falsified the underlying data in that breakthrough book. In an article in the December issue of *Fast Company*, Peters writes: "This is pretty small beer, but for what it's worth, okay, I confess: We faked the data."

Peters may consider it small beer, but this confession is a doozy. *In Search* was the ultimate cult business book. It had a lock on the best-seller list for over three years and eventually sold more than 3 million copies. "Excellence" became a buzzword even after *Business Week* debunked some of the hoopla in a 1984 cover story entitled "Oops!"

"GET OFF MY CASE." For years, many assumed that the authors employed rigorous research and stringent financial screens to identify "excellent" companies. Peters now maintains that he and Waterman simply asked their McKinsey colleagues and other "smart people" for the names of companies doing "cool work." Then, they screened that initial list of 62 organizations for financial performance over a 20-year period. That whittled the list to 43 companies, ranging from Johnson & Johnson to Intel Corp.

Even more peculiar than Peters' confession of inventing data is the author's insistence that his published admission is actually untrue. "Get off my case," he grouses. "We didn't fake the data. It's called an aggressive headline."

That's one way of looking at it. The explanation the authors gave in the book of how they picked their role-model companies is almost exactly the same as the version Peters gave in the magazine. So why the "confession"?

The article resulted from a six-hour interview with Alan M. Webber, a founding editor of *Fast Company*. In the writing and editing of the story, says Peters, Webber inserted the line about faking the data. Peters, one of ten early investors in *Fast Company* who has since cashed out, was shown an advance copy of the article and didn't object to the addition. Then, Webber promoted the story on the magazine's cover with the tag line "The Confessions of Tom Peters: 'We faked the data.'"

Peters says he was "pissed" when he first saw the cover. "It was his [Webber's] damn word," he says. "I'm not going to take the heat for it."

For his part, Webber says: "Tom is being too generous in giving me credit. It was hyperbole. It's in service of a bigger point, which is to trust your gut. Anyone who takes this seriously should be tested for the disappearance of their sense of humor."

Relying on instinct was one of the book's important lessons. It was published at a time when Japan severely challenged Corporate America's dominance. Many believed entire industries were vulnerable to the Japanese onslaught. The book attacked the management-by-the-numbers mindset and sent a positive message that there were many American companies that had got it right. Peters and Waterman claimed the best ones shared eight attributes, such as being "close to the customer" and having organizational cultures that emphasized "autonomy and entrepreneurship."

From the start, there was controversy. Academics sniffed that the work was superficial and lacked rigor. And as *Business Week* pointed out, many of the companies extolled as best fell on hard times soon after publication, including Amdahl and Data General.

The latest controversy has Waterman none too pleased. "It's Tom being Tom again," says Waterman, who remains friends with his old partner. "He loves to be outrageous. But I'm sad he did that because we got criticized after the book was published for being flippant."

Is Peters sorry he let Webber use the line? "If there is a firestorm, I'll regret it," he says. This is one case where following your instincts might not have been such a good idea.

By John A. Byrne in New York

IT'S A DOOZY: *Peters says his interview with Webber (above) wasn't so explicit*

> ❝ This is pretty small beer, but for what it's worth, okay, I confess: We faked the data ❞ — TOM PETERS, *Fast Company*

Oops! Tom Peters admits data from In Search of Excellence *was faked.*

How to eliminate half your work force.

Get the other half to use your software!

The worst piece of high-tech collateral ever created

The Jerry Seinfeld of software: SoftRAM did nothing

The author learns how to sell the original IBM PC.

The PC Junior with its "chiclet" keyboard destroyed IBM's aura of hardware invincibility.

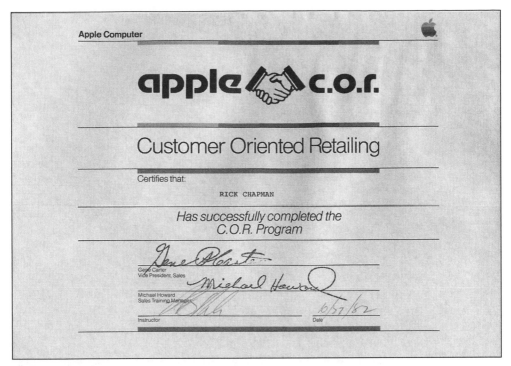

Apple Computer

apple C.O.R.

Customer Oriented Retailing

Certifies that:

RICK CHAPMAN

Has successfully completed the
C.O.R. Program

Gene Carter
Vice President, Sales

Michael Howard
Sales Training Manager

Instructor

Date

Ready to sell some fruit

IBM

Personal Computer Training Program

This certifies that

RICK CHAPMAN

has attended the course in

MARKETING THE PERSONAL COMPUTER

and in recognition thereof is awarded
this certificate.

10/14/82

Date

Training Manager

The author's PC marketing "diploma"

The "Two Nags" ad from Microsoft: Which horse loses?

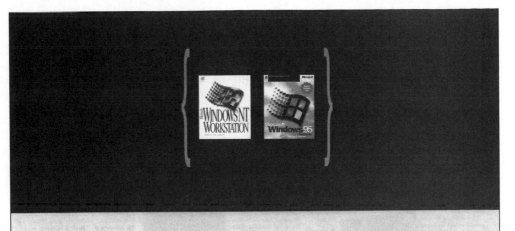

A lot of other companies do, too. They're running both the Windows® 95 and the Windows NT® Workstation operating systems.

Why? Because they want to realize the benefits of a more reliable, more manageable operating system. They also want to run the latest

versions of their applications* and take advantage of exciting new Internet technologies. That's why seven out of ten organizations**

have deployed (or are planning to deploy) Windows 95 and/or Windows NT Workstation: They know that both are safe bets.

The reason we developed both operating systems is twofold: First, to achieve maximum compatibility with our customers'

existing hardware and software, and second, to provide them with an even more reliable and secure operating system.

Today, customers can run most of the same applications across both Windows 95 and Windows NT Workstation. And soon,

with the release of Windows NT Workstation 4.0, both products will share the same user interface.

What's the right mix for your organization? That depends on what you need. **Windows 95** is the easiest way to migrate

to 32-bit Windows. It not only supports a third more hardware devices than Windows NT Workstation, it also has lower system

requirements. Windows 95 also offers greater compatibility with certain MS-DOS* applications. What's more, it has two

functions that Windows NT Workstation, for the time being, does not: Plug-and-Play, and Power Management for mobile users.

Windows NT Workstation, on the other hand, offers greater reliability and security, thanks to its advanced microkernel

architecture. It's simply one of the most powerful and robust 32-bit desktop operating systems you can get.

So if you thought you needed to hedge your bets, you don't, because this is no horse race. In fact, we will continue to

support and update each product in the future since our customers continue to want both the broad compatibility of Windows 95

and the power of Windows NT Workstation.

For more help determining the best mix for your company, visit www.microsoft.com/windows/mix4/

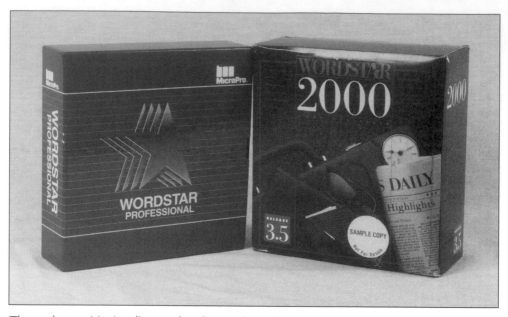

The product positioning disaster that destroyed MicroPro

The Internet's biggest celebrity looking for a new job

MicroPro International Corporation 33 San Pablo Avenue, San Rafael, CA 94903 · (415) 499-1200 · Telex 340-388

MEMORANDUM

TO: Dick Churchville

FROM: Adriana Slager
           Betts Disney

DATE: August 19, 1983

RE: Rick Chapman
           Field Support Class
           August 1 - 12, 1983

We in Marketing Services and Training were very impressed with
a Field Support Specialist like Rick. He excells in the
categories of product knowledge, industry knowledge, and sales
presentation techniques.

Both presentations were smooth, professional, and meticulously
presented. Rick is an excellent addition to the New York office.

Recommendations lie in the area of Rick's continuing the sharing
of his product and industry knowledge with his peers.

cc: Rick Chapman

The first step on the road to product manager and WordStar "glory"

Ashton-Tate's very own underground comix

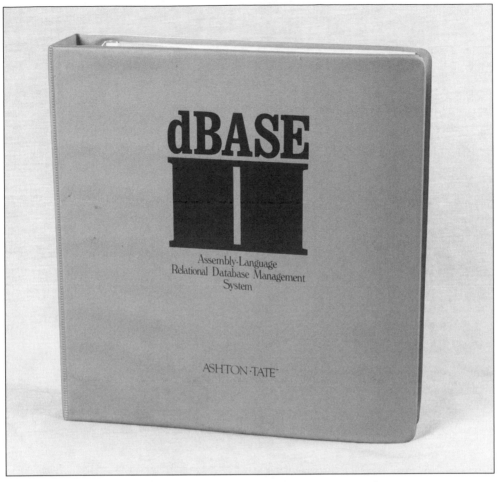

The author's personal copy of dBASE II, the product that built Ashton-Tate

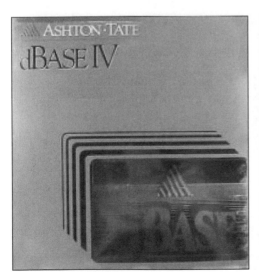

dBASE IV: The product that destroyed Ashton-Tate

The second-worst piece of high-tech collateral ever created

Something everyone with Windows should look into.

OS/2 eats a potential customer.

Ads like these helped destroy the market for Borland's Quattro spreadsheet.

MAY 1993, VOLUME 1, NUMBER 3

OS2
PROFESSIONAL

THE BORG IS HERE

$6 U.S.
$8 Canada

0 74470 82884 6   05

OS/2's Star Trek themes led to the Warp naming fiasco.

eight

BRANDS FOR THE BURNING:
Intel and Motorola

THE CONCEPT OF BRANDING has always held a special allure for marketers in all industries, and high tech has by no means proved immune to its siren call. Throughout the 1990s, numerous articles, seminars, books, gurus, and Web sites all proclaimed the "magic of brands." An unending supply of PowerPoint presentations placed before the High Priests of Investment Wealth, the venture capitalists (VCs), fervently declared their fealty to the brand in different ways, some promising to "establish brands," others to "drive brands to the market," and yet others to create "universal brands." The Internet frenzy led to the brand's ultimate apotheosis in the late '90s as millions of innocent dollars were burnt on the altars of sock puppets, consumed in the name of just-in-time snacks for slackers too busy to shop for themselves, and sacrificed in uncounted numbers at America's supreme religious rite of marketing, the Super Bowl.

The benefits of brand worship are said to be many. Brands are supposed to be able to

- Make sure everyone knows who's selling the stuff they're buying (brand *identity*).
- Allow you to charge and sell more of your stuff (brand *premium*).
- Help you sell new stuff (brand *extension*).

But alas for the Brand Acolytes, as in many cases the Gods of Branding seemed to not hear the piteous cries for profits emanating from their frenzied followers. Millions of their dollars vanished down the maws of the Gods with no measurable return on investment (ROI). The Pets.com Sock Puppet ended up being recycled as footwear for the homeless. The slackers and their attendant love handles were forced back to the bricks and mortar stores, where they resumed laboring joylessly at the task of buying and bagging their own sustenance. Hundreds of thousands of eager-eyed dot-com twenty-somethings were detoured off the fast path of success to employment opportunities in food courts and retail service. The Gods of Branding had failed them all.

Much agony and disillusionment could have been avoided if the people had understood more about the nature of the deities they worshipped. For although brands can be powerful and mighty, they suffer from many weaknesses and limitations, and they often turn on those who fail to understand their fickle nature. The Gods often turn out to have feet of clay.

~

The Nature of Brands

To ensure a sojourn at the branding altar free from sin, it's vital to understand what a brand is. First, it is not, nor can it ever be, a product or service. This is a concept difficult for many marketers to grasp. Yes, you can buy a company. And you can buy its brands. However, you can never sell these brands to the customer. All you can ever sell is products or services.

This basic fact was ignored time and again during the dot-com and application service provider (ASP) boom of the late 1990s. Branding exercises were substituted for sustainable business models. Billions of investment dollars were lost as companies poured money into expensive media and PR campaigns without first analyzing or testing whether anyone would actually buy their offerings.

The reason brands can never be sold is that they're symbols, intangible entities created and charged by dint of product excellence, unceasing PR, advertising, and good collaterals with **positive** equity. Brands live in a symbiotic relationship with products and services. If a product or service offers value and utility, a brand "rides along" with the purchase decision, whispering a soothing string of assurances into the buyer's soul that he's done the right thing. The ultimate goal of investing in a brand program is the ability to charge a premium for a product or service, to increase market share, or both.

Please note the emphasis on positive equity. It's quite possible for a brand's equity to change from positive to negative, and when this occurs, you no longer have a brand. Instead, you have a liability or an *antibrand*, if you will. WordStar is a classic example of a product's brand equity changing from positive to negative. At the beginning of the 1980s, WordStar represented power and market dominance; by the 1990s, WordStar stood for hard-to-use and out-of-date.

A more recent example of this phenomenon is the gruesome fate of the aforementioned Pets.com Sock Puppet. The Sock Puppet is an example of creating a *brand component* to support a corporate branding program. The Sock Puppet followed in the footsteps of his ancestors, Speedy Alka-Seltzer and the Pillsbury Doughboy, and was a huge PR success. Everyone loved that stuffed bit of cloth with buttons attached, so much so that when Pets.com collapsed, the company announced it was selling the rights to the Sock Puppet and listed it as one of the company's assets.

This was, of course, ridiculous. Some pundits claim that brands and brand components don't die. They're wrong, and sometimes something even worse happens. The brand component upon death undergoes a horrible transmogrification and emerges from the grave in a decayed, decrepit state. This awful fate befell the Sock Puppet. He became a mortuary icon, a symbol of death and failure, an antibrand. His decayed remains showed up in a Super Bowl commercial. He appeared in numerous mocking cartoons, his pathetic body subjected to all manner of indignities (run over, squashed, dismembered, torn apart) to illustrate the foolishness of the Pets.com (and the entire "dot-bomb") strategy of pursuing brand recognition and bigness while ignoring business realities.

What was the marketing value of the Sock Puppet? Nothing. Unless, perhaps, you're in the business of selling coffins. (He finally did get employment in a comparable industry: selling auto loans to people with bum credit.)

~

The Sins of Branding

But even those who have learned that a brand is a symbol often fall into error by failing to understand that a brand can only arise from two sources. The first is as a result of product success. Most brand identities spring from this source. For example, Proctor & Gamble transformed Crest from just another contender to America's leading toothpaste for decades after persuading the American Dental Association that Crest really did help prevent cavities. For a time, Crest was the only toothpaste able to make this claim, and the moms and dads of America flocked to buy a product that could objectively back up its claim to be "better." Building upon this success, Proctor & Gamble was able to build a brand around Crest, introducing over time an entire family of related Crest-brand products including mouthwash, dental accessories, and variants of the toothpaste.

In high tech, most brand identities have also been built upon product success. Apple's powerful brand image flows from its introduction of the Macintosh computer in 1984. From this point until the early 1990s, the Macintosh was clearly superior to other systems in ease of use and functionality,[1] and many argue this superiority continues. And though it has became common practice for many to denigrate Microsoft technology, during the 1980s and early '90s most of the company's applications, particularly Excel, Word, and PowerPoint, received favorable press mentions and often beat (or at least equaled) their competition in head-to-head comparisons.

The second source of brand identity is a branding program. This type of program is a deliberate attempt to create brand identity and recognition via massive PR and marketing campaigns. Such efforts are expensive, and usually only large companies with established product lines can afford them. Remember, you can't sell a brand—you can only sell a product or service. That means every dollar spent on their creation comes out of your marketing and sales budget. It can be difficult, though not impossible, for even large companies to calculate how many incremental dollars a branding program is generating. But if you have the resources and money to execute one, over time a corporate branding campaign can build tremendous market awareness for your products and company while also acting as a formidable barrier to market entry for your competition.

A second great error many marketers fall into is failing to understand the limitations and requirements of brand creation. For example, just because your products have high name recognition doesn't mean people will automatically buy them. Once Windows-equipped PCs had caught up to the Mac (or had at least become good enough) in terms of ease of use and flexibility, Apple's market share rapidly dwindled. In place of technical superiority, Apple has substituted "coolness" and innovative design. But this only carries you so far in high tech. Apple's current worldwide 3 percent to 4 percent market share in sales of new hardware attests to this. Everyone knows about Apple; not everyone buys a Macintosh.

The PC market also taught IBM the limits of branding. The Silicon Beast the company unleashed in 1981 made many of IBM's brand

---

[1] However, this wasn't true in terms of stability and reliability. By the mid-1990s, Windows NT was widely acknowledged to be superior to the aging Mac OS in this regard.

intangibles—reputation, safety, and market leadership—less important. Over time, the ability of former college student Michael Dell, who started his business assembling PCs in his dorm room, to manufacture desktop computers more cost-effectively than IBM has proved to be a more powerful market incentive than IBM's lofty reputation. IBM had the point driven home by the collapse of its PS/2 effort.

Nor do brands allow you to simply raise prices at will. Many companies learned this lesson the hard way. Throughout the 1980s, Porsche and Mercedes raised the prices of their products seemingly in defiance of the laws of economics as consumers developed a thirst for German engineering. When they were done, by the early 1990s a fun little two-seater, such as the Porsche 944, that you could have bought for $14,000.00 in 1982 cost almost $50,000.00, and a small family sedan, the Mercedes Benz 190, that initially went for $15,000.00 cost $45,000.00. Then Mazda introduced the Miata for about $15,000.00 and Porsche's sales disappeared. Toyota and Nissan introduced full-sized luxury sedans for $30,000.00 and Mercedes gave up U.S. market share and profits by the bucketful. IBM also learned this lesson when it introduced OS/2 in 1987 with a price tag of $340.00, a sticker-shock contrast to the $60.00 price tag buyers had become accustomed to seeing for the current version of DOS.

The ability to extend brands can also be sharply limited. On the software side of high tech, companies such as Lotus, WordPerfect, Borland, and most notably Microsoft have built brand strategies focused on superior products and then attempted to extend their success to other products and markets. This isn't to say that the process is always successful. If your product isn't judged by the market to be equal or superior to the competition, brand identity is no guarantor of success. For instance, do you think that because you've (Lotus) created the market's best-selling spreadsheet (1-2-3), you can sell a new word processor (Manuscript)? Or because you're selling word processors (WordPerfect) like there's no tomorrow, you can also sell a database (DataPerfect)?

Finally, brands must be defended. This sounds logical and easy, but high-tech companies are often too arrogant to want to bother. Don't people understand that all this technology is . . . well . . . complicated? Don't they realize America's geeks are smarter than they are and understand this stuff? Haven't they learned that they need to be guided by an elite corps of intellectuals who had difficulty getting dates in high school and danced with themselves at the senior prom? In 1994, Intel thought so.

By the early 1990s, the commoditization of the computer market, sparked by the unleashing of IBM's Silicon Beast, was almost complete. Prior to this, if you'd started talking about "microprocessors" to computer buyers, you'd often as not have gotten a blank stare. People bought an IBM or a Mac, not a "chip." But purchasers were increasingly focusing on the functionality of the computers they bought, not intangible brand attributes. If a computer was fast, cheap, and reliable enough, and the company selling it provided decent service, people would buy it. Who really cared what company made it?

~

The Great Pentium Bunny Roast: Intel Inside

In this environment, semiconductor giant Intel spotted an opportunity. Earlier in its history, the company had launched a marketing campaign aimed at IT types that was designed to convince them they should be concerned about whether their computers were built around Intel's 386 processor. The program had been fairly successful and now Intel believed it was time to be more ambitious and make Intel a household name. Though people increasingly cared less about what company manufactured their PC, they still wanted to compare their purchases and brag about them. As a consequence, computer owners had begun to worry about the specifications and speed of their processors[2] in much the same way that car owners obsess over the horsepower and cylinder specs of their respective buggies.

Intel reasoned that if people were going to worry about their microprocessors, the company might as well make them worry about not having one made by Intel. And while Intel was at it, the company should provide disincentives to computer manufacturers in the rapidly growing

---

[2] This obsession led to the phenomenon of *overclocking,* the unauthorized (by the manufacturer) boosting of a microprocessor's speed by ratcheting up its designated clock speed. The first modern overclockers were purchasers of the original IBM AT, who discovered they could open up their units and easily replace the 5 MHz crystal that governed the AT's 80286 chip with an 6 MHz unit. The author occasionally indulges in this nefarious practice and has a collection of fried chips and motherboards to prove it.

home market for PCs from using anything other than Intel microprocessors inside the boxes being purchased by Joe and Josephine America. These dual motivations gave birth to the *Intel Inside* program, the most massive consumer branding campaign high tech has ever seen. The Bunny People were released on an unsuspecting world.

Intel Inside consists of two key components. The first, and perhaps most significant on a long-term basis, is the marketing development funds (MDF) (or bribe, depending on your point of view[3]) aspect of the program. Largely hidden from public view, Intel's MDF systems work by kicking back to manufacturers an average of 6 percent of the total average selling price of the company's worldwide monthly microprocessor shipments. In return, computer makers agree to display the Intel Inside label on their computers and in their advertisements.

The accrued MDF funds don't go directly back to the vendors. Instead, Intel deposits the money in an Intel-managed MDF that the manufacturers must use to pay for print, Web, TV, or radio advertising for their Intel-based systems. If they don't use the funding within 12 months, they lose it.

All Intel Inside participants must **submit every ad, regardless of medium,** to Intel for approval. Ads are checked for compliance with Intel corporate identity standards for

- Size
- Color
- Prominence of Intel's logo
- Verbiage in the accompanying taglines
- Click-throughs to Intel Web sites for Web advertising

Intel also "manages" the percentage of the funds that vendors must use for advertising in each medium. Helping Intel manage the process is a 100-page manual of regulations that even dictates how ad copy must be written. Failing to follow Intel's guidelines and committing even a minor infraction can lead to all MDF funds being frozen. Adding a product that uses a non-Intel chip to an existing line leads to forfeiture of all Intel MDF for that line. The vendor must establish a new product line to maintain access to its Intel Inside funds.

---

[3] MDF plays a similar role in the software industry. In 1988, I spent a day in Buffalo, New York, handing out what are called *spiffs* (cash payments) to telemarketers at computer distributor Ingram Micro every time they sold a package of WordStar 2000.

Intel Inside has proved very successful in locking Intel's competitors out of the top end of the market. Of the top ten PC makers, only HP currently uses non-Intel chips in its business desktop lines, though nine of the ten top PC makers use non-Intel chips in brands targeted at the consumer and small office/home office (SOHO) markets. Giant Dell Computer, despite nonstop flirtations with Intel's main rival Advanced Micro Devices (AMD) that are designed to keep Intel honest, remains an Intel-only shop.

Invasion of the Bunny People

The second and far more visible aspect of Intel Inside is a massive media campaign consisting of a series of ads and commercials featuring all sorts of jiggly jiving critters. The first generation of Intel media pitchmen were known as the "Bunny People": dancing "technicians" who leaped around in the "clean suits" worn by the people who work in semiconductor fabrication plants. Just like real rabbits, the Bunny People have been supplanted by numerous descendants, including the Blue Man Group and animated aliens who look like Bunny People whose genes have been subjected to nuclear radiation in a hidden lab. In addition to the Bunny People, Intel also created a jingle (the company calls it a "signature ID audio visual logo") placement program—that ubiquitous 3-second tad-dah-tad-DAH song snippet millions of Americans have had pounded into their subconscious during a Dell or Gateway TV ad.

The main thrust of Intel's media campaign was to convince people that computers are more fun, exciting, and colorful if they have Intel inside and, after spending a great deal of money, Intel succeeded in doing just that. Millions of people knew about Intel (though many weren't precisely sure what they knew), bought computers that had Intel inside, and were confident that in doing so they had assured themselves of the very best computing experience they could have. That's because their computers had Intel inside and that was a good thing because . . . Intel had spent a lot of money to hire dancing Bunny People to say so . . . and because it costs a lot of money to hire dancing Bunny People, lots of people must be buying Intel . . . so Intel has lots of money to spend on dancing Bunny People and that's . . . a good thing!

By 1994, the Intel Inside program had built up a full head of steam and that was a good thing, too, because Intel was about to introduce its Pentium chip, a major product and marketing milestone for the company. Prior to the Pentium, Intel had identified chips via a series of numbers that also corresponded to the chip's ancestry. The 286 was the second generation of the 8086 line, the 386 the third generation, and so on. However, Intel had been told by a very unsympathetic trademark office that it wouldn't be granted a trademark on a series of numbers, and that anyone could call their chip a "486" if they felt like it. Intel promptly renamed its 586 the "Pentium" and the Bunny People were instructed to leap about with enthusiasm to celebrate the event.

People responded favorably to all of this frantic dancing, and new Pentium-based computers flew off the shelves. The computers all seemed to work very well, undoubtedly because of the Intel inside them, and America was a happy, happy place. And then a disturbing serpent appeared in Intel's sales paradise as a rumor spread through the Internet and the media about a flaw in Intel's latest microprocessor. It appeared the Pentium inside in your computer couldn't . . . well . . . count.

The Rabbits Fail Math

The problem was with the Pentium's *floating-point unit* (FPU). An FPU speeds up the operations of software that does extensive calculations involving decimal-point math. Unlike previous Intel microprocessors, all new 58 . . . er . . . Pentiums integrated an FPU directly into the chip itself. Prior to this, if you wanted to obtain the benefits of an FPU, you often had to purchase a separate chip, usually called a *math coprocessor,* and install it inside your PC. Most people didn't bother; only a handful of software packages made much use of FPU math operations.[4] But people who were concerned about math operations did buy them or bought chips that had FPU capabilities and, being math types, they tended to be quite picky about the answers the chips provided.

One of these picky people was Thomas Nicely, a math professor at Virginia's Lynchburg College. In the summer of 1994, while checking the sum of the reciprocals of a large collection of prime numbers on his Pentium-based computer, Nicely noticed the answers differed significantly from the projected correct values. He tracked the error down to the Pentium by running his calculations on an older system that used a previous generation 486 chip. This unit spit out the right answers.

---

[4] Foremost among the applications supporting the Intel's FPU chips was 1-2-3 from Lotus. For the first several years of its existence, 1-2-3 almost exclusively drove sales of Intel math chips. Interestingly enough, Intel also had a text coprocessor it periodically marketed to the word-processing companies, but none of them ever developed for it.

Confirmation in hand, Nicely promptly sent off some inquiries to Intel about his results. Intel, wrapped up in the care and feeding of its Bunny People, ignored him. Nicely thereupon posted a general notice on the Internet asking for others to confirm his findings. Intel, after realizing Nicely was not going away, talked of hiring the professor as a "consultant," and Nicely signed a non-disclosure agreement that basically said he wouldn't discuss further developments on the issue. The cat, however, was out of the bag—to Nicely, and Intel's, great surprise.

What was actually happening inside the Pentium was fairly obscure (except to picky math people). The Pentium contains what are called *lookup tables,* rows of values embedded in the chip that speed up math calculations. When creating these tables, someone had put a zero in one of the columns. What should have looked something like this:

123456789

looked something like this instead:

123456089

The real-world results of that misplaced zero were that the Pentium would give incorrect answers on numbers that went past four decimals. What should have read

5505001/294911 = 18.666651973 *(486 with FPU)*

instead came out as

5505001/294911 = 18.66600093 *(Pentium)*

Making matters worse for Intel was that as the investigation into the Pentium's problems continued, other, even more obscure problems surfaced with the chip's math processing.

As Intel was quick to tell everyone, a bug in a microprocessor's embedded code or data isn't a new phenomenon. An *errata sheet,* a document listing known problems with a chip, accompanies practically every major CPU released by Intel, Motorola, AMD, and so forth. Engineers are used to dealing with these problems and devising workarounds. Usually, the chip's maker issues a software patch to deal with any programming or application issues, the fabrication plant makes an inline change to its manufacturing process, and that's that. After all, these things happen and Intel had never promised you a rose garden.

Um, well, yes it had. Somehow, as the Bunny People had leaped and cavorted on the screens of America's TVs, they had failed to mention errata sheets. Software patches. Workarounds. They hadn't mentioned those at all! Millions of computer buyers were confused and amazed.

Intel's actions subsequent to the disclosure of the Pentium's FPU faux pas epitomized techno-geek stupidity at its worst. As news about the problem spread, Intel announced that

> *". . . an error is only likely to occur [about] once in nine billion random floating point divides . . . an average spreadsheet user could encounter this subtle flaw once in every 27,000 years of use."*

Critics responded by noting that although it might be unlikely you'd get a wrong answer, if your calculation met the right conditions you could be **sure** of getting a wrong answer. And worse, there was no way of knowing **if** you'd gotten a wrong answer. In the meantime, IBM halted shipment of Pentium-based computers (which wasn't that big a deal because they were still selling more of the older 486 units) and told everyone that "Common spreadsheet programs, recalculating for 15 minutes a day, could produce Pentium-related errors as often as once every 24 days." Wow! That sure sounded more often than 27,000 years!

Then it was disclosed that Intel had known that the Pentium flunked math before it shipped and hadn't bothered to tell the public. OK, it would have been odd to have the Bunny People dancing around with signs on their chests that proclaimed "1 + 1 = 3," but still! We the people expected our Intels inside to be able to count, for God's sake.

Not content to leave bad enough alone, Intel then compounded what was a rapidly growing PR nightmare by having Intel CEO Andrew Grove issue an apology over the Internet while the company was simultaneously telling everyone it wasn't planning a mass recall of the Pentium and intended to sell its existing inventory of math-challenged chips until it was exhausted. After which you could presumably buy a computer that counted correctly. At this point the Bunny People were leaping about to the point of cardiac infarct, but not many people were watching them anymore. People were starting to get really angry or were telling mean jokes about the Pentium. Jokes like this:

Question: How many Pentium designers does it take to screw in a light bulb?

Answer: 1.99904274017, but that's close enough for nontechnical people.

Question: Complete the following word analogy: Add is to Subtract as Multiply is to

a) Divide

b) Round

c) Random

d) On a Pentium, all of the above

Top Ten New Intel Slogans for the Pentium

9.9999973251 It's a FLAW, Dammit, not a Bug

8.9999163362 It's Close Enough, We Say So

7.9999414610 Nearly 300 Correct Opcodes

6.9999831538 You Don't Need to Know What's Inside

5.9999835137 Redefining the PC—and Mathematics As Well

4.9999999021 We Fixed It, Really

3.9998245917 Division Considered Harmful

2.9991523619 Why Do You Think They Call It *Floating* Point?

1.9999103517 We're Looking for a Few Good Flaws

0.9999999998 The Errata Inside

Intel didn't think these jokes were funny at all, but the company wasn't yet done exploring the depths of marketing stupidity. Shortly after Grove's unconvincing Internet mea culpa, Intel announced that yeah, OK, for all those whiners out there, yeah, the company will swap out your Pentium if you're prepared to explain why you need a computer chip that can count right. And buddy, the explanation had better be good.

By now the Bunny People were achieving leaps of absolutely stratospheric heights, but no one was watching, no one at all. A new joke about the Pentium began making the Internet rounds. It wasn't that funny, but to a great many people, it sounded highly accurate:

Question: What's another name for the "Intel Inside" sticker they put on Pentiums?

Answer: Warning label.

The Dark Bunny Dream of Andy Grove

At this juncture, rumors began to spread that members of Intel's PR and marketing groups, perhaps even Andy Grove himself, were suffering from a recurrent dream, a terrible nightmare that some began calling "The Dark Bunny Dream of Andy Grove." They described it like this:

> *"In the dream I am always Andy Grove and the dream always begins the same way. I am looking at a typical American town on a typical American day. The yellow sun shines brightly in a royal blue sky spread over a sea of prim tract houses of varying tasteful hues, each placed with geometrical precision in the center of a perfect green lawn. A neat white picket fence surrounds every home and each garage holds two cars, at least one being a sensible and reliable Japanese import. (Yes, we're all Americans here, but we need to make sure we get to work on time every day!)*

> *"In each perfect house is a perfect PC, all of which have Intel inside. This is a good thing because . . . Intel had spent a lot of money to hire dancing Bunny People to say so . . . and because it costs a lot of money to hire . . . well, we already covered this. In any event, each perfect PC has become an integral part of each perfect family's productive and happy life. As the dream continues, I (Andy) realize I am floating above the home of Joe and Josephine America and their son, Joe America Jr. I have taken the form of a techno-ghost, an unseen spirit who can hear and see everything that is going on in the Americas' home. But today all is not well. I feel more than see the ominous dark cloud that appears on the horizon and rushes toward their snug little abode. Quickly, before the black billows can reach me, I sink through the roof of the home below me.*

> *"Once inside I see that, like everyone else on their block, the Americas have a PC with Intel inside. Dad comes home each night to use the PC to catch up on some office work and check sports scores across the nation. Mom uses the PC to store recipes and manage her family's busy social calendar. Junior uses the PC to help him in his schoolwork as he prepares to become the sensitive and caring yet assertive and forceful high-wage earner his parents know he can be.*

"As I drift through the Americas' home I pass by the kitchen and see a woman sitting at the table of a dinette set with her head in her hands, shoulders shaking from the silent sobs that rack her body. It is Josephine America. On a table beside her is a letter she has just opened. What news can it contain to cause her such grief?

"At the same time, I hear the wheels of Joe America's Honda crunch on the gravel driveway, then the slam of the car door and the sound of Joe's footsteps proceeding to the front entrance. When Joe returns home from work he normally comes bounding into the house to greet Josephine with a hug and a kiss, but today he hesitates to enter, his hand frozen on the doorknob as some unseen force, some unknown instinct, warns him that something is wrong. Very wrong. Inside, Josephine has heard him. Gathering up the letter, she steels herself for the ordeal ahead. The next few minutes will be hard, terribly hard, but she must be strong. For him. (Outside the home the day darkens as thunderclouds build rapidly above the Americas' home.)

"Gathering up his nerve, Joe turns the knob and enters his house to see a grave-looking Josephine facing him, holding the letter by her side. Neither says a word for several seconds. In the stillness, the distance between them seems to stretch like Turkish taffy. Finally, Joe breaks the silence.

Joe: *(Quietly)* Hello, Josephine. What is it?

Josephine: Hi, Joe. We need to talk.

Joe: *(Again, quietly)* I can see that. *(Long pause.)* What's the problem? What's wrong? I assume it has something to do with that letter?

Josephine: Yes, Joe, it does.

Joe: What does it say, Josephine? Are you ill? Has someone died?

Josephine: No, Joe. It's about Joe Junior.

Joe: Joe Junior? What's wrong, Josephine? Has **he** been hurt? Is he ill?

Josephine: No, Joe, he's OK. Physically, he's OK.

Joe: Then what is it, Josephine? For God's sake, tell me.

Josephine: *(Hands Joe the letter.)* Joe Junior can't count, Joe. This report from school says he has the mathematical abilities of algae. A potato can multiply better than Joe Junior. The only thing Joe Junior can subtract is food from our refrigerator. His teacher feels that to allow him to add his genes to the pool would be a crime against computation. *(Thunder crashes outside the Americas' home as the storm begins.)*

Joe: *(Hoarsely)* My God, Josephine! How could this have happened? Who is responsible?

Josephine: It's the computer, Joe. It can't count.

Joe: You mean, our state-of-the-art PC with Intel inside? The computer that Joe Junior uses to do his homework and spends all his spare time playing *Alien Invasion* on? That computer?

Josephine: Yes, Joe. It's the Pentium inside the computer. It can't count. It's in all the newspapers. On TV. Everyone's talking about it. It's made our boy dumber than DOS.

Joe: My God. My God. I can't . . . quite . . . comprehend this. Not yet. That boy had all the talent in the world. I always knew Joe Junior was destined for greater things, bigger things than I could ever aspire to. He was going to graduate from an Ivy League school. Get his graduate degree, maybe an MBA. I hear there's something big coming along, something called the Internet. All the guys at work are talking about it. They say it's huge, really huge. They say it's going to change everything, that one day we'll all be buying toys, groceries, furniture, even pet food on the Internet. I thought Joe Junior might be part of that, get rich, retire young, buy us a retirement home in Florida, make the old man proud.

But none of that is going to happen now. What can a boy who can't count aspire to? A life in middle management at Taco Bell overseeing the chalupa and chimichangas stations? A permanent spot in french fry preparation at McDonald's? A job as an apparel folding and hanger specialist at The Gap?

(Joe walks over to the living room couch, sinks down in despair, and buries his head in his hands, a broken man. Josephine sits next to him and puts her arm around his shoulders. They are silent for a minute. Suddenly Joe sits up, resolve stiffening his spine.)

Joe: Well, we're not going to sit here like the other sheep and take it, Josephine. Not the Americas! Those callous, coldhearted corporate bastards, putting the almighty buck over our son's opportunity to be one of America's top one-percent wage earners! They're not going to get away with selling us a computer that can't count! They're not going to get away with destroying our son's future! I tell you, Josephine, we're going to get justice. We're going to fight for what's right! We're going to sue!

"And I wake up screaming."

Joe and Josephine were as good as their word and several class action lawsuits were filed against Intel. At this point, someone at the company finally yanked the IPU (idiot processing unit) out of the company's PR and marketing machine and Intel capitulated. It agreed to replace its faulty Pentium unconditionally to anyone who asked and announced that the flawed chips[5] were heading to the landfill. By the time it was all over, the whole mess ended up costing Intel about $500 million.

The Bunnies Hop to It

It didn't have to happen this way. But Intel had embarked on a corporate branding program aimed at consumers without understanding the ramifications of its actions. The company had spent millions of dollars promising people that having an Intel inside their computers would make their machines, and by extension their lives, better. Once publicity and perception had compromised this promise, it was incumbent upon Intel to react immediately to redeem itself. Taking refuge in technical minutiae and engineering doublespeak wasn't an option. Instead, Intel had to chart a course of

Groveling

Groveling mixed with effusive apologies

Immediate promises to make it all better

The ritual execution of several middle managers, if necessary

---

[5] Well, most of them. For a while there was a lively gray market for cheap "defective" Pentiums.

If absolutely necessary, the ritual execution of several selected members of upper management, up to and including the CEO (think Enron)

Intel could have saved itself tens, perhaps hundreds, of millions of dollars if the company had immediately offered to replace any "defective" chip, no questions asked. Far fewer people than the number who actually did ask for new chips would have bothered, but the hysteria whipped up by the whole mess roiled the market and raised awareness and concern over the issue.

Still, when it was all over, Intel seemed to recover rather nicely from the whole fiasco. In 1994, people were buying PCs like there was no tomorrow and Intel had the millions available to learn its lesson. These days, the company's Web site brags that

"Today, the Intel Inside Program is one of the world's largest cooperative marketing programs, supported by some 1,000 PC makers who are licensed to use the Intel Inside logos. Since the program's inception in 1991, well over $7 billion has been invested by Intel and computer manufacturers in advertising that carried the Intel Inside logos. This has created an estimated 500 billion impressions, while building Intel's worldwide name. Today the Intel brand is one of the top ten known-brands in the world, in a class with Coke, Disney and McDonalds, according to various rankings."

It's hard to argue with success like that! And, after all, though bunnies know how to multiply, whoever said they could count?

~

Digital DNA:
A Day in the Life of Alfred E. Motorola

It's a hard fact of life for the hardware guys and gals of high tech that it's usually the software geeks who get most of the glory. When software people code a software failure, they usually look like their reach exceeded their grasp; when hardware types build a flop, they look like dorks. With software, a timely patch can often erase the ugliest blemish; with hardware, mistakes are set in silicon, so to speak.

The Loneliness of Being Hardware

A recent example of this principal in action occurred with the release of Palm, Inc.'s m130 handheld computer. Before it released its latest personal digital assistant (PDA) in March 2002, Palm bragged that the device's 16-bit screen could display more than 64,000 different colors, but it turned out the m130 could actually show far fewer. Exactly **how** many fewer was a matter of some dispute. A spokesperson for the company was quoted as saying that by "blending techniques," such as combining nearby pixels, the m130 could display 58,000 "color combinations," which isn't quite the same thing as 64,000 colors. Palm profusely apologized for its mistake but made no offer to take its drabber-than-expected PDAs back despite the screams of some annoyed buyers. It **did** tell everyone it was busy thinking about some way to make it up to its disappointed customers. Industry wits immediately suggested that every m130 be shipped with a big box of Crayola crayons.

No, it's not fair, but that's the way it is.

Oh, there are a couple of exceptions. A few people know who Michael Dell is, though most people think he's that young guy who says "Dude!" in all those TV commercials. But Dell is really a boring company once you get to know it. Its main business is selling large numbers of square beige computers shipped in square white boxes. It's a great business, and Dell is a very, very successful company, but there's not much glamour there. Dell isn't cool and it isn't glorious.

Then there's the guy (Ted Waite of Gateway) who talks to the cow, but cows aren't very cool (though the cow is kind of funny). And his company is losing a ton of money. That's not very glorious.

And maybe Scott McNealy of Sun Microsystems? Well, that's a tough one. He spends most of his time talking about Java and the Internet, though the company actually makes its money selling expensive computers running some incomprehensible OS called UNIX. Isn't Java software?

There **is** Steve Jobs of Apple. Jobs has a genius for hiring people who can design wonderfully colored and shaped computers that about 4 percent of the market wants to buy. He's the guy who brought us the movie *Toy Story* and Buzz Lightyear, and he also looks pretty sharp in Nehru shirts. Some guy from the television show *ER* even played him in that interesting but completely inaccurate movie, *The Pirates of Silicon Valley*. Yeah, Steve Jobs is pretty cool. Too bad more people don't use his computers.

But after that it all becomes kind of fuzzy. Who's the Father (or Mother) of the Palm Pilot? Who's the Disk Drive King? The God of Monitors? The Queen of Keyboards? The Prince of Uninterruptible Power Supplies? The Master of Removable Media?

No one knows. No one cares. It's tough to be in hardware.

On the software side, however, superstars abound. There's Bill Gates. Paul Allen. Steve Ballmer. Larry Ellison. Marc Andreessen. Steve Case. Peter Norton. Dan Bricklin. Ray Noorda. That Linux guy from Sweden—or is it Norway?—Linus Torvalds? Some incomprehensible Englishman named Tim Berners-Lee whom everyone calls "the father of the Web." Heck, even Gary Kildall is famous just for failing big time. Michael Cowpland of Corel used to be pretty well-known too (though most people remember him for that wedding-day picture of his trophy wife draped across a Lamborghini[6]).

There is, however, one hardware company that has some major media mojo attached to it. After years of dancing Bunny People, the Blue Man Group, and hyperactive space aliens, that company is Intel. Microprocessors are the hardware heart of the technology revolution and Intel makes them. Most people aren't exactly sure how a microprocessor works, but they do know Intel produces a lot of them and

---

[6] She looked marvelous.

many know they have an Intel in their computer. Intel is the semiconductor industry's ultimate glamour boy, hardware's Ken doll.

But as we all know, envy exists in this world. Our Ken has a jealous rival, someone who looks at our clean-cut builder of CPUs from the periphery of the admiring throng and grinds his teeth in frustration. "Why is everyone so crazy about him?" our hardware Iago wonders. "I make CPUs too. I'm a multi-billion-dollar company. My technology helps drive commerce and industry worldwide. Why doesn't anyone care about me?"

Too frustrated to watch anymore, the observer turns away and strides by us. A quick glance at his countenance confirms his identity. Who else possesses that peculiar combination of dull stare, pockmarked skin, sandy hair, prominent dental gap, and eternally vacant expression?

Yes, that's him all right. Alfred E. Motorola.

Memories of a Crushing Blow

Motorola has envied Intel its marketing prowess since the companies first clashed in the early 1980s during the rollout of their respective 16-bit microprocessors. Motorola had the better chip, but Intel had "Crush," a prototypical kill-the-competition campaign put together by William H. Davidow. Described in Davidow's book, *Marketing High Technology*, Crush integrated PR, marketing communications, and advertising in a comprehensive effort to convince customers that Intel's ability to outdevelop, outsupport, and outsell the competition made an investment in Motorola's technology a bad bet regardless of technical merit. Motorola was caught flat-footed by Crush and could never develop a credible response. The company ended up ceding the bulk of the glamorous and profitable market for general-purpose microprocessors to Intel.

Motorola has never forgotten Crush, and the success of Intel Inside only rubbed salt in the wound over the years. In 1999, the company decided it couldn't stand it anymore and that it too needed to have a big corporate branding program. Thus was born Motorola's "Digital DNA" program, a waste of $65 million that demonstrated the company had learned little from the body slam Intel dealt it years before.

Bad, Bad Genes

The first problem with Digital DNA was that Motorola never deigned to pay anyone to stick the Digital DNA logo, a sticker that read "Digital DNA from Motorola," on their hardware. This alone was enough to doom the program. Motorola didn't want to pay out MDF because of the expense but was missing the point. Intel's MDF campaign allowed it sell and charge more for its chips over rivals such as Motorola and AMD. The calculation was simple: For every dollar spent on MDF, Intel saw two dollars back via chip sales and profitability. The lack of an MDF component to the campaign also robbed Motorola of the ability to direct the marketing and advertising efforts of Digital DNA participants à la Intel Inside.

The second problem was the program's target audience: Motorola's customers, not the customers of their customers. Motorola's advertising for the program was thus aimed at phone makers, car manufacturers (big buyers of embedded computer systems), and electronics makers, not the buyers of phones, cars, and electronics. This strategy ensured no consumer demand for products with Digital DNA inside them would be generated. It also put Motorola in direct competition with those companies to whom it supplied chips, such as cellular phone manufacturers. Companies such as Nokia and QUALCOMM regarded the prospect of putting a Motorola logo on their phones with little enthusiasm. Again, Motorola had completely missed the point of the Intel approach, which was to make **consumers** demand computers with Intel inside, thus pressuring manufacturers to buy more Intel chips.

The third problem was schizoid execution. Having made the decision to target its customers, the company also diverted precious advertising budget dollars to running print-based consumer advertising as well. This wasn't money intelligently spent; an effective corporate branding effort requires a massive and extensive media blitz carried out over an extended period of time. A few million dollars spent in newspaper and magazine ads wasn't going to create any significant consumer interest in Digital DNA.

After a couple of years of wasted time and money, it became clear that Digital DNA was genetically defective. The program generated no end-user demand for Motorola products, no increased awareness of Motorola, and no increased demand other than that dictated by normal business necessity for Motorola products among its customers. Digital DNA was allowed to quietly wither away into obscurity.

The last time Ken passed Alfred on the beach he kicked sand in his face.

nine

FROM GODZILLA TO GECKO:
The Long, Slow Decline of Novell

MOST PEOPLE HAVE always had a sneaking love for those cheesy Japanese movies in which vast areas of Tokyo were always being subjected to large-scale urban renewal via the efforts of a huge, irradiated prehistoric creature with a bad attitude.

The undisputed king of the Japanese movie monsters was always Godzilla. Anyone who messed with this supercharged lizard that liked to spit radioactive phlegm was guaranteed a bad day. In various encounters he squashed Mothra the Giant Bug, blew away the Smog Monster, pulled the wings off of Rodan the Giant Pterosaur (or whatever), and kicked King Kong's giant chimp butt. (Yeah, yeah, in the version shown in America the monkey wins, but in the **real** version shown in Japan, Kong gets a face full of nuclear halitosis and goes down for the count.) He never even paid attention to the plastic tanks and model airplanes the Japanese army threw against him.

Novell was once like that. The company started off its life in 1979 as Novell Data Systems, a Utah-based computer manufacturer and developer of proprietary disk operating systems. Its main offering, Sharenet, was a very expensive proprietary mix of hardware and software, and Novell had little success in selling it. By 1983, Novell was on the verge of collapse, but before the lights were turned off for the last time, the company brought in one of its investors, a gentleman by the name of Ray Noorda, to see if anything could be salvaged from the mess. Noorda was not a technologist, but he was a shrewd businessman with an eye for value and an almost pathological focus on keeping costs down.

After poking about a bit, Noorda focused on the network operating system (NOS) that was Sharenet's software heart and decided Novell's redemption lay in this product. The NOS, soon to be christened "NetWare," was the pet project of the "Superset", a small group of contractors led by Drew Major and hired by Novell. It would serve as the foundation for what would become, for over a decade, one of the industry's most powerful and influential companies.

NetWare's unique value was in how it allowed users to share files and resources on a network of connected PCs. Prior to NetWare's creation, competing NOSs for the PC market from companies such as 3Com simply partitioned a server (the remote computer on which the NOS ran) into virtual drives. You could store files remotely, but they were inaccessible to others. NetWare was far more sophisticated. The remote hard disk was treated as a common resource available to all users of the network. Individual users were granted rights to subdirectories on the server, and if the user had permission from the network administrator, he could easily transfer files across the network to others. In addition to its file-sharing capabilities, NetWare also made it easy for multiple users to share printers, an important issue in an era when a primitive dot-matrix unit cost about $600.00.

Another strength of NetWare was its independence of any particular vendor's hardware. NetWare could run over ARCnet, Ethernet, or Token Ring. Most of its competitors were tied to specific LAN types or LAN adapters. To communicate between the server and the desktop PC, the company relied on its proprietary Internetwork Packet Exchange (IPX) protocol. For a brief period in high-tech history, IPX became the de facto industry standard for network protocols. This would change as the Internet and TCP/IP gathered momentum in the 1990s.

Noorda initially offered his new NOS to some of the major players in the industry, most notably 3Com. Headed up by Robert Metcalfe, the coinventor of Ethernet, 3Com was the early leader in the NOS and networking environment. In a meeting at COMDEX in 1982, one that typifies the friendly, hail-fellow-well-met attitude so prevalent in high tech, Metcalfe threw Noorda out of the 3Com booth.[1] Metcalfe's reward for his intelligent behavior was to help ensure 3Com's eventual departure from the NOS market.

From this inauspicious beginning, Novell soon bulked up to become the Godzilla of PC networking. In a brilliant marketing move that could have been thought up by Bill Gates, Novell bought several network interface card (NIC) vendors and helped drive hardware prices down. Having ruined margins for several companies but expanded the market for NetWare, Novell dumped most of its hardware business to focus on its OS.

By 1987, Novell was the baddest of the bad in the NOS arena. NetWare crushed Corvus, another early market leader in the industry. Plucked Banyan's VINES. Body slammed 3Com. Kicked sand in the face of Microsoft's LAN Manager and IBM's LAN Server. From the early 1980s to the mid-1990s, Novell's dominance in LANs and NOSs was unchallenged.

---

[1] Noorda liked to tell this story in social situations, and I first heard it from him at the New York rollout of a fault-tolerant version of NetWare in 1985 and in 1986 at a gathering in COMDEX.

Playing to its strengths, Novell also established itself as a major player in the "groupware" category with GroupWise. Noorda also drove the development of Novell's reseller education and certification programs, and made a Certified Novell Engineer (CNE) certificate the most valuable networking designation in the industry from 1985 to 1995. Novell's CNE program was widely admired and copied in the industry. When Microsoft rolled out Windows NT, it made no secret of the fact that its Microsoft Certified Systems Engineer (MCSE) training regimen was based on Novell's program. The company was big, powerful, and profitable. By 1994, yearly revenue exceeded $2 billion at "Big Red."

And then, just like in a Japanese movie, a nerd with glasses and a questionable haircut developed an incredible radioactive shrinking ray and turned it on the rampaging monster. When the ray had wreaked its incredible effect, the beast had been shrunk to gecko-like proportions.

To add insult to injury, the nerd didn't even bother to reach for a tank or a missile or a jet to apply the coup de grace to our miniaturized monster.

He used a cereal box.

$$\sim$$

Crunch Time for Novell

Novell's moment of truth came in the form of an aggressive direct marketing campaign Microsoft launched against the company in 2001. By then, Novell was a wounded lizard in the marketplace, losing market share to Microsoft almost on a daily basis while the press and the industry questioned the company's relevance in a server world dominated by Windows NT, Linux, and the Internet.

Desperate and clearly in over his head, a shotgun marriage was arranged by Novell's then CEO Eric Schmidt. The company merged with Boston-based Cambridge Technology Partners, a large but money-losing consulting and system integration firm. The company's corporate headquarters was officially shifted from Provo, Utah, to Cambridge, Massachusetts. Jack Messman, CEO of Cambridge Technology Partners and former president of Novell from 1982 to 1983, became the head of the newly merged entity. It all felt very unnatural, as if Godzilla had married Mothra. Normally, Godzilla **eats** Mothra.

Microsoft, never reluctant to kick an opponent when it's down, wound up and tossed a "Microsoft Server Crunch" Novell's way. "Crunch" consisted of a clever bit of marketing collateral designed to look like a cereal box. The piece's copy made several statements about Novell and NetWare designed to tempt even the most devout of the company's many Mormons (a faith that discourages the use of coffee) to reach for a cup of java and some strong aspirin. The choicest nuggets in Crunch were

"What's the expiration date on that NetWare platform?"

"You're left with a server platform without the full support of its manufacturer. Which means increasing costs as it rapidly becomes obsolete, forcing you to implement time-consuming retrofits."

"As a result of the recent Cambridge Technology Partners merger, Novell is shifting its focus from software development to consultancy services."

When I read about the Microsoft campaign I flashed back to the mid-1990s. Shortly after the merger of Novell and WordPerfect, I was invited out to Provo, Utah, to train a combined group of Novell and former WordPerfect product managers on software marketing. During the training, the attendees ran up with an ad I now think of as "The Ship Slowly Sinking While the Band Plays On" piece.

The ad showed a picture of a person in a rowboat heading toward a sleek yacht in the distance. The rowboat was meant to symbolize WordPerfect; the yacht, Microsoft. The raison d'être for all this rowing was better service, as represented by the yacht. At its core, Microsoft was claiming it offered better customer service than Novell, a company that at the time was continuing WordPerfect's famous policy of offering 800 (that's toll-free) support to anyone who bought its products.

"This is outrageous," the trainees wailed. "What should we do?"

~

Famous Cheapskates

"**W**ell," I said, "let's think this through. You could call Microsoft and complain that the ad is misleading and unfair and stuff like that, but, you know, while all that's going on you're not answering the charge that Microsoft is making. And I don't think they'll be very moved by your plight.

"**Or,** you could employ that famous marketing nostrum that proclaims replying to a negative ad gives it credibility and draws attention to the competition. Of course, that theory was propounded by someone who entered a sealed time capsule in the 1960s [when Godzilla was at his peak] and missed the development and refinement of the attack ad, which seems to work just fine, **especially** when you fail to answer the charges made by the other party.

"**Or,** you could consider answering the charges the ad makes in a strong and powerful way that makes Microsoft think twice about developing this type of ad in the future. What do you want to do?"

Everyone seemed to think the third choice was the best alternative, so we went to work.

"Well," I said, "how about this? I've been teaching you in the course that Microsoft has built a powerful brand element around the persona of Bill Gates. Gates is presented as a nonthreatening guide to computing for the masses. In public he usually dresses informally, he talks glowingly about the benefits of technology, and he never ever ever mentions money. Despite the fact that he's one of the richest guys on the planet. Why? Because no one likes rich guys, usually. It's the 'Nobody roots for Goliath' syndrome described by master marketer Wilt Chamberlain.

"So let's create the following ad. We'll call it 'Famous Cheapskates.' We'll have a picture of King Midas, Scrooge, and that Getty guy, the one who put pay phones in his home to prevent guests from making toll calls at his expense. We'll put a caption under each cheapskate that tells his or her tale. And heading up the Hall of Cheapness will be a picture of Bill Gates. Next to Gates's picture we'll put a phone with a coin slot on the dial pad. Next to the phone will be a dime. The caption for the ad will read: 'Bill Gates has $30 billion [the approximate count at that time], but when his word processor doesn't work right, he wants you to spend **your** dime to get help.'

"What do you think? Microsoft isn't going to like this: It musses up the company's most important branding symbol. It's accurate. It's funny. And it accesses certain primeval emotions in the mind of the audience. Heck, show it to them before you run it. I bet they'll yank that boat ad if that's what you want."

There was a long silence in the room. I did notice one senior product manager from the WordPerfect side of the company giggling to himself and frantically taking notes. Finally, another senior product manager from the Novell side looked at me with a Utah-deer-caught-in-the-glare-of-the-headlights-of-an-18-wheel-semi-from-Seattle-bearing-down-on-it gaze and said, "Oh, Novell could never create an ad like this."

And so they did nothing, except finally sell WordPerfect to Corel at a loss of about $1.2 billion.

Now, to Novell's credit, new CEO Jack Messman went ballistic when the Crunch campaign appeared and called in the lawyers. Microsoft professed the proper amount of abashment, sent out a correction to the ad, said it was sorry, etc., etc., but all in all it was pretty weak tea. The ad had been sent, the accusations made. What was Novell's answer to these charges? And how would the company respond in front of the appropriate audience (and that audience wasn't found in a courtroom)?

The 1990s were full of similar crunch times for Novell and the company rarely seemed able to rise to the challenge. No single problem led to Novell's loss of market leadership. Rather, a series of interlocking problems sapped the company's strength and drained the fire from its belly.

~

The Big Lizards

Novell from its inception was fundamentally a technology-driven company with a sales-oriented CEO. Like many such firms, Novell tended to regard its marketing operations almost as a problem to be managed, not a generator of opportunity. The problem was exacerbated by the position of the Superset within the company. This group consisted of a small group of elite programmers that had total control over the development of the NetWare kernel, the OS core, and it functioned almost independently of the rest of Novell. Over time, the Superset came to be regarded with almost religious reverence by the rest of the company, with Drew Major playing the role of chief pontiff to its small and self-governing techno-priesthood. You could suggest something to the Superset, but even Ray Noorda didn't give the group orders. For years the members of the Superset weren't even company employees.[2]

One result of the complete ascendance of technology over marketing at Novell was that the company's product management system was weak. Product managers had little ability to impact NetWare's product development cycle. For example, for years the Superset ignored the screams of users demanding a GUI for NetWare. At one juncture Drew Major proclaimed that there would never be a GUI for NetWare[3], and for years, as Novell's product looked increasingly creaky and out-of-date in a GUI-driven world, he had his way. Another clue to marketing's weakness was its inability to provide compelling ROI arguments for purchases of NetWare and other Novell products. The company was good at developing long checklists of technical improvements to NetWare, but it made few attempts to tie these improvements to real-world benefits and savings.

Marketing's weakness carried over to other areas in Novell, particularly its GroupWise products. A powerful competitor to both Outlook and Notes, with over 35 million users (an interesting fact that Novell was excellent at keeping secret), by the millennium GroupWise had a mid-1990s interface badly in need of updating. Novell's product marketing group had known this for years but was unable to persuade the GroupWise development team to provide a modern look and feel for the product line.

~

Island of Lost Souls

Another issue was culture. Until its merger with Cambridge Technology Partners, Novell, as noted, was headquartered in Provo, Utah. Utah is a land of decency, polygamy, and theocracy, all courtesy of the country's most successful homegrown religion,

---

[2] Robert X. Cringely, *Accidental Empires* (New York: Addison-Wesley, 1992), page 278.

[3] Major made this statement before a group of Novell resellers, including Pierre Chamberland of FaxTeam Software.

Mormonism. The state is an anomaly in the United States; it's a place of remarkable cultural, religious, and political uniformity. Mormons make up 63 percent of Utah's population and hold most statewide elective offices. Politically, white Republican males dominate the state legislature. Utah's entire U.S. congressional delegation is Mormon, as are both senators.

The result of this cultural and religious homogeneity proved a subtle problem for Novell as the company grew. Although Utah has fine universities that turn out decent numbers of programmers and sales and marketing types, Novell never held much appeal for people outside the Utah and Mormon milieu, nor did the company make strong efforts to attract them. For instance, though Mormonism doesn't technically ban the use of caffeine, it doesn't look on its use with particular favor either. As a result, obtaining a cup of coffee at Novell headquarters wasn't an easy thing to do. This proved a minor problem in an industry that uses various java brews and caffeine-laced concoctions such as Mountain Dew and Jolt Cola to increase programmer productivity and happiness. After Novell's merger with Cambridge Technology Partners in 2001, new CEO Jack Messman made a point of handing out cigars (Mormons also don't believe in smoking) at a meeting of Novell resellers. Brigham Young may have been spinning in his grave, but Messman's point that the company was going to have to break out of its old mindset wasn't lost on many.

The lack of acceptable sodas mirrored a more subtle intellectual issue that also dogged the company as it grew. Internally, Novell lacked the fizz and ferment of new ideas and concepts that the cross-pollination of employees coming and going generates in high-tech companies. As a result, Novell often seemed to regard itself as above the grimy realities of business. One clue to this attitude could be seen in Novell's intelligence-gathering operations. Industry observers have long noted that if you go to one of the various company-sponsored shows, such as a Microsoft's Exchange conference, you'll find IBM personnel (or their surrogates) in attendance and vice versa for an IBM Domino/Notes show. However, you would rarely find a Novell GroupWise contingent sneaking about at a competitor's conference garnering information. It was just not the sort of thing Novell did.

Novell delivered a more subliminal message about its attitude toward the outside world with its infamous hotel, known informally in the industry as "Noorda's Nightmare[4]." For years, weary travelers who visited Novell at its corporate headquarters in decidedly unglamorous Provo were forced to sojourn at this "inn," as it was the only place for miles around where you could park your head in the evening. Novell's "resort" featured mediocre food, carpeting of a dubious color, threadbare towels, and much scratchy off-white linen drooped over tired mattresses. One corporate type who visited Novell to attend a high-level dog-and-pony show discussing the future of NetWare left Provo vowing to buy NT simply to repay Novell for the lethal case of heartburn he'd developed eating the Nightmare's food.

And, of course, years of success also played a factor in Novell's insular attitude. When a company has done so well for so long it's hard not to think it's got it all under control. But, as Bill Gates has always known, in a modern capitalistic society, they really **are** all out to get you. Properly channeled, paranoia is a useful management tool, but Novell for a long time seemed to lack any.

~

How to Miss Tokyo

The preceding two problems led to the development of a third: Novell's continuing inability to execute product-marketing fundamentals. Positioning and product naming seemed to be Novell's particular bêtes noires. In March 1993, with the introduction of NetWare 4.11, Novell decided to change the name of NetWare to "intraNetWare" in a clumsy attempt to take advantage of all the Internet excitement. No good marketing group would have made such a mistake; the confusion this action generated was completely predictable. Everyone immediately assumed that Novell had discontinued NetWare and began to ask what had happened to the product. After all, there was still a huge market for conventional LANs, and it seemed Novell no longer stocked such an item. After a year or so of trying to explain to the market that, yes, Novell still sold LANs and that intraNetWare was also a LAN product, but with intranet capability as well as all those terrific LAN capabilities traditionally associated with NetWare, Novell gave up and returned to

---

[4] I speak about the charms of the Nightmare from personal experience.

the tried, true, trusted, and blessedly familiar "NetWare" (now with intranet capabilities) name.

More deadly have been Novell's ongoing positioning mistakes. In a reprise of MicroPro's fatal course, Novell created two competing groupware product lines, GroupWise and Novell Internet Messaging System (NIMS, a development alliance with Netscape). Both products are close enough in functionality and audience to generate the dreaded "What's the difference?" question when prospective buyers are considering a purchase, instead of the desired "Why should I buy?" inquiry your sales force needs.

Of course, Novell would have survived all these problems handily but for a single pivotal event: the introduction of Windows NT in August 1993. Despite Novell's earlier success in stomping down Microsoft's LAN Manager, Windows NT was a tougher beast. Microsoft had studied Godzilla carefully and learned from its earlier mistakes. Its radioactive ray guns were primed and ready to take advantage of the beast's weaknesses.

~

Godzilla Meets NT, the Three-Headed Monster

Perhaps Godzilla's toughest opponent of all time was Ghidrah, the Three-Headed Monster. Launched by a team of bad Japanese special effects experts, Ghidrah was a tough dragon-like beast from outer space with, uh, three fire-spitting heads, perhaps worse breath than Godzilla, and, like his pseudo prehistoric rival, the same desire to crush any plastic-and-balsa-wood Tokyo city models it could reach.

In the movie, Godzilla finally chases Ghidrah back to space with some help from Mothra the Giant Bug and Rodan the Monster Who Wanted to Be in *Jurassic Park* but Was Too Rubbery. Like Ghidrah, Microsoft's Windows NT attack on Novell was basically a three-headed affair. Unfortunately for Novell, no giant rubber allies were to be found in Utah at the time, and when the battle was over, Novell, from a sales and market share perspective, resembled Tokyo after Godzilla had completed one of his periodic sojourns through the city.

Ghidrah Does Demos

NT stood for "New Technology," and in contrast to NetWare, it looked like it. By 1993, 9 years after the introduction of the Macintosh and 3 years after the release of Windows 3.0, everyone was tired of command-line interfaces and X:\ prompts. Everyone, that is, except technology-driven Novell and the Superset. In Provo, command-line interfaces remained just the thing, and Novell didn't intend to allow some ridiculous obsession with pretty pictures on a PC screen to mar their NOS's speed and stability.

The consequences of this decision were far reaching. The Windows NT interface made the product much easier to use and cheaper to deploy, and it reduced training and maintenance costs. This was an important point in an early 1990s world in which the principal purchases of LANs took place at the departmental level. As Microsoft gained control of the corporate departments, it positioned itself to attack the enterprise market, Novell's profit heart.

Sweet-Talking Lips

One of the least understood aspects of Microsoft's success over the years is its prowess in working with and communicating with the development community. Microsoft has always been good at making it easy and comparatively cheap to build Windows applications. It provides good-quality utilities, compilers, and frameworks on a timely basis. In line with its earlier efforts, it supported the rollout of Windows NT with several initiatives designed to encourage the development of new client/server applications for NT.

By contrast, developing products for NetWare in the critical 1993 time frame was difficult. Novell's tools were expensive and primitive. Developing an application for NetWare required a programmer to almost reprogram the OS itself. And despite numerous promises, Novell's widely heralded AppWare development framework never seemed to be available. Novell's attitude toward many NetWare developers was a mixture of equal parts distrust and disdain. The corporate zeitgeist at Novell was "If anyone is going to develop applications for our product, it should be us. We understand it and cherish it. If we allow just any hoi polloi to develop for our baby, they might change and deform it horribly." Sort of what happened to Godzilla when progressive aliens attempted to clone him as Mechagodzilla.

Novell helped drive this point home to developers with the shutdown of its Austin, Texas–based third-party development support center in 1994. This group consisted of over 300 employees and was responsible for evangelizing software publishers to build NetWare-specific applications (called NetWare Loadable Modules or NLMs). It has become a standard mantra to proclaim that NetWare was just a file and print server, but despite the obstacles the company threw in the way of programmers, a large and growing market of applications native to NetWare flourished through the mid-1990s.

Novell was particularly well represented in the accounting and database markets, software that fits naturally into a network environment. Companies supporting NetWare included Great Plains, Macola, Peachtree, Oracle, Sybase, and Borland, to name a few. The Austin center supported Novell's ISVs with technical assistance and sold them development tools and utilities. Its marketing efforts encompassed helping companies reach customers via direct marketing campaigns, co-op advertising, and trade show appearances in partnership with Novell.

With the Austin center gone, most of Novell's third-party outreach programs went into limbo. Preoccupied with its purchase of WordPerfect, Novell didn't bother to fully reconstitute its Austin center in Utah for years. The development community, cast adrift, was thus primed to be receptive to Microsoft when it came calling with promises of NT development and marketing support.

Novell's contempt toward its development community also had serious long-term consequences as the Internet tide swept through high tech. Few new Internet applications were released for NetWare as the company spiraled toward irrelevancy. Novell's combination of high development costs, poor support, and shrinking customer base held little appeal to programmers and companies looking to enter new markets. Instead, Microsoft, with its history of providing inexpensive development tools and access to a huge market, and open source, with its even cheaper development costs and rapidly growing community of "anybody but Microsoft" acolytes, garnered the lion's share of new product investment. By end of the 1990s, Novell had succeeded in converting the impression that NetWare was just a file and print server into a fact.

At the same time that Microsoft was stripping away Novell's development support, it was simultaneously wooing the top corporate executive community with a series of nationwide presentations. These presentations focused on highlighting

- NT's spiffy new look (and the fact that it was now actually possible to demo the product to upper management with the hope they'd understand something of what they were seeing)
- NT's underlying functionality and stability (which was inferior to NetWare's when the product was first released, but it was a Microsoft representative doing the talking)
- NT's nice price (an NT departmental solution was far less expensive than its Novell counterpart)
- The fact that Microsoft had more money in the bank than many developing countries and was a safe and smart purchase

Bite and Hold On

Novell's response to Microsoft's relentless attack was initially to do . . . nothing. In this, it resembled those movie scenes in which one large Japanese monster is whaling on another downed Japanese monster that isn't fighting back, just sort of twitching in place like a pinned WWE wrestler. The company was sure the technical superiority of NetWare would speak for itself. The company **did** spend a lot of time telling IT types who reported to the CEOs and CFOs that Novell used far less hardware than Microsoft. Of course, as has happened only about a hundred times in the past, Moore's Law made this argument moot. As hardware prices plummeted, Novell's real and perceived pricing disadvantage only increased.

Godzilla Goes Ape

It took about 6 months for Novell to realize that, no, it looked like difficult-to-demonstrate technical superiority wasn't going to be enough to answer Microsoft's NT challenge. Something more was needed. Novell pondered the situation, then decided the answer was . . . UNIX. In December 1993, the company announced it was acquiring UNIX System Laboratories from AT&T along with the UNIX trademark. Its strategic reason for the purchase: SuperNOS. A grand merger of NetWare with UNIX that was supposed to result in an NT killer. Due date: 1995.

The decision made no sense. As with MicroPro's WordStar and WordStar 2000, NetWare and UNIX on the server did basically the same things for the same people with the same hardware. Yes, AT&T's version of UNIX could also be used on the desktop, but Novell had neither the time nor the inclination to try to develop desktop UNIX for PCs. It couldn't sell the Windows applications it already had. "Combining" the best of the two OSs often meant no more than adding multiple ways of doing the same thing for an audience that had already decided on how things should be done.

And, as with MicroPro, Novell promptly broke into internal warring camps. Key members of the NetWare development group looked down on the UNIX side of the company and made no secret of their desire to see the end of UNIX. The UNIX side of the business resented being treated like second-class citizens and liked to rub UNIX's technical superiority in areas such as preemptive scheduling and virtual memory in the faces of the NetWare folks. To which the NetWare folks liked to retort with a ripping "Oh, yeah?" (a popular comeback among Mormons because they like to avoid swearing). Compounding it all, Novell released an interim version of UNIX it called "UnixWare" which wasn't SuperNOS and wasn't NetWare, but sure sounded like it was some sort of mix of the two.

After about 2 years of this, Novell had enough. In 1995, it sold UnixWare and the rights to the UNIX operating system to SCO and that was the end of that. Along the way, Novell made yet another attempt to provide developers with more useful development tools via an object-oriented programming effort called Serius, but that venture went down the same black hole as AppWare.

Then Novell completely lost its head and in 1994 purchased WordPerfect for $850 million.

To industry observers, the purchase by Novell of one-time word-processing leader WordPerfect Corporation never made any sense, and it was difficult at the time to find anyone even in Novell who would privately provide a convincing rationale for the deal. Publicly, the company stated it was buying Novell to prevent it from "losing the desktop," but as Novell had never had a significant role to play in selling desktop and retail software it was an unconvincing story. The most logical answer anyone could come up with was that because the two companies were located in Utah just a few miles from one another, it was a case of one Mormon-dominated company coming to the rescue of another.

WordPerfect had entered the 1990s in seemingly fine shape, but from 1991 to 1993 it had deteriorated rapidly. Since its inception as Satellite Software in 1979, the company had possessed one of the industry's oddest managerial systems. Ostensible CEO Pete Peterson[5] was actually one member of a governing triumvirate that included founders Bruce Bastian and Alan Ashton. Peterson acted in the role of tiebreaker in the event of a disagreement within the troika and played the role of stern daddy, keeping expenses under control and attempting to build a durable management structure for the fast-growing company. Under Peterson's regime, WordPerfect kept costs low and developed a fairly effective sales and marketing organization. The company was aided in its growth by the fact that then market leader MicroPro was bleeding to death internally over its self-inflicted WordStar versus WordStar 2000 wounds.

Despite his CEO title, Peterson didn't have responsibility for development at WordPerfect; that was under the purview of Alan Ashton. In 1992, Bastian and Ashton, tired of Peterson's stern-daddy management style, decided they were ready to fly free on their own. Peterson was sent packing, and Ashton and Bastian promptly began to spend WordPerfect to death, raising employee head count from about 3,300 in 1992 to 5,500 by the end of 1993, a 40 percent increase. Simultaneously, WordPerfect's sales growth began to slow, though the company did see an increase in revenue from $570 million for 1991 to about $700 million for 1992. This increase wasn't enough to offset the tremendous rise in expenses engendered by WordPerfect's rapid expansion, and the company began to bleed cash. The problem became worse as sales growth continued to slow in 1993.

The main reason for the sales slowdown can be traced back to the first release of WordPerfect for Windows in late 1991. Despite the market's mad rush to Windows, WordPerfect had sent in the second team to develop its first Windows word processor. The company's best project

---

[5] Peterson's brother Andre also worked for WordPerfect and was one of the company's best public speakers. He was legendary for his performances at SoftTeach, an industry-specific seminar series held by computer distributor Merisel. Andre's presentations began with a slide of his wife and multiple offspring and were enlivened by the wads of candy he threw into the audience.

managers and coders had preferred to stay with their tried-and-true DOS product, and Ashton, a "consensus" builder, had been unwilling to knock heads together in order to ensure the product's success. The result was that the first release of WordPerfect for Windows was slow, buggy, lacked key competitive features, and received mediocre reviews. It was a critical mistake at a crucial juncture and WordPerfect would never truly recover from it.

Compounding the problem was the release of Microsoft's Office suite. WordPerfect had lost its bragging rights to best-of-breed word processor, and the Office suite represented a tremendous value. WordPerfect had no Windows database or spreadsheet with which to build its own suite and sales slowed even further. An attempt to cobble together a solution to Microsoft's challenge in concert with Borland, which did have a spreadsheet and database, received a poor reception from the market. The WordPerfect/Borland suite lacked Microsoft Office's integration and its individual products weren't clearly perceived as market leaders in their respective categories.

Instead of a cash cow with promised sales of $880 million and an estimated $100 million in profits, WordPerfect proved to be a bum steer that showed up with rapidly declining sales and a tag on its ear that read "$100 million loss." Compounding its problems, Novell promptly fired most of the WordPerfect sales and marketing personnel. Novell, left with no expertise in the retail software business, was completely unprepared to fix the situation and ended up selling what was left of WordPerfect at the fire-sale price of $158 million to Corel in 1996 (the actual deal had very little cash up front attached to it).

In the meantime, Microsoft's deadly radioactive shrinking rays were steadily cutting Godzilla down to size.

Novell also missed an opportunity to exploit the positioning problem Microsoft had created for itself with the introduction of NT. At this point, Microsoft had created two 32-bit operating systems with the same name, similar pricing (at the desktop level), and almost identical interfaces. One was reliable and hard to use, and one was easy to use and hardly reliable at all. An astute marketing organization could have given Microsoft severe heartburn over this positioning conflict, but Novell didn't.

There were no moves to upgrade NetWare's look and feel with a modern GUI. No high-level seminars that pointed out that Novell also had a lot of money in the bank, a huge installed base, and a better and more stable product. No pricing moves. No serious push to finally provide a competitive development framework for NetWare. Ultimately, Novell relied on the assumption that NetWare's superiority would speak for itself. And another assumption that people went out and bought a big expensive server with a pricey NOS installed and **then** thought about what to put on it—the exact opposite of real-life thinking.

Instead, for over 3 years, Novell fought back by burning cash via pointless acquisitions while Microsoft kept demonstrating its up-to-date-looking product with its attractive price to decision makers. Several new CEOs were brought in to tidy things up, but Novell successfully resisted all change. In the meanwhile, its sales shrank and profitability went away. In 2001, Novell earned revenues of $1.04 billion, down from 2000's $1.16 billion, and lost $273 million.[6] Finally, the company decided the only way to deal with the situation was to sell out to Cambridge Technology Partners and move its headquarters to just outside of Boston, a place where they drink lots of Sam Adams beer, smoke, and swear quite a bit. And quaff Jolt Cola.

Now, to be fair, Novell finally woke up. Today, its pricing is competitive. It's now easier to develop NOS- and server-based applications for NetWare (though support for this effort lags far behind Windows NT/2000). The product now has a GUI. And many people who moved to Windows NT later regretted it. Although the Superset members weren't good marketers, they were wonderful programmers, and NT has yet to match NetWare's stability and robustness.

But you have to wonder. The remake of Godzilla flopped at the box office in 2000. The movie was terrible. (Though this is perhaps not a fair criticism. All the Godzilla movies were terrible.) It just may be that Ghidrah has returned from outer space and triumphed at last.

Certainly Novell thought so. On April 14th, Novell chairman and CEO Jack Messman announced the next version of NetWare would be built on NetWare and Linux. Then, remaining true to Novell's history of ham-handed marketing, he called Linux "an immature operating system" and infuriated the open-source community. He later apologized for calling Linux immature.

Somewhere, Ghidrah is laughing.

---

[6] Novell press release titled "Novell Reports Fourth Quarter and Full Year Fiscal 2001 Results," November 29, 2001.

ten

RIPPING PR YARNS:
Microsoft and Netscape

The high-tech industry has never grasped the dichotomy that exists between its vision of Microsoft and the public's. To industry insiders, Microsoft and Bill Gates are tough, ruthless, and predatory foes. To the public, they're something else entirely. This difference in perception is no accident. It's the result of almost 20 years of an unrelenting and masterly PR campaign. To comprehend and understand this campaign is to begin to grasp the Zen of Marketing.

Before you can proceed down the path of enlightenment, you must first undergo a purification ritual. Clear your mind of illusions and foolish cant. Sit down, assume the lotus position, and meditate. Allow your mind to become a limpid pool of clarity and reason.

~

The Zen of Marketing

As your gaze begins to pierce this world's veil of deception, you see three great myths lying about you. These myths take the form of great sayings. Approach one and its false words will ring in the air about you. Draw near the first myth and hear its cry:

MICROSOFT PRODUCTS ARE OF POOR QUALITY AND HAVE SUCCEEDED ONLY BECAUSE OF THE COMPANY'S MARKET MONOPOLIES

This is untrue. Since the early 1980s, Microsoft products have usually been well reviewed and received by both the press and the public. It's true that like every other major software publisher, Microsoft has preannounced products; practiced fear, uncertainty, and doubt (FUD) tactics whenever it could get away with them; and shipped products late.

However, Microsoft's products, when finally delivered, have usually been of decent quality and feature rich. The first version of Microsoft Word introduced style sheets to PC word processing, a concept since picked up by every desktop publishing product and most competing word processors. The DOS version of Word usually came in a close second to WordPerfect in product reviews and sometimes surpassed it. This state of affairs reversed itself after the release of the first version of Word for Windows in 1989. Word for Windows began to regularly beat DOS-based WordPerfect and all DOS products in the reviews; the advantages inherent in Word's GUI interface were just too compelling to ignore.

The Excel story is similar. When the 1.0 version shipped in 1987, *PC Magazine*, at the time the most influential PC-oriented publication in terms of the impact of its reviews, stated that "Microsoft Corp. has just unleashed a spreadsheet that makes 1-2-3 look like a rough draft." Most of the other reviews were just as laudatory, and all made much of the WYSIWYG functionality of the product.

PowerPoint at the time of its acquisition by Microsoft in the late 1980s was regarded as one of the top presentation products for the Macintosh. Once translated to Windows, the product received similar favorable reviews. Ironically, the purchase of PowerPoint was controversial within Microsoft, as the company had forked over the "incredible" amount of $12 million for the software. A cornerstone of the Office suite, it would have been cheap at twice the price.

Microsoft Access when first introduced in 1992 competed primarily with Paradox for Windows. The first release of Paradox for Windows was eagerly awaited by the development community, but it shipped months late and was extremely buggy. By contrast, the first version of Access was regarded as competitive with Paradox for Windows in terms of its feature set and a bit more stable. It quickly established itself as a major contender in the DBMS arena, assisted by an aggressive upgrade promotional price of $99.95.

In the tools and language arenas, Microsoft's products have also been competitive. Since the 1980s, its C and other language compilers have usually received favorable reviews and have often won best-of-breed awards in their respective markets. Even those who dislike Microsoft concede that Visual Basic has been a powerful force in introducing object-oriented and visual programming to a wide audience. Despite Microsoft's public wrestling match with Sun Microsystems over Java, its first Java development system was universally acknowledged as one of the best tools available for the new wonder language. Microsoft has always been solicitous of the development community, providing it with tools, products, and information at attractive discounts. As a result, a huge ecosystem of third-party add-ons, training, and services has developed around the company's panoply of software. Millions now rely on Microsoft for their daily income.

At the enterprise level, Windows NT was designed from the ground up in an effort led by technical god Dave Cutler of DEC fame. Although the product has always had its critics, it has also been widely praised for its overall stability, ease of use, and flexibility. Its SQL database, derived from relational DBMS pioneer Sybase, gives Larry Ellison of Oracle nightmares as it steadily improves in power and functionality. Its Internet offerings, though heavily criticized for security problems, are nonetheless flexible, relatively easy to configure, and powerful. And they're often free.

Microsoft has been widely criticized for not being an "innovative" publisher, but in this it differs little from its major competitors. Apple hijacked the GUI interface concept from hapless Xerox and made it a commercial success. Lotus became a major power via 1-2-3, a high-powered knockoff of the original VisiCalc. Borland made its initial splash in the industry with Turbo Pascal, a low-priced, high-performing language derived directly from .NET father Anders Hejlsberg's COMPAS Pascal. Borland grew rapidly during the 1980s on the strength of Turbo Pascal but then became a major player by buying the Paradox database and the Quattro spreadsheet. Satellite Software was by no means a pioneer in word processing and never succeeded in building a significant product other than WordPerfect. Ashton-Tate's dBASE was "derived" from the Jet Propulsion Laboratory's JPLDIS language. A third party developed its most innovative product, Framework. Linux is a UNIX derivative for Intel-based systems.

Microsoft has, of course, suffered its share of flops. Microsoft Access, a communications program (not the database of the same name introduced years later), was released in the early 1980s to scathing reviews. Microsoft quickly withdrew the program from the market and now boxes of the product are considered minor collector's items. Microsoft Bob was another major faux pas, though analysts of the product have never criticized the product's feature set per se, and some believe it might have achieved some success if it had been marketed to children as a friendly front-end for Windows. And though everyone hated Clippy the talking paperclip, they kept buying Microsoft Office nonetheless.

Now draw near the second myth to hear its equally misleading claim:

Microsoft Has Always Been Feared and Hated by the Industry

Also untrue. Until the 1990 release of Windows 3.0, it was Apple, not Microsoft, that played the role of high tech's OS heavy. The success of the Mac OS, derived from Xerox's seminal Alto computer, gave Apple a tremendous competitive advantage for several years in the 1980s. Apple wasn't shy about using every legal tactic it could to defend its lead in GUIs, and for several years the company seemed to be on the hunt for every trash-can icon and drop-down menu it could sue.

Apple's first target was Digital Research's graphics environment manager (GEM). The GEM shell mimicked closely the look and feel of the Mac, though because it sat on top of DOS, it lacked much of the underlying functionality of the Mac OS. Regardless, Apple sued Digital Research shortly after the release of GEM in 1985 and forced the company to pull the product from the market for months. After the surgical removal of the GEM trash can from the desktop and minor changes to the menu system, GEM reappeared, but its enforced hiatus had cost the product precious time and momentum.[1] Everyone felt sorry for poor little Digital Research and very upset with big bully Apple.

Next up on Apple's legal agenda was Microsoft and by extension IBM. There had been labyrinthine look-and-feel negotiations between Apple and Microsoft over Windows 1.0 and the release of Windows 2.0 in 1987. This led to even more arguments about icons, graphics, and GUIs, and more legal threats. It was in this context that IBM and Microsoft invited a group of software publishers to come down to IBM's PC headquarters in Boca Raton, Florida, to preview the 1.1 release of OS/2, the one that would ship with the "Presentation Manager" interface. They were also asked to demonstrate their current OS/2 offerings to an internal conference of IBM employees. As the then product manager of WordStar 2000 for OS/2, I was sent to the event, where I spent a gloomy day showing off an OS/2-compatible character-based word processor and remembering TopView.

---

[1] GEM developed a fair amount of international support, particularly in Germany. However, the Windows wave eventually swept over Europe and GEM sank out of sight.

The day after the show, a series of presentations on the future of OS/2 were held for the ISVs. Attending from Microsoft were Scott Oki and Bill Gates himself. Gates gave an unremarkable speech on the coming glories of the new OS, and then Oki stood up to take the group on a tour of OS/2 1.1. Pointing to a spot on the Presentation Manager desktop where an Apple user would expect to find the trash can, Oki made a quip about how OS/2 would lack this most vital of features.

There was a long pause, then the room exploded in laughter and appreciation for funny Scott and wonderful Bill and plucky-but-brave little Microsoft. How dare that big bully Apple push everybody around and build a litigation fence around a crummy trash can, for Pete's sake? Icons should be free.

You could feel the love. By 1991 the loving was over, but that's another matter.

Now it's time to approach the third myth. It proclaims the greatest falsehood of all, and once you study this great deception many things will become clear to you. Listen carefully as it proclaims:

People Don't Like Bill Gates

A great untruth. The software industry doesn't like Bill Gates. The public at large likes him just fine. It used to like him even more, but there **is** the matter of that U.S. Department of Justice (DOJ) deposition and 1997 lawsuit that Microsoft lost, an issue you'll learn more about as you proceed down the path to enlightenment.

~

Bill Gates vs. the DOJ: Sometimes We All Go a Little Bit Crazy

The public's affection for Bill Gates isn't an accident. It's the result of a long-term and brilliantly crafted PR effort that has paid off enormous dividends over the years. This effort was begun in the early 1980s by PR specialist Pam Edstrom, and since then Microsoft has spent years crafting Bill Gates's public image and using it as its chief branding symbol.

Building the Perfect Bill

Three major components have gone into the building of Bill Gates's public persona: dress, demeanor, and financial humility. In terms of his personal appearance, inordinate amounts of ink have been dedicated to Bill Gates's clothing and personal appearance. He wears glasses, not contacts. His sweaters are usually described as tattered and worn. His hair is often a "rat's nest" and usually untidy. It used to be widely reported he didn't bathe often enough (but his wife took care of that). He tends to fidget when his picture is taken. He wears lots of jeans and worn khakis. He almost never used to wear a suit and looks a bit uncomfortable when he does. (And you never saw in him those annoying master-of-the-universe, 1980s-style suspenders.) And that's a smart thing, because people always tend to distrust a man in an Armani suit with a yellow tie, red suspenders, helmet hair, and perfect nails.

Of course, as the years have passed, we've learned Gates has changed. Dandruff, wild hair, and greasy clothing have given way to more reasonable coiffures, better clothing, and even sometimes a suit if conditions demand it (like testifying in federal court during the penalty phase of an antitrust case). The ugly geekling has undergone a transformation into a mature elder-statesman-of-technology swan. It's a story with a nice arc. People respond to it.

Then there's Gates's demeanor. Over the course of his career, he's always avoided talking about or criticizing other companies and people (in public). There have been lapses, but not many. Gates has never indulged in such Sturm und Drang pronouncements as Larry Ellison's infamous "It's not enough we (Oracle) win, everyone else must lose."[2]

Gates is at his best when he's talking about the impact of computing on the future and its potential to enrich us all. He's not a good public speaker by conventional measures. His voice tends to be thin and reedy, though he is a disciplined presenter and always covers his main talking points. But Gates is a passionate speaker, one who believes in what he says, and this quality overcomes most of his technical deficiencies.

He wrote a book of deep thoughts about the future of technology, *The Road Ahead*. It's not a very good book, but people are OK with that. Richest man in the world, smart little geek, and talented writer might be a little too much to bear. And the book is just bad enough to

---

[2] Gary Rivlin, *The Plot to Get Bill Gates* (New York: Times Books/Random House, 1999).

convince people that Gates really tried to write it himself and didn't hire some slick ghostwriter to churn out more corporate propaganda. Gates wrote his **own** propaganda and he believes it. People like sincerity combined with the right dash of self-effacing ineptitude.

Finally, there's the matter of money. It's hard to ignore the fact that Bill Gates is the wealthiest man who has ever lived. But that doesn't mean you need to talk about it and Bill Gates never does. Over the years Gates has acted like all this money just . . . happened. And Gates has done conventional humble millionaire things like taking coach flights instead of riding first class (and of course let everyone know it). He owns tons of Microsoft stock, but his executive compensation is moderate by current corporate standards. Americans like that. A dash of Uriah Heep and 'umbleness go a long way in creating a pleasing corporate persona.

Gates's personal rectitude has also helped reinforce his image. He didn't buy a yacht or sponsor one (always a bad PR move). Unlike Larry Ellison, who tried to buy a Russian Mig-29, he's made no attempt to buy any discarded military ordinance. He did buy a jet or two, but he doesn't talk about it. He does like fast cars, but what American boy doesn't? There have been no multiple succession of Mrs. Gates'—just the one with whom he's had three children. No discarded starlets and semifamous personalities dishing dirt to the tabloids. Before his mother's tragic early death from cancer, Gates called her every week.

He did spend a lot on his house ($50 million plus), but Microsoft PR spent a lot of time positioning Gates's Xanadu as both a giant geek toy and a multimedia laboratory. Those built-in electronic wall displays that can be programmed to project an endless variety of artistic images, you know. A bit of a stretch, but given Gates's past history they got away with it. And the man **does** have three kids. That's a big family in today's world and you need a big house. Prodded by Mrs. Gates, he's caught on to the charity game and the noblesse oblige expected from the very rich. The Bill and Melinda Gates Foundation has subsequently given away hundreds of millions of well-publicized dollars. All the bases have been covered.

And Gates has also shared the wealth! No Enron-type scandals here, no poor bedraggled corporate drones deprived of their retirement funds and stock options earned from the exhausting task of depriving the state of California of power. Not only has Microsoft created more millionaires than any company in history (current estimates peg the number at about 12,000), but it has also created more **billionaires**: Gates, cofounder Paul Allen, Steve Ballmer, and Scott Oki. And Microsoft the company also gives away millions of dollars of stuff, mostly Microsoft software, valued at full retail price. (Normally, industry marketers call this "building an installed base," and no one pays full retail, but the stuff **is** free.)

There has also been a series of nice touches added over the years. In 1996, Microsoft initiated a program of private getaways (called "pajama parties") for journalists who get to spend personal time with the world's richest man and find out he's a regular guy after all. The theory behind this is that after you've met a fellow, shared a beer with him, and talked about the kids, it's a bit difficult to shove the journalistic knife in up to the hilt. You'll do your duty and nick him if that's what's called for, but you'll probably avoid homicide. The theory is, in the main, correct.

Combined, these components form the amalgam that is the foundation of Bill Gates's image. Once it was in place, the real selling of Gates could begin and Microsoft pursued its mission with a vengeance. Despite all the talk about how Bill Gates dislikes taking time away from running (now technically guiding) Microsoft, he has somehow managed to spend a lot of time in front of various cameras during his career. Throughout the 1980s and '90s it became difficult **not** to see pictures of Bill Gates holding a floppy disk, Bill Gates standing in a grove of redwoods, Bill Gates gazing into a monitor, Bill Gates talking about the information age (hastily revised to be the "Internet age" as events overtook the old buzzword), Bill Gates posing as A Handsome Guy on the cover of a women's magazine, etc., etc., all the while expounding on the future of the PC marketplace. The image Microsoft's PR effort finally succeeded in creating for Gates was of a friendly, nonthreatening technical wizard—a kind of high-tech elf. Completely harmless.

If you competed against Microsoft in the 1980s and were an astute observer of what was going on, you began to see Microsoft's PR effort beginning to pay off in the mid- to late-'80s. In 1987, *PC Week* published an article that claimed "Microsoft doesn't understand marketing, they just want to create great products."

Later that year, as Excel was being launched, Jerry Pournelle, influential columnist for *BYTE* magazine, commented that a Microsoft demo team was eager to show off the product because "they thought it was a neat hack." A "neat hack." Yes, the boys and girls of Microsoft weren't interested in all the money to be made in the market's second most lucrative segment (word processing being the first). They were just a group of friendly, naive hackers eager to show the world their latest trick.

To achieve this type of press is to master the Zen of Marketing.

Gates's public persona was, of course, completely at variance with his PC-insider reputation. A 1987 *Wall Street Journal* article detailing the 1985 negotiations between Apple and Microsoft over renewing Apple's license for Microsoft BASIC on its Apple II systems was one of the first to probe beneath the surface of Gates's carefully constructed public image. The article revealed a tough-as-nails negotiator and ultra-shrewd businessman who didn't hesitate to press an advantage over anyone he perceived as standing in his way. The deal's outcome led to Apple scrapping its innovative MacBASIC and many hard feelings between the two companies. But that was one article, and the press had people like Ed Esber to divert its attention. No one paid much attention to the *Journal*'s revelations.

The next several years saw Microsoft reap rich dividends from its PR effort as the company became the industry's 1,200-pound gorilla. The big dividends started in 1993. By then the high-tech industry was learning that Microsoft was every bit as brutal a competitor as IBM had ever been and much smarter. The OS wars, despite IBM's desperate attempts to make a comeback, seemed to be over. Microsoft Office, the company's marketing bet that combining a series of high-quality business applications into a semi-integrated suite would beat the best-of-breed approach still advocated by its competition, was paying off handsomely. WordPerfect, Lotus 1-2-3, Quattro, Paradox, dBASE, Harvard Graphics, and other competitors were all fast retreating into irrelevancy.

As you might imagine, everyone was screaming for the government to do something. (It's a truism that capitalists all believe in free markets until they have to live in one.) After all, Microsoft did have a monopoly in the desktop OS market. The company did engage in questionable business practices, such as forcing computer hardware manufacturers to buy licenses for DOS and Windows for every machine they made, thus effectively locking competitors such as Digital Research out of the market. Everyone in the industry had known for years that Microsoft was always ready to engage in a price war because it could use its DOS revenues to endure losses on any single product line for an indefinite period of time. A low-level probe of Microsoft's business practices had been launched in 1990 and was still burbling away out of sight of the general public's gaze. Important people were sure that the DOJ was going to pounce on Microsoft any moment and wrestle the gorilla to the ground.[3]

And, of course, Bill Gates was Satan. Everyone knew that!

Well, everyone didn't. In the United States the government reflects the will of the people and the people were willing to leave Bill Gates alone. Sure, the lawyers wanted to sue him, but lawyers like to sue everybody and they don't make people rich. Bill Gates had made a lot of people rich and a lot of people knew it. And who was the government running to the rescue of? Big stupid IBM? No one felt sorry for that company. That French guy, Philippe Khan? Boy, we sure hate the French. Those Mormons from Utah? Don't they all have 6 wives and 30 kids? No wonder they need more money.

And Microsoft Office sure was a bargain! Imagine, where once you paid $279.00 (street price) for a word processor or a spreadsheet by itself, with Office you got Word, Excel, PowerPoint, and lots of other goodies for the same $279.00! Just how was John Q. Public being hurt by that?

And were any of the other companies any different from Microsoft? Jim Manzi of Lotus had spent years trying to hunt down Borland's Quattro spreadsheet with legal hit men. Apple had spent years suing anyone who put a picture of a trash can on a computer. Ed Esber of Ashton-Tate had sued people for using the dBASE language. In point of fact, everyone in the industry is constantly suing someone else over something: patents, false advertising, because it's Tuesday. Why should the U.S. taxpayer's time and money be wasted on trying to sort this all out? Let nature take its course and may the best geek win.

The Clinton White House, a poll-driven machine, took a look at Bill Gates's popularity ratings and reigned in its legal hounds. In 1994, the U.S. government arrived at a fairly toothless settlement whose provisions wouldn't take effect until 1995. Microsoft agreed not to require hardware manufacturers to buy an OS license for every machine they made, regardless of whether the machine used Windows or DOS. This was a rather pointless restriction, as by the time the decree went into

---

[3] In April 1994, I had a lively discussion panel exchange with several IBMers at the OS/2 Technical Interchange in San Francisco during which I predicted the government wouldn't press its case against Microsoft.

effect there wasn't much else left to buy. Microsoft also agreed not to integrate new features and capabilities into its products if they were intended to "crush" the competition. Presumably, a gentle mauling would have to be sufficient.

Gates, however, in an action that signaled he had finally started to grow too big for his britches, made a mistake at this point. Having maneuvered a dream deal out of the DOJ's lawyers, Gates proceeded to hurt their feelings by swaggering about telling everyone that nothing had changed and that Microsoft would continue with business as usual. It was stupid behavior. Microsoft is big and has a lot of money, but the U.S. government is bigger and has **all** the money. Soft words and a humble attitude would have been the smart move. The political appointees at the DOJ didn't pay much heed to Gates's mouthing off, but in the eyes of the department's career attorneys, Bill Gates was a marked man.

Still, that was all in the future. In the meantime, a state of meaningless mutual satisfaction having been reached, everyone got back to watching Microsoft build its next monopoly in the applications market. The job was pretty much complete by 1995, just in time for the Internet and Netscape to show up.

Bill Strikes Back

It's no secret that the Internet caught Microsoft and Bill Gates flat-footed. Seemingly overnight, everyone was talking about new paradigms, the new economy, and new technologies. Microsoft, to its chagrin, wasn't perceived as a leader in any of them. Instead of Windows and Microsoft Office, proven and profitable monopolies, everyone was focusing on upstarts such as Netscape and recycled programming concepts such as Sun Microsystems's Java. Loud voices in the press announced that Microsoft was yesterday's news, old code, technology's new Edsel. Chained to the desktop, confined inside Windows, pushing "yesterday's" languages such as C and C++. Pundits proclaimed the company faced the imminent disappearance of its markets and a quick journey to irrelevancy.

Stimulated in part by fear and in part by the immensely big mouth of Netscape cofounder Marc Andreessen, Gates responded to the threat by focusing his complete attention and paranoia on all things Internet. In May 1995, he released a companywide memo instructing Microsoft employees to focus their energies on understanding the different opportunities and challenges presented by the Internet to Microsoft and Windows. On December 7 of the same year, he made a speech the industry nicknamed the "Pearl Harbor Day Manifesto" and announced that Microsoft was an Internet company. The software giant's legions of developers and marketers immediately began to change course and march inexorably toward a Web-based future. Almost immediately, the press and the pundits changed their tune, and instead of obloquy they now heaped praise on Gates's ability to "turn Microsoft on a dime" and move the company in its new direction.

Time has shown that the praise, like the initial criticism, was overblown. Microsoft's counterattack was ham-handed, generated enormous public ill will, and led to a finding in favor of the U.S. government that the company had violated the nation's antitrust laws. Yes, Netscape was laid low in the end. But a marketing and development campaign that ends up with your company having the federal government playing the role of active partner in your business behavior for the foreseeable future isn't a triumph.

The company's development efforts can't be faulted; in this respect Microsoft performed superbly. Starting from nowhere, its Internet Explorer (IE) browser quickly caught, then surpassed, Netscape's Navigator and Communicator products in functionality and stability. By 1998, most reviews were giving the nod to Microsoft's product over Netscape's. Netscape, in a case of a company falling for its own propaganda, helped cut its own throat by going off on a half-baked quest to rewrite its market-leading browser in Java, a course that helped ensure the company would fall permanently behind Microsoft in the development race.

What did break down during the last half of the 1990s was Microsoft's PR machine. The decade began with Microsoft receiving, with very few exceptions, glowing media coverage and enjoying high public esteem. It ended with a slew of articles, books, and TV specials springing up dedicated to discovering the dark side of Bill Gates and Microsoft. A truly awful movie, *Antitrust*, was filmed with actor Tim Robbins playing an ersatz Gates, an evil billionaire who runs around killing lovable open-source programmers. (By the end of the film, most people are rooting for the evil billionaire.) As unflattering comparisons to earlier titans of industry such as Andrew Carnegie and John Rockefeller surfaced in the press, Gates began to undergo a public transformation from golden geek to gilded-age robber baron. And because Microsoft's PR machine had worked so assiduously to present Gates as Microsoft's official face, any blemish to his image reflected directly on his company.

This is all the more ironic when you realize that Bill Gates's initial reaction to the Internet was more prescient than people had realized. Microsoft has always been run as a real business that makes real profits, and in 1994 Gates immediately spotted the obvious: None of the Internet "business models" being bandied about described how anyone was going make any money on the Internet. The one place where profits could be found was in selling software that would allow **other people** to build Web sites where you could buy 30-pound bags of pet food at a loss. Microsoft promptly went out and did the intelligent thing and bought the leading Web development package, FrontPage, from Vermeer Technologies. The acquisition led to Microsoft immediately becoming the leader in this new market category. But despite this initial display of good sense, Microsoft ended up buying into much of the Internet non-sense of the mid-1990s and allowed its behavior to spiral out of control.

Microsoft's first overreaction was to the development of Java. The new language was the brainchild of Sun Microsystems, a company that has released some interesting software technology over the years but has made little money doing it. Java was designed as a "Write Once, Run Anywhere" environment. It achieves this by allowing developers to write to a Java Virtual Machine (JVM), a software-based computer that's ported to different computer platforms. In theory, if your software meets the JVM specification, you can write a software program once and have it run on any machine with a JVM. Java wasn't specifically a part of the Internet's infrastructure, but the language's applicability to developing server-based software soon tied the two technologies together in the public's mind.

"Write Once, Run Anywhere" programming isn't a new idea. The concept had been tried before in the early 1980s, only then it was called the UCSD p-System[4]. You wrote p-System programs to the virtual p-System microprocessor and, in theory, your software would run on any computer with a virtual p-System machine. The problem with the

---

[4] The product was sold commercially by a company called Softech and later Pecan Software.

p-System and Java is that they require you to write to any particular piece of hardware's lowest common denominator, thus ensuring that a program's performance and interface are always far less than optimal. Developers could never resist tweaking their p-System programs just a bit to support a particular bit of silicon, but once they did, cross-platform compatibility disappeared. The primary difference between the two approaches was that a JVM could run in your browser, giving you access to a new universe of slow-performing Web-based applications with standardized primitive interfaces running on all your computers. The p-System quickly faded as customers demanded applications optimized for their real, not virtual, machines. Java's "Write Once, Run Anywhere" claim proved just as chimerical as the p-System's, though the language is widely used to develop server-based applications.

Overwhelmed by the Internet roar, Microsoft made the mistake of licensing the Java language from Sun Microsystems, a move many saw as an acknowledgment that the company needed to play catch-up with its competition. Microsoft didn't need a license to provide "Java" compatibility and capabilities in its products, the Java language was highly cloneable. But use of the Java trademark **did** require that license.

Once the deal was struck, Microsoft promptly released a Java IDE that was widely praised for its performance and possessed, to no one's great surprise, "hooks" that, if used, optimized your Java programs for Windows (and made them incompatible with other platforms). Sun Microsystems and Microsoft promptly got into a noisy catfight about the purity of the Java language and cross-platform compatibility. Given that Java was proving to be about as cross-platform as the p-System, there didn't seem to be much point to the squabbling, but the episode damaged Microsoft's reputation in the press and with the public.

Microsoft's second, more important mistake was in allowing itself to be goaded into stupid behavior by Netscape's noisy declarations about browsers replacing Windows as an application portal. Netscape needed to make these grandiose claims for what was, and still is, primarily a viewing technology, because a browser is what Netscape had to sell. The idea that anyone was going to use Netscape or any other browser anytime soon to write documents, lay out publications, build budgets, store files, and design presentations was a fantasy. (The people who made these breathless predictions apparently never tried to actually perform any of these tasks in a browser.)

What has actually occurred is that desktop applications are slowly extending "out" across the Internet. For example, although it makes little sense for a word processor to be Web based, it makes a great deal of sense for that word processor to be able to access a *Web service* that allows multiple people to view a document, comment on it, and then distribute the revisions back to everyone on a distribution list. Prior to the Internet, proprietary products such as Lotus Notes provided this kind of functionality, but the Internet now allows these types of capabilities to be more broadly distributed. But building the software plumbing and infrastructure to support these capabilities is a development effort that's only now beginning and will take years to complete. Netscape had difficulties enough in building a competitive browser; its ability to construct a robust infrastructure of Web services was nonexistent.

An Offer You Can't Refuse

Nonetheless, Microsoft, intent on its mission to destroy Netscape, rolled out across the industry with all the subtlety and attendant goodwill of Germany invading Poland. The first thing the company did after building IE was bundle it with the OEM version of Windows 95 and announce it was free. To be fair, this wasn't as aggressive a move as it appeared. Though the Netscape browsers (first Navigator and later Communicator) did have a theoretical SRP of $49.95, they were released on a trialware basis. You could download a fully functional copy of the browser and make full use of it without cost, though you were ostensibly supposed to pay up after an evaluation period. The products weren't crippled or time-locked in any significant way, and few individuals ever bought a copy, though Netscape did briefly make a nice living selling corporate licenses for its browsers.

But after this opening thrust, Microsoft ran rampant through the industry. The company threatened IBM and Compaq with the loss of their Windows licenses[5] if they offered Netscape instead of IE on their machines. It threatened Apple with the cancellation of a critical upgrade of the Mac version of Microsoft Office, the system's principal business

---

[5] Gary Norris of IBM testified during the Microsoft/DOJ trial that IBM, Compaq, and Hewlett-Packard feared loss of their Windows licenses if they considered offering OS/2 on their systems.

application suite, if it didn't yank the Netscape browser.[6] It offered "inducements" to companies such as KPMG to break volume purchase agreements they'd signed with Netscape.[7] It approached the major online services such as AOL, CompuServe, and MCI and cut deals with them to replace the Netscape browser with IE.[8] About the only thing Microsoft didn't do was kidnap the children of executives of companies using Netscape products and hold them hostage until their parents agreed to stop using Netscape's browser.

Microsoft employees also developed a bad habit of saying stupid things in public. In 1996, for instance, Microsoft Vice President Paul Maritz was quoted proclaiming that "We are going to cut off Netscape's air supply."[9] Although Maritz later denied saying it, the phrase nonetheless became particularly beloved at Microsoft and was repeated endlessly in internal e-mails, at company meetings, in conversations with the press, on online forums, etc. It all sounded tough and macho to the employees at Microsoft and rolled off the tongue in a satisfying fashion.[10] Netscape was going to suffer the same fate that befell Luca Brazzi and that treacherous little weasel of a brother-in-law in the movie *The Godfather*. But if Netscape was Luca Brazzi, what did that make Microsoft?

In Microsoft's defense, as with legal threats, tough talk in the industry is nothing new. Jim Manzi, after winning a look-and-feel judgment against Borland over its Quattro spreadsheet, had announced that he was going to perform a "cashectomy" on his foe.[11] (The judgment was overturned on appeal and Lotus never got a dime.) Ed Esber of Ashton-Tate had publicly bellowed "Make my day!" to companies daring to write dBASE language compilers. (Ashton-Tate never saw a dime either.) The difference is that when Jim Manzi and Ed Esber were shooting off

---

[6] Transcript of the videotaped deposition of Bill Gates, 1998, pp. 32–35.

[7] Rivlin, op. cit., pp. 198–199. This announcement was made in 1997 and involved KPMG pulling out 1,800 Navigator seats in favor of IE.

[8] Ibid, p. 198.

[9] Steve McGeady, a senior vice president at Intel, originally attributed this statement to Maritz at a 1995 meeting between the two companies.

[10] "US Takes on Microsoft." *The Boston Globe*, May 19, 1998.

[11] *Technology Update*, January/February 1994 (http://www.abanet.org/lpm2/magazine/tu941.html). This statement was perhaps the most famous of Manzi's entire career and was widely reported in every major PC and business magazine at the time of its utterance.

their mouths, they didn't have a bunch of resentful U.S. attorneys looking for an excuse to launch a federal antitrust action against their firms.

Viewed tactically, the Microsoft campaign was a success. By the end of 1998, Netscape and Microsoft were almost dead even in browser market share. Netscape was on the ropes and was saved from inevitable extinction only by being acquired by AOL.

Strategically, the campaign was a disaster. Microsoft had somehow convinced itself that its actions wouldn't bring down another DOJ lawsuit on its head, a calculation of almost incomprehensible idiocy. The feds came down with both feet on the company and Microsoft found itself back in front of a federal judge explaining its behavior.

If Netscape represented the "Poland" phase of Microsoft's campaign, Gates's 1998 video deposition during the government's antitrust case was its "Stalingrad." The deposition was conducted in Microsoft headquarters over 3 days and featured a wan-looking Bill Gates nervously rocking back and forth and twitching while answering questions from David Boies, the government's lead attorney. His demeanor was a cross between that of Norman Bates in *Psycho* discussing "Mother" with Janet Leigh and Martin Short's Sweaty Nervous Guy of *Saturday Night Live* fame. (Sweaty Nervous Guy, a recurring character on the show, was a chain-smoking lawyer with an eternal caught-with-his-hand-in-the-cookie-jar expression who was constantly being interviewed by a Mike Wallace–type interlocutor about his various sleazy business deals.)

Gates demonstrated he had Sweaty Nervous Guy down to a "T" during the deposition. He never smiled during the sessions, nor did he talk about the wonders of technology and all the good Microsoft was doing for humanity. He made few attempts to disagree with the premises of the questions, something you can do during a deposition. (He also seemed to feel sorry for himself, forgetting that no one feels sorry for billionaires.) Instead, he rocked back and forth, avoided making eye contact with his interrogators, and gave answers that were every bit as evasive, inane, and hilarious as Short at his best.

As Gates hit his stride, he had trial spectators and Judge Thomas Penfield Jackson guffawing in disbelief and amusement. One of the most widely reported gems was this:

David Boies: Do you recall speaking to anyone about the meeting referred to here between Dan Rosen and Jim Barksdale?

Bill Gates: No.

DB: The e-mail goes on to list six working goals, which are one, launch STT, our electronic payment protocol. Get STT presence on the Internet. Two, move Netscape out of the Win32 Internet client area. Three, avoid cold or hot war with Netscape. Keep them from sabotaging our platform evolution. Do you understand the reference to Win32 Internet client to be a reference to Windows 95?

BG: No.

DB: What do you understand it to be a reference to?

BG: Win32.

DB: And can you describe what that is.

BG: Thirty-two-bit Windows.

DB: Is Windows 95 a 32-bit Windows product?

BG: It's one of them.

Then there was this rib tickler:

David Boies: Does Microsoft have software that competes with QuickTime?

Bill Gates: Since QuickTime's a free runtime, you can answer that either yes or no. It's not a revenue source for Apple. But there is an Apple technology that has some common things with some Microsoft technologies.

DB: Do you believe that QuickTime software competes with any software distributed by Microsoft?

David Heiner (Microsoft attorney): Objection.

BG: Depends on what you mean by compete.

And this particular exchange practically brought down the house:

David Boies: Well, let me show you a document that has previously been marked as government exhibit 268. This is a document bearing Microsoft document production stamps ms 98 0110952 through 53. The first part of this purports to be a copy of an e-mail from Dan—Don Bradford to Ben Waldman, with a copy to you, Mr. Maritz and others, on the subject of, quote, Java on Macintosh/IE control. Did you receive a copy of this e-mail on or about February 13, 1998?

BG: I don't know.

DB: Do you have any reason to doubt that you received a copy of this e-mail?

BG: No.

DB: The first paragraph reads, quote, Apple wants to keep both Netscape and Microsoft developing browsers for Mac—believing if one drops out, the other will lose interest (and also not really wanting to pick up the development burden). Getting Apple to do anything that significantly materially disadvantages Netscape will be tough. Do you agree that Apple should be meeting—it reads, do you agree that Apple should be meeting the spirit of our cross-license agreement and that MacOffice is the perfect club to use on them. Do you have an understanding of what Mr. Bradford means when he refers to MacOffice as, quote, the perfect club to use on Apple, closed quote?

BG: No.

Judge Jackson paused from his enjoyment of this sidesplitting bit of theater just long enough to find Microsoft guilty of antitrust violations and recommend the company be broken up. Although Jackson was later removed from the case for injudicious conduct (i.e., telling anyone who would listen he thought Microsoft was guilty as hell), the finding was upheld on appeal and the guilty verdict sustained. All that remained to be determined was the punishment the company could look forward to.

The answer seemed to come when the government announced a settlement with Microsoft in which the company now agreed to

- Allow people to yank things such as IE out of Windows (or hide it from view) if they so chose (Microsoft had previously announced this was "impossible," but apparently a guilty verdict in a federal antitrust trial can achieve miracles that would impress even Moses waiting to cross the Red Sea).
- Play nice in the OEM market and not threaten trembling reeds such as HP and Dell with loss of their Windows licenses if they bundled products that competed with Microsoft on their PCs (and this time the government really really meant it).
- Provide technical information on Windows APIs and protocols the company had previously kept proprietary.

- Approve the payment of "billions of dollars" to the market in compensatory "damages," though much of said compensation seemed to consist of coupons that allowed people to buy Microsoft products at attractive discounts. Microsoft's sales and marketing group were said to be delighted with the concept.

- Agree to allow the court to inspect Microsoft's business activities via a committee set up by the court for at least 5 years.

- And in general play nice in the future and act the part of good corporate citizen.

A group of spoilsport states and companies promptly announced they were unhappy with the agreement and spent a great deal of time trying to persuade U.S. District Court Judge Colleen Kollar-Kotelly, who had taken over upon Judge Jackson's abrupt departure from the case, to treat Microsoft far more harshly, but in November 2002 Judge Kollar-Kotelly issued a ruling that largely affirmed the initial settlement. The pundits promptly proclaimed Microsoft's total triumph in the case, and that seemed to be that.

Such proclamations were demonstrated to be premature a couple of months later when U.S. District Court Judge J. Frederick Motz decided in a separate lawsuit filed by Sun Microsoft that Microsoft had to bundle a spiffy, up-to-date version of Java in Windows instead of the obsolete hulk it had grudgingly agreed to stick into the OS in an out-of-the-way corner. Judge Motz was mightily impressed by the concept that Microsoft had been already found guilty of acting as an illegal monopolist and seemed inclined to kick sand in the face of the Redmond bully. When Microsoft objected and noted that Judge Kollar-Kotelly hadn't required this remedy in the government's case, Motz noted tartly that that was a different judge and a different case. He granted a preliminary injunction in Sun Microsystems's favor and ended up giving Microsoft 3 months to see the court's ruling implemented. At this point, Microsoft and others began to understand the long-term impact of losing an antitrust case to the U.S. courts: The company was now in many respects a 98-pound legal weakling who could be picked on by any judge having a "bad robe day." Over time, Microsoft could look forward to being nicked in courts again and again.

And it wasn't just Sun Microsystems looking for a pound of profits and revenge. Other companies, such as Be[12] and Burst also had ongoing suits against Microsoft, and even a few diehard states, such as Massachusetts, announced they were going to continue worrying the software publisher's heels with sharp little legal teeth until they had extracted their own "justice" from the situation. And every time Microsoft lawyers walked into court, they could expect to hear an earful about how the company had been found "guilty" in the awful majestic eyes of the U.S. government of acting like a reincarnation of a nineteenth-century robber baron. (IBM, which managed to successfully fend off the U.S. government's similar charges, can give Microsoft some pointers on how this can affect a company's business environment over time.) The company had removed a thorn from its side in return for an anaconda around its neck.

Another casualty of Microsoft's Netscape blitzkrieg was Bill Gates's public persona. By the trial's end, Gates had become so closely associated with Microsoft's competitive knife work that he was in danger of becoming the high-tech version of Martha Stewart. It was judged necessary to ease him out of the company's CEO position by replacing him with second-in-command Steve Ballmer and settling him into the less visible role of company "chief technologist." Here, the scars and cracks Gates's behavior and comments during the deposition and trial had left on his carefully crafted and burnished corporate image could be slowly mended and repaired. In the meantime, Microsoft's PR machine went to work transforming Ballmer's attack-dog persona into something more warm and personable. Pictures of Ballmer's stout, bald-pated countenance sporting a beneficent expression soon began appearing on the front covers of business magazines everywhere. In the place of a high tech elf, Microsoft now offered the world a high-tech teddy bear.

---

[12] Of all the companies baying after Microsoft, Be was perhaps the best example of a firm baking its own croissant but being unwilling to eat it. Be was the brainchild of Jean-Louis Gassee, who had spent much of the 1980s at Apple as vice president of engineering fighting any and all attempts to license the Mac OS to third parties. Gassee's efforts to keep the Mac OS proprietary were successful, ensuring Apple's descent from industry leader to niche player. After leaving Apple, Gassee founded Be, which briefly tried to replicate Apple's integrated hardware/software strategy before becoming a software-only firm. After failing to sell the Be OS back to proprietary Apple at the mind-boggling price of $300 million, Gassee underwent something of a conversion and attempted to position Be as an "open" OS. Not many people ever bought the company's products despite their considerable capabilities, and Be was eventually sold to Palm in 2001 for $11 million in stock, the high-tech equivalent of a handful of baguettes.

There was another path Microsoft could have traveled. Realizing the government was keeping a close eye on its every move, Microsoft could have moved forcefully but far more judiciously in its effort to compete. The company was on fairly safe ground in bundling IE with Windows and even offering it for free: Netscape was basically giving away its browser as well. The tie-in to Windows 95 in and of itself gave Microsoft a long-term advantage over Netscape that ensured it would pick up significant browser market share. And because it had bought and was successfully selling the market's leading Web development package, FrontPage, Microsoft was in a position to leverage use of its browser on this front as well.

Where Microsoft needed to move carefully was in establishing its partnerships and picking the spots where it would apply maximum pressure. Blackmailing Apple was pointless; the company had all of 4 percent market share worldwide, and if every Mac user on earth had sworn to commit ritual suicide on behalf of Netscape it didn't really matter. It wasn't necessary for Microsoft to chase Netscape off of **every** major online service; the AOL deal by itself was a major coup and ensured a huge pickup in user desktops. Threatening IBM and Compaq with loss of their Windows licenses if they didn't remove Netscape from their computers was an open invitation to an antitrust suit; simply ensuring that IE received equal billing on their PCs was more than enough to maintain the shift toward Microsoft.

It would also have been a smart move for everyone at Microsoft to have had an electronic collar fastened around their necks that gave off a severe shock anytime they said something mean about Netscape in public. Microsoft failed to understand that the public liked Netscape. It thought blonde, roly-poly founder Marc Andreessen was rather cute, kind of a high-tech panda bear. Netscape reminded them of another hot young technology company whose main spokesperson was also blonde, though he was now not so young and not so cute. And people hate it when other people are seen being mean to cute things. If you're going to club a baby seal to death, make sure you do it when the cameras aren't rolling.

Rather than sending out its unending series of blood-curdling announcements, Microsoft should have been lavish in its praise for cute young Netscape. It should have complimented the company on its cleverness and bright thinking while making sure everyone knew that IE was now being rated higher than Netscape's competing products. It should have praised the value of competition and welcomed Netscape as a "partner" in providing all Americans with access to the exciting new world of the Internet while simultaneously working to ensure IE's market share grew.

Microsoft should also have considered whether it was useful for Netscape to survive as a viable, but distant, number two competitor. It's no secret that it's currently in Microsoft's best interest for Apple to stick around. While it does, Microsoft can make at least a semiserious claim that there's some competition in the OS market. Intel, another company that has from time to time felt the hot breath of the federal regulatory serpent, has also learned this lesson. The company has the power to crush long-time rival AMD in the microprocessor market if it chooses, but it has chosen not to. As with Microsoft and Apple, while AMD exists Intel can credibly claim that it faces real industry competition.

Still, it all could have turned out worse for Bill Gates and Microsoft. The change in administration in 2001 put a new, more business-friendly regime in power at the White House and some of the pressure on Microsoft eased. Of course, having Judge Motz drop a new Java into Windows was the technical equivalent of having a big black fly expire in the middle of your fresh bowl of potato salad, but it seemed unlikely that the federal anaconda would squeeze the company into one or more parts. At least not right now. But it would stick around to keep an eye on its new friends, Bill Gates and Microsoft.

And Gates had clearly learned his lesson. The madness that had seized him during the 1998 deposition was nowhere in evidence when he testified on Microsoft's behalf in early 2002 at the remedy phase of the antitrust trial. He came to court dressed in an understated suit with a purple tie (a very spiritual color). His wife, Melinda, pregnant with their third child, accompanied him to court and held his hand.

During his testimony, in contrast with his Norman Bates/Sweaty Nervous Guy demeanor of 4 years ago, Gates was relaxed and under control, and he smiled genially and often. He even cracked a few jokes. He talked about how Microsoft had contributed to America's welfare with its technology. He portrayed the company as being at the center of a new industrial revolution. He reminded everyone that Microsoft played by the same rules as every other company it competed with.

Bill Gates doesn't often make the same mistake twice.

~

Netscape and Marc Andreessen: Will You Please Just Shut Up?

If you like to go horror movies, you know the cast usually sports a character you've come to think of as The Idiot Who Deserves to Die. He's the knucklehead who runs screaming into the path of Godzilla just as the giant reptile is heading out to spend a relaxing afternoon destroying Tokyo, and gets squashed like a bug. The dimwit who sticks his noggin out of the deserted cabin in the woods and yells out "Mad slasher? What mad slasher?" just before the mad slasher decapitates him. The space-bound fumble-fingers who always manages to drop his blaster right when the Tentacle of Doom is zeroing in on him as lunch.

If Marc Andreessen, cofounder of one-time wonder company Netscape, ever gives up high tech for a career in horror movies, he'll play that character.

In 1993, Marc Andreessen, a computer science major at the University of Illinois at Urbana-Champaign, posted the first version of the Mosaic browser for download on several Internet sites. Mosaic was primarily the joint creation of Andreessen, who functioned as the product architect and idea guy, and Eric Bina, a programmer at the university who did most of the actual coding. Mosaic represented a radical step forward in browser design. It had, for the time, an easy-to-use graphical interface that a newcomer to the Internet could master in about an hour. It used HTML to display both text and pictures within the browser environment. Versions of it were available for UNIX, Windows, and the Mac. Mosaic, which would serve as the spiritual foundation of Netscape Corporation, swept through the Internet like a virus, only with a happier outcome. By the end of 1995, millions of copies of the product were in use, and to the general public the World Wide Web **was** the Internet.

In the interim, Andreessen, deprived of what he felt was his proper share of the glory for Mosaic's creation,[13] headed out west to make his fortune as a generation of high-tech expatriates had done before him. He quickly fell in with Jim Clark, one of the founders of Silicon Graphics,

---

[13] Charles H. Ferguson, *High Stakes, No Prisoners* (New York: Times Books/Random House, 1999), p. 52.

Inc. (SGI), and the two founded Netscape. The company promptly wrote a new browser that was eventually entitled Navigator to avoid legal problems with the University of Illinois, which owned the rights to Mosaic. Netscape's new baby was released over the Internet in December 1994.

Far more functional and feature packed than its competitors, including its Mosaic predecessor, Navigator quickly became the de facto market standard and by 1995 had approximately 80 percent of the browser market share. Netscape went public in the summer of 1995 (2 weeks before the rollout of Windows 95). The stock, pegged at a pre-IPO value of $28.00 per share, opened at $71.00 and closed at $58.25. Overnight, Netscape was a media sensation and Andreessen, its vice president of technology, became one of the industry's latest on-paper multimillionaires. Even better, Andreessen also found himself at the tender age of 25 playing the role of spokesman and poster boy for the Internet company at a time when all anyone could talk about was the Internet.

It was a disaster.

The New Bill, Not the Same As the Old

On the face of it, it could have all worked out. Andreessen is a big, soft-looking fellow with stocky blonde good looks. Yes, he was young, but Bill Gates was still drinking Shirley Temples when he founded Microsoft and he was only 26 when he negotiated the famous IBM deal. Andreessen is fairly literate and very intelligent. He looks good in pictures and is comfortable on camera. People naturally warm to him and he has a good speaking voice. On the face of it, a nice PR package. Unfortunately, what was missing from the package in the mid-1990s was even an ounce of common sense.

Once he'd gotten a taste of the limelight, Andreessen, along with the rest of Netscape, promptly decided that very smartest thing they could do was to bait and threaten Microsoft. Andreessen began his big push to guarantee his company's destruction at the hands of Microsoft by taking an early look at Java in 1995 and telling the world that this new language, in conjunction with Netscape's browsers, was the application platform of the future and would replace Windows. This immediately got Bill Gates's full attention. Windows is Microsoft's most valuable franchise and what threatens it threatens the company. Not one to let an opportunity slip by, Andreessen proceeded to ensure Gates would stay fully focused on him and Netscape for the foreseeable future by allowing himself to be quoted in the trade press predicting that Windows would be reduced to a "poorly debugged set of device drivers."

After his immortal "device drivers" bon mot, Andreessen was hardly through. Over the next few months he proved to be an endless source of witty and memorable observations, all of which were widely reported on in the press and collected by Microsoft, the owner of those poorly debugged device drivers. Some of his most pithy comments included the following:

"It was like a visit to Don Corleone. I expected to find a bloody computer monitor in my bed the next day."[14]

"We're gonna smoke 'em."[15] (Microsoft being the intended smokee.)

"No horse head in the bed yet."[16]

"Those idiots up in Redmond."[17]

"The beast from Redmond."[18]

"They can't keep up."[19] (Referring to Microsoft's inability to out-code the tyros from Netscape.)

"The Evil Empire."[20]

"Godzilla."[21]

---

[14] Ibid, p. 52.

[15] Rivlin, op. cit., p. 195.

[16] Rivlin, loc. cit.

[17] Rivlin, loc. cit.

[18] Rivlin, loc. cit.

[19] Rivlin, loc. cit.

[20] Transcript from *Nightly Business Report*, WPBT, September 21, 2000.

[21] Ibid.

Andreessen also discovered that, like Bill Gates, he had an affinity for the camera. In a 2-year period he appeared in or was profiled by every major news and business magazine. He appeared on the cover of *Time* magazine seated on a golden throne. George Gilder, prophet of everything high tech, pronounced Andreessen earth's most supercalifragilisticexpealidotious person. A *Forbes* article proclaimed Andreessen was the "next Bill Gates."

Merry Pranksters

Inspired in part by Netscape's irrepressible vice president of technology, AOL, another fierce Microsoft competitor, embarked on a path of merry pranksterism. The company flew a blimp over the rollout of Windows 95 with the word "Welcome" emblazoned on its side. (This stunt had a shining precedent: Steve Jobs's condescending 1981 newspaper ads "welcoming" IBM to the microcomputer industry. Today, Apple and Netscape [now owned by AOL] each hold about 4 percent shares in their respective markets. As Marx noted, history **does** repeat itself.) All the while Netscape was indulging itself in displays of high spirits, the company was developing a reputation of being just as arrogant and hard to deal with as Microsoft.

Meanwhile, back in Redmond, Washington, the real Bill Gates, not the simulacrum from Netscape, paid Andreessen the very highest compliment of all. He took him seriously and dedicated all his time and energy to destroying Andreessen's company. The Netscape cofounder personally earned celebrity dartboard status at Microsoft, an honor that had previously been reserved for such luminaries as Philippe Kahn of Borland. By 1998 it was all over, as shrinking revenues and market share forced Netscape to trade high-tech heaven and independence for the low-tech haven of AOL and subordination.

It's impossible to overestimate the rank stupidity Andreessen demonstrated in his choice of public words and attitude vis-à-vis Microsoft. He'd committed the strategic equivalent of walking into the cage of a hungry tiger, turning around, taping a sirloin steak to his butt, and executing a slow bump and grind. It should have come as no surprise that when he left the cage he had no ass.

The harsh truth is that Netscape wasn't in a position to go head-to-head with Microsoft on anything in 1995. After its IPO, Netscape had

$203 million in the bank; Microsoft had $10 billion. Netscape's core products, browsers, weren't hard to build and Microsoft had the resources to build them. Nor, despite Andreessen's boasts, was Netscape a stronger development organization than Microsoft; in fact, the reverse was true. As already noted, by version 3.0 of IE, Microsoft was winning the product review battles in the press.

The release in 1997 of Netscape Communicator, designed to be an IE killer, drove the point home. Communicator quickly developed a widespread reputation for being slow, flaky, and overloaded with features such as an e-mail manager that never really worked. Netscape's server-based programs were also regarded as second-rate efforts, and many of the products the company claimed to have under development were vaporware. Java as a replacement for Windows proved to be a fantasy. Nor was Netscape smart enough to develop or acquire a robust Web design tool à la FrontPage, one of the few places in the Internet bubble where real and sustainable profits could have been made.

Netscape, of course, faced an incredibly difficult challenge. Its initial strong success with Navigator and highly visible IPO guaranteed the company would attract Microsoft's attention. The intelligent thing for Netscape to have done during the period when Microsoft was considering what to do about the Internet would have been to immediately sew Marc Andreessen's lips shut and be as meek and unassuming as possible. Company executives should have publicly fainted when anyone suggested that Netscape technology would ever replace Windows as an applications platform. Netscape should have pledged eternal fealty to Windows, offered to partner with Microsoft (with the full understanding that Microsoft would eventually turn on them), and bought enough time for the company to cement its third-party relationships, make money, and build a more unassailable market position. In point of fact, Netscape **did** try to do this as the full weight of Microsoft's marketing panzers bore down on it, but after Andreessen's series of trenchant observations, Microsoft wasn't buying. What Netscape needed to survive the inevitable Microsoft onslaught was to buy as much time as possible, but the moments allotted by circumstances of its own making turned out to be not enough.

After the sellout to AOL, Marc Andreessen found his role in the industry had changed from young Internet über-man to personal geek assistant to Steve Case. After realizing his career at AOL was going to consist mainly of teaching members of the executive staff how to program their VCRs, he left to form a new Internet services and infrastructure company called Loudcloud. In view of Andreessen's previous performance at Netscape, it was perhaps an unfortunate choice of name. The company finally changed it to Opsware.

eleven

___

PURPLE HAZE
ALL THROUGH MY BRAIN:
The Internet and ASP Busts

When the Internet exploded on the public consciousness in 1994, one of the reasons for the early excitement was that it seemed so fresh and new. This freshness was, as much else about the Internet proved to be, illusory. The Internet was a child of the 1960s finally all grown up, and it was about as new as LSD. And, like the notorious psychedelic elixir of the era of free love, flower power, and peace, those who partook of the Internet's dot-com drug in the late 1990s experienced an amazing and mind-bending experience that often detoured into a bad trip of bankruptcy, unemployment, and day-after flashbacks of disbelief.

~

Child of the '60s: The Internet

The Internet received its conceptual send-off in the early 1960s from the research and work of Paul Baran and Bob Taylor. Baran, a Rand company employee and computer scientist, wrote a series of papers for the Pentagon dealing with the problem of the U.S. military control and command structure during a major war. During this period, the nation's communications networks were highly centralized. A first strike on the system by either conventional or nuclear forces could have decapitated the military's communications command and control structures, rendering it unable to coordinate an effective retaliation.

To deal with this problem, Baran proposed building a distributed network based on digital technology at a time when all U.S. communications were based on analog systems. This system would pass messages from node to node via "message blocks." No one node would be responsible for end-to-end communications; instead, each would have a store and forward capability, allowing the message blocks to travel via the best or only path available. Using Baran's work as a foundation, in 1965 Rand proposed to the U.S. Air Force that it build a prototype of Baran's network, test it, and then go operational. The Air Force's different radio and TV experts took a dim view of all this talk of "digital transmission" and shot the idea down.

While Baran was working on preparing for nuclear apocalypse, Bob Taylor, head of NASA's Advanced Research Projects Agency (ARPA) unit was wondering why the three computer terminals in his office couldn't talk to one another. ARPA had been started in 1958 as an Air Force project designed to help the United States pick up the technical gauntlet thrown by the Soviet Union with its successful launch of Sputnik I. The agency was moved over to NASA later that year, and though most of its attention was focused on the space race, there was still plenty of money floating around to fund some interesting research into communications.

Taking advantage of the opportunity, Taylor scooped up millions of taxpayer dollars to fund the development of a system that would allow his terminals to chat and hired MIT graduate Larry Roberts to lead the effort. Roberts began the design and implementation of what was soon to be known as ARPANET, the Internet's direct ancestor. In October 1969, the system went live when a message from the second node on the system to the first caused a system crash. The Internet had been born.

From this inauspicious beginning, the Internet grew from its original two nodes to over 100,000 hosts by 1989. In 1983, MILNET, reserved for military use, was spun off from ARPANET. In 1990, ARPANET was transferred over to the National Science Foundation (NSF) and renamed NFSNET. ARPANET was officially shut down and replaced by the Internet.

The Internet received its first taste of front-page publicity in 1988 courtesy of wiseacre Robert Morris, Jr., a Cornell graduate student in computer science who released a worm onto the Internet. A *worm* is a form of digital virus that infects a system, replicates, and then transmits itself to other systems where it attempts to repeat the cycle.

Morris may have gotten good grades at school, but the world soon found out he wasn't much of a programmer. His worm had a big bug in it, one that allowed the virus to replicate and spread much faster than he'd anticipated. Site after site on the Internet crashed as the worm overloaded hard drives and jammed transmission lines at facilities that included universities, military sites, hospitals, and government offices. The estimated cost of clearing out the virus from infected systems reached into the millions. Morris was convicted of violating the newly hatched Computer Fraud and Abuse Act and promptly became an iconic figure to subsequent generations of socially inadequate, smarter-than-you geeks who today follow in his inglorious footsteps by making everyone's life miserable via the regular creation and release of new Internet-transmitted viruses.

Despite the hullabaloo surrounding Morris's exploit, many people who read about him weren't sure what it was he'd actually done. Despite its rapid growth, the Internet had failed to catch the public's fancy. The various software programs used to browse the system employed primitive interfaces, and though standards had been developed for transmitting data across the Internet, none existed for locating files and documents. As a result, the Internet remained a semiprivate reserve used mainly by academics, the military, and IT workers in a variety of different industries.

The British Invasion

The Internet took a giant step forward in usability with the development of the World Wide Web by British software engineer Tim Berners-Lee. Berners-Lee was a regular Internet user but found the organization of information on the system fragmented and cumbersome. To overcome the problem, he developed a series of protocols and technologies that provide a foundation for what is now called the Web.

Berners-Lee designed the Web to sit on top of the Internet and to use its existing protocols and infrastructure. The Web added three new facets to the system:

- Hypertext Transfer Protocol (HTTP), a methodology for jumping directly from one file to another on the Internet

- The concept of the uniform resource locator (URL), a virtual "address" that can be assigned to any file on the Web

- Hypertext Markup Language (HTML), which controls text formatting for viewing an Internet site

Berners-Lee also created a primitive Web browser to help test his initial work, but interestingly enough, browsing technology wasn't a part of his original specification.

The world's first Web site, http://www.info.cern.ch, went live in 1990, and Paul Kunz of the Stanford Linear Accelerator Center (SLAC) posted the first American Web site in August 1991. That same year, the U.S. government made the decision to turn over NFSNET to commercial companies and open the system up to commerce. In 1993, CERN, which owned the rights to Berners-Lee's work, announced anyone could use the Web's protocols and underlying technology royalty-free.

By the end of 1992, the Internet had over a million users, but only 1 percent of that traffic represented Web usage. A final element was needed before the Internet's formula for mass-market acceptance was complete: an easy-to-use graphical interface that would make the system attractive and accessible to the millions of PC users still using bulletin-board systems and proprietary services. The earliest Web browsers were clunky, character-based systems; the Berners-Lee browser, for example, could display only one line of text at a time. More sophisticated UNIX-based programs were available, but they were difficult to install and UNIX was regarded by many PC and Mac users as a tool of Satan. Marc Andreessen's aforementioned (see Chapter 10) release of the Mosaic browser provided the final piece to the puzzle, and the modern Internet was born.

Up to this point in time, the Internet story made sense. A complex communications network first conceived of in the 1960s is slowly built and extended over the decades. Piece by piece, new capabilities and features are added to improve the system's performance, reliability, and usability. Public participation steadily grows until the technology reaches a critical mass. When it does, businesses jump into the new market to take advantage of new commercial opportunities. Some make a great deal of money and others fall short and fail.

The Netscape IPO in August 1995 changed all that and sparked a speculative bubble focused on dot-com companies and their stocks the likes of which hadn't been seen since the late 1960s, when investors had lost their heads and portfolios over "technology" companies such as National Video[1] (they were going to build video players for the masses over a decade before this was actually feasible) and conglomerates such as Ling-Temco-Vought (they were going to build everything). Within a year of the Netscape IPO, thousands of companies were being formed to create the "new economy," a world of Web-based e-commerce ventures that seers and visionaries proclaimed would uproot and replace every existing business model and distribution system. The resulting mania drove the Dow Jones Industrial Average (it tracks the average value of 30 large, industrial stocks) from 5,000 to almost 12,000 and the technology-focused NASDAQ (it tracks many of those "dot-bomb" stocks that ruined your portfolio) from the 1,000 range to over 5,000.

---

[1] My father worked as a stockbroker during the 1960s and '70s, and I can remember him discussing National Video in the same terms people discussed the dot-com companies of the late 1990s. National Video was an early "high tech" high flier that sucked up great wads of investor cash before disappearing from the scene.

Magic Carpet Ride

The book that best describes the late twentieth century's dot-com bubble was written in the nineteenth century by Charles MacKay, thought by many to be the Nostradamus of marketing. MacKay's opus is entitled *Extraordinary Popular Delusions and the Madness of Crowds*[2] and it chronicles a long series of manias and speculative booms that have afflicted Western society since the Crusades. Reading through this classic treatise, you can find descriptions of events and circumstances that both presage and prophesy the dot-com boom. For instance, consider alchemy, the centuries-old belief that different substances could be transmuted to gold. Many think that MacKay was trying to warn future generations of the folly of buying stock from TheGlobe.com. When the company went public in November 1998, the stock opened at an incredible $87.00 and reached a high of $97.00. The company's assets? A not-very-quick nor comprehensive search engine, Web pages filled with warmed-over links, and a revenue model that lost $4.00 for every $1.00 it earned. Fool's gold, and TheGlobe.com turned back into lead with its shutdown in August 2001.

In a similar vein, others believe *Extraordinary Popular Delusions and the Madness of Crowds'* description of the craze for exotic tulips that spread throughout seventeenth-century Holland was a warning of another sort. The chapter on "Tulipomania" describes how in the space of a few months the cost of a rare bulb skyrocketed from the merely expensive to the incredible. For a brief period, the sale of a single pretty flower was enough to enable a person to retire wealthy for life. Scholars believe this tale was intended to warn us about Amazon.com stock, which at the height of the bubble reached a high of $113.00 per share, while at the same time the company was bleeding copious amounts of red ink and company CEO Jeff Bezos was telling everyone he had no idea when Amazon would ever turn a profit. By August 2001, the stock was trading at around $9.00 per share, less than the single bulb price of many collectible tulips.

MacKay also cast a jaundiced gaze on witchcraft and the persistent human belief in spirits and the supernatural. When he wrote that chapter,

---

[2] As a young man my father had worked for Farrar, Straus and Giroux, the American publisher of *Extraordinary Popular Delusions and the Madness of Crowds*, and he brought home a copy. I first read through the book as a young boy and still have it in my family library.

he may have been inspired by a future vision of Kozmo.com, the best known of several dot-com delivery services that sprang up during the boom. Kozmo's original business model consisted of sending people on bicycles to deliver videos, condoms, gum, and Twinkies to lazy New York City yuppies and hungry potheads. This particular venture sucked up over $250 million in investment capital and almost made it to an IPO. Because it cost the company an average of $10.00 in labor and overhead to fulfill the $12.00 average Kozmo order, a sum that didn't account for the company's cost of goods and marketing expenditures, it truly would have required supernatural intervention for Kozmo to have ever turned a profit.

One thing that *Extraordinary Popular Delusions and the Madness of Crowds* doesn't do is explain the root causes of these speculative bubbles. No one ever has. They usually share factors such as good economic times, easy access to credit, and sometimes the development of new technology, but the combination of all these circumstances usually **does not** generate a bubble. Many reasons for the dot-com boom have been offered, but all are somewhat unsatisfactory. The most common explanations postulate the following:

Major technological breakthroughs often spark speculative fever. Perhaps, but the introduction of the airplane, TV, CB radios and, most recently, the personal computer did not. And it could be argued that the Internet, although a significant advance in communications, was hardly a technology breakthrough even on the scale of refrigeration, which transformed the American South from a backwater into the country's most vibrant economic region. On other hand, railroads, the high-tech darlings of the nineteenth century, triggered a speculative mania that helped contribute to a depression, as Charles Kindleberger points out in *Manias, Panics, and Crashes: A History of Financial Crises* (the second best book ever written about the dot-com boom). But why trains and not TVs?

The number of people investing in the stock market had increased tremendously over the past 30 years, making the market more volatile. This contradicts mathematics and experience. The larger markets become, the more overall stability they tend to achieve. In the post–Civil War era, "robber barons" such as Jay Gould and Jim Fisk were able to attempt to corner the U.S. gold market (and were only prevented from doing so by President Grant's direct intervention).

The Hunt brothers would attempt to reprise this feat with silver in the 1980s. But by the early 1990s, public participation in the stock market put such an enterprise beyond the power of any individual or even any group of speculators.

The stock market had undergone continuous expansion since the Reagan recovery of 1982. Unfortunately for this theory, few stock market expansions spark speculative bubbles.

Everyone who had lived through the stock market crash of 1929 was now dead and the U.S. school systems do a rotten job of teaching children about important events in American history and why they occur. This theory makes a lot of sense.

The Internet, a technology child of the 1960s, functioned not only as a communications medium but also as a virtual magic mushroom that clouded the brains of people worldwide. Though somewhat metaphysical, this theory also makes a lot of sense.

Wall Street is full of idiots. This theory is both popular and has a lot going for it.

The people who bought stock from the idiots on Wall Street were also idiots. What?! Are you implying that the failure of the American people to, when confronted with IPOs that reeked of red ink and gobbled on about idiotic schemes to sell 30-pound bags of pet food directly to consumers at a guaranteed loss (Pets.com), not fall laughing hysterically to the floor before kicking these IPO turkeys out the door were somehow responsible for their own losses? This sort of speculation isn't even worthy of a reply!

Whatever the precise reasons for a particular speculative bubble, its life cycle follows a set course, though it's difficult to predict the exact timing of the sequence of events. First, there's an initial boom period during which insiders get rich and the public "discovers" what's going on. The bubble then grows larger as early skeptics enter the maelstrom and make money while sensible people stand on the sidelines scoffing at their foolishness. The speculators then turn around and make fun of the naysayers, who, embarrassed at their failure to "get it," rush in to scoop up their fair share of the plunder before the opportunity vanishes. At this point, the bubble reaches it maximum expansion and seems to pinch off from normal reality to become a universe of its own. The normal rules of profit and loss no longer apply in this alternate realm; all that matters is supply and demand.

At this point, the smart money tries to bail out before the inevitable crash. A few do succeed in escaping with their riches, and their exit begins to deflate the bubble. The rest of the occupants become uneasy and begin to edge toward the exit as well. For a while, the bubble seems to reach a state of equilibrium as the last group of idiots on the outside rush in to search for now nonexistent profits within the doomed alternate universe. Then contraction occurs, suddenly, and the bubble bursts. Seemingly overnight, profit, wealth, and happiness are replaced by loss, poverty, and misery.

Reflecting the morality of another age, *Extraordinary Popular Delusions and the Madness of Crowds* doesn't waste much pity on bubble participants. In his examination of the South Sea mania, a weird eighteenth-century scheme that involved buying shares in companies that were going to do business of some sort on the coasts of South America, Mackay writes

> *"Nobody seemed to imagine that the nation itself was as culpable as the South-Sea company. Nobody blamed the credulity and the avarice of the people—the degrading lust of gain, which had swallowed up every nobler quality in the national character, or the infatuation which had made the multitude run their heads with such frantic eagerness into the net held out for them by scheming projectors. These things were never mentioned. The people were a simple, honest, hard-working people, ruined by a gang of robbers, who were to be hanged, drawn, and quartered without mercy."*[3]

Although such observations are not politically correct in an era of universal victimhood, they're fair. As the dot-com bubble grew and swallowed increasing volumes of innocent cash, the fact that many of the original business assumptions associated with Internet and Web commerce were proving invalid was no secret. At least one prediction about the Internet and e-business was proving true: When things happened, they happened quickly.

---

[3] Charles MacKay, *Memoirs of Extraordinary Popular Delusions and the Madness of Crowds* (New York: Farrar, Strauss and Giroux, 1932), p.72.

The Web's hyperlinked architecture made measuring response and results fairly straightforward and ensured you could learn the depressing news quickly.

The Pusher Man

Banner advertising was e-commerce's first bad trip. Most sources credit the Coors Brewing Company with placing the first Web banner. The ad, a bit larger than the 468×60 pixel form factor that would become a Web standard, was one element in a national campaign on behalf of Zima, a new clear malt "beverage" (otherwise known as "beer") Coors hoped it would attract barhopping urban professionals everywhere. The banner was placed in October 1994 on the HotWired site, at the time one of the Web's most active, and was a hit. Response rates (measured by how many times people clicked the banner) averaged between 5 percent and 10 percent over the life of the campaign.

Unfortunately for Coors, its ad campaign was so successful that many people actually ran out and tried Zima,[4] only to find the stuff had about as much taste and charm as a glass of warm bathwater. Worse, the initial response to the banner encouraged e-commerce fans to predict that the Zima campaign would be representative of future Web banner performance. It wasn't. Once the novelty of banners had worn off, response rates plunged. By 1998, average banner hit rates had dropped from figures of 3 percent to 5 percent to numbers that ranged between one-tenth to one-quarter of a percent on average.

This drop was entirely predictable. A standard 480 × 60 pixel Web banner consists of about 5 square inches and takes up less that 5 percent of the real estate on a 17" computer monitor. Colors, animation, and interactivity are limited by the bandwidth of the ad server system and the need to ensure that Web pages load quickly. Complicating things further is the easy availability of technology capable of blocking most ads, though they're so easy to ignore most people don't bother. By contrast, an ad on a 25" TV consists of about 400 inches of uninterrupted pulsating pixels that talk, sing, and dance while imploring you to buy something. Channel surfing to avoid ads doesn't help, as most stations run their commercials at the same time. Another option is to learn how to

---

[4] I drank a glass of the stuff once. Ugh.

program your VCR, DVD, or similar recording device, but most people prefer the ads.

The Internet's next psychedelic nightmare was *frictionless* e-commerce. On the face of it, this was the most intriguing argument made to justify the existence of many dot-com ventures. Web-based companies, the theory went, would "disintermediate" the middlemen (i.e., distributors and resellers) because people could simply buy products directly via their browsers. One writer for *NewMedia* magazine breathlessly predicted that the Internet would soon replace the country's malls and retail stores. In their place would be a vast sprawl of distribution centers and warehouses serviced by fleets of vans designed to deliver purchases to your door within 4 to 6 hours.

This was truly stupid stuff. If we've learned anything from history, it's that new methods of distribution and payment rarely supplant existing systems; either they're integrated into the existing system or they become an additional enhancement. If you doubt this, take a coin out of your pocket and inspect this product of Bronze Age technology carefully. Coins are heavy, hard to store, and difficult to transport. Are they obsolete? Ask a vending-machine operator or a Las Vegas casino. Scattering vast new warehouse complexes around the country sounded nice to some, but where were they going to be located? There are areas of the country where building a new gas station or restaurant is reason enough for environmental angst.

And direct marketing with overnight delivery was nothing new. Not surprisingly, people who enjoyed direct shopping via the mail also enjoyed direct shopping on the Web, and there are few complaints about the current efficiency of the delivery system for goods.

Another obvious problem with the concept of disintermediation was that people like to go out and shop. We've enjoyed the experience for several millennia, and we're not going to drop the habit just because the Internet showed up. In 1998, total retail sales on the Internet were $15 billion and projected to reach $1.3 trillion by 2003. A healthy figure, but contrast this number with the 2.3 trillion in-store shopping dollars targeted by Sears and Wal-Mart **alone**. In the United States, and increasingly in the rest of the world, shopping is a necessity and entertainment all rolled into one. Rather than replace retail channels, the Internet is being integrated into the existing system. Web-based kiosks, for example, allow shoppers to browse through a store's inventory and special-order items not found on the floor. New advertising "billboard" displays make use of Web technology to dynamically change their content based on the time of day, promotions, and even estimates of current store demographics.[5]

The rise and fall of ValueAmerica.com, one of the Internet's most storied e-tailers, best exemplifies why the pursuit of frictionless e-commerce was a chimera. If you traveled regularly on business trips in the late 1990s, you probably stayed at one those hotels that likes to shove a copy of *USA Today* under your door at 5:00AM. As you staggered down to breakfast with McPaper under your arm and waited for that first cup of coffee to kick start your day, you may remember seeing full-page ads on the back pages of the paper for portable computers, desktop PCs, consumer electronics, barbecue grills, and so forth. If you do, that was your introduction to Value America (which, by the way, generated most of its sales from those newspaper ads).

Value America was the brainchild of sell-your-mother sales wunderkind Craig Winn. Earlier in his career, Winn had built a successful home-lighting business, Dynasty Classics Corp., and then promptly turned around and drove it into the ground. Dynasty's collapse revolved around Winn's managerial incompetence combined with his continued insistence on butting heads with major distributors and resellers such as Wal-Mart. Like many other entrepreneurs before him, Winn resented the distribution system's power to dictate prices, margins, and even packaging to vendors and suppliers.[6] Value America, in addition to making Winn very rich, was also intended to be his revenge on the U.S. distribution system.[7] It would be the system, however, that would have the last laugh.

Value America's business model was both simple and unworkable. The company presented itself as a giant online store. In truth, it was simply a

---

[5] To get a sense of what awaits you in the future, I strongly suggest you see *Minority Report*, the 2002 sci-fi thriller starring Tom Cruise. The film depicts personalized digital advertising displays that greet you by name via scans of your retinal patterns. To depress you further, you should also see *Gattaca*, a scary and prophetic look into a biometric future. Much of *Gattaca* was shot at the Marin County Civic Center, a leaky edifice that was designed by Frank Lloyd Wright and known only semiaffectionately by the natives as "Frank Lloyd Wright's last erection." To many people, the building resembles a giant . . . well . . . you get the idea. I passed this building every day on my way to my job as a product manager at MicroPro corporate headquarters on North San Pedro Road.

[6] Winn blamed Wal-Mart for the bankruptcy of his first company, Dynasty Classics, in an interview in 2000 with *Business Week* magazine.

[7] J. David Kuo, *Dot.Bomb: My Days and Nights at an Internet Goliath* (New York: Little, Brown and Company, 2001).

middleman between buyers and manufacturers. Value America's plan was for the company to never to have shelves or warehouses and the costs that accompany them. When a customer placed an order, Value America passed the request on to a manufacturer, which shipped the item directly to the consumer. Buyers were instructed to ship returned items directly back to the manufacturer. Value America was ostensibly supposed to make money by "reselling products" at a 1 percent markup over cost. For a bricks-and-mortar retailer this is a suicidal price structure, but Value America's inventory-free model supposedly made it possible to achieve profitability with this microscopically thin margin.

Despite the patina of high tech the Internet threw about Winn's creation, nothing he was attempting was new. The manufacturer-direct-to-customer approach has been tried before, and it has failed before. Many, many times. The reason for this is simple: Distribution systems congeal out of businesses and industries not because of desire or opportunism but out of sheer necessity. Unfortunately for the poor souls who loaded e-tail stocks into their portfolios, few people advocating inventory-free retailing had much understanding of how and why distribution systems exist.

The usual function of a distributor or reseller is, in the vernacular, to "break bulk" and reduce the many to the one. These entities are experts in receiving orders from multiple sources and fulfilling them via complex and highly automated systems that provide warehousing, credit checking, tracking, fulfillment, returns management, etc., etc. Creating and efficiently managing such systems requires years of acquired expertise and is expensive. Just how expensive is something Amazon.com discovered as it attempted to create in a few years warehousing and fulfillment systems it had taken companies such as Wal-Mart decades to implement and perfect.

Vendors and manufacturers are naturally drawn to the idea of cutting out the middlemen and selling their products and services directly to customers, but few ultimately succeed. In high tech, business-to-business companies such as IBM and Microsoft have in the past attempted to bypass major hardware and software distributors such as Ingram and Tech Data. Eventually, all have been forced to abandon the attempt. Companies discovered that as they added increasing numbers of resellers, the cost of attempting to replicate the specialized expertise of a distributor became prohibitive. It was more cost-effective to simply ship large quantities of product X (the bulk) to distributor Y (the one) and let them worry about the logistics of shipping the stuff out to various resellers (the many). In consumer retailing the same logic constantly repeats itself, with the sheer volume of companies and customers making the need for a distribution channel even more critical.

There are companies that are able to buck the system, computer manufacturer Dell being one of high tech's most notable. Dell's direct-to-consumer model has flourished because computers are comparatively high-dollar purchases, possess a highly standardized form factor, and are easy to ship via mail. The majority of Dell customers are more interested in price and availability than brand equity and service and, because Dell assembles its own inventory, the company can closely manage demand and fulfillment. With all these contingencies in its favor, Dell's direct business approach can succeed.

None of these aforementioned factors applied to Value America, however. Because it stocked and built nothing, once an order was received and transmitted to a manufacturer tracking and delivery was out of Value America's control. And, as a business-to-consumer enterprise, it carried the additional burden of coordinating the sales of hundreds of thousands of orders from customers with thousands of manufacturers. Value America never developed inventory management systems that came close to the power and sophistication needed to manage such a complex task.

This wasn't the only drawback to the company's inventory-free model. Manufacturers that sold only a few items via recommendations from Value America gave those orders low priority. In some cases, once they realized that Value America wouldn't be selling significant amounts of product, they didn't bother to fulfill them at all. (In point of fact, many manufacturers required Value America to buy their products from distributors, because they had little interest in attempting to become distributors themselves. This in turn helped undermine the company's "1 percent over manufacturer cost" revenue model.) And though vendors receiving higher volumes of orders from the company were quicker to respond to customer issues, Value America's primitive order tracking and fulfillment systems often made finding and fixing problems difficult, if not impossible.

The company also didn't understand that when you sell something to a customer, you "own" that customer and all the customer's associated problems, including the problem of customer dissatisfaction with a purchase. Despite its claims to have no shelves and no warehouses, Value America soon acquired both in order to manage product returns.

J. David Kuo, in *Dot.Bomb: My Days and Nights at an Internet Goliath*, his I-was-there description of the rise and fall of Value America, described how the situation developed:

> *"When Winn created Value America, an important part of the model was not holding any inventory, anywhere, at any time. But a strange thing began to happen as the company sold more and more merchandise. When people didn't like a product or changed their mind, or when the product didn't work, they returned the product to Value America. Despite the fact they were **told** to send it back to the manufacturer, they did what shoppers everywhere do. They returned it to the place they purchased it."* [8]

At one point Value America found itself managing hundreds of pallets of returned goods sitting in a rented warehouse. And as products aged, many manufacturers refused to take them back, requiring the inventory to be dumped at a loss.

The result of all these problems was that before its inevitable demise, Value America was perhaps the Internet's most reviled e-store. Credit-card returns could take as long as 45 days to process. Items listed as in-stock on the Web site often weren't. Holds on customer service phone lines averaged 45 minutes. Chat rooms and discussion sites that rated online shopping experiences reviled Value America and the company's online popularity rankings were bottom of the barrel.

Value America, which went public in April 1999 and saw its stock shoot to $73.00 per share on its first day of trading, was in bankruptcy by August 2000. Type in Value America's domain name on the Internet today and you'll get a DNS error.

The strength of America's shopping habit was illustrated by the rapid rise and just as rapid demise of Webvan and eToys. Webvan was the brainchild of Louis Borders, founder of the Borders bookstore chain, who conceived it as a national grocery delivery service that would ship food to the domiciles of hungry, time-starved yuppies. The company's debut in Oakland, California, showcased Webvan's commercial heart: a state-of-the-art warehouse festooned with refrigerators, conveyer belts, and lots of plastic baggies (each green pepper sold, for instance, was assigned its very own plastic pouch). The warehouse in turn serviced a

---

[8] Ibid., p. 59.

fleet of vans that delivered your vittles supposedly within 30 minutes of receiving an order. The whole system took $1.2 billion to build.

For a number of people, Webvan was a godsend and they were happy to pay a premium for their food in return for the convenience of not having to go out and shop. (Not coincidentally, a high percentage of Webvan customers were themselves dot-com types, a nice example of drinking your own triple espresso chocolate latte mocha.) Unfortunately for Webvan, this number of people was small. A warehouse designed to service 8,000 orders per day was fulfilling a few hundred. It turned out most people still preferred to go out and pick out their own peppers for consumption, even if they didn't come wrapped in plastic. Before the company went public in 1999, its prospectus revealed Webvan had lost $35 million on sales of just $395,000.00. This grim financial fact didn't prevent the market from bidding the stock up from $15.00 to $26.00 per share on Webvan's first day of trading.

Another problem with Webvan was the fact that anyone who'd ever gone to a supermarket knew that a reliable infrastructure for the delivery of home groceries already existed. Depending on where you grew up, it might be a kid on a bike with a basket hanging off the front of the handlebars or someone driving a beat-up jalopy with a large trunk, but this system worked and still does. But it didn't seem to occur to anyone that spending $1.2 billion to reinvent a highly functional wheel didn't make a lot of sense.

Webvan stopped wrapping veggies in plastic and closed its doors for good in July 2001. Before the end, its stock was trading for around $.50 per share. About the cost of a single ripe green pepper, sans plastic baggie.

This isn't to say that online shopping for groceries on the Web is extinct. Today in New York City, you can order food on the Internet from upscale stores such as D'Agostinos and Gristede's via your browser. In some cases, you drive to a local store to pick up your order; in others, the supermarket drops your food off at your house. If you're a mensch,[9] you give the delivery kid a nice tip.

In contrast to Webvan, eToys, the now defunct online toy store, had far more success in selling mass quantities of Barbies and LEGOs to America's youth; sales at its peak reached about $200 million. Unfortunately, to ensure the on-time delivery of all that brightly colored plastic to kids the world over, particularly during Christmastime, the toy

---

[9] A Yiddish term for "nice guy."

industry's make-or-break season, the company had to invest in building a $900 million warehouse and fulfillment system. Shipping individual toys presents a particular challenge as they come in a maddening variety of shapes and sizes, and vary widely in durability, ranging from incredibly fragile to simply very easy to break.

And though the eToys Web site was widely praised for its interface and usability, it proved unable to replace the experience of bringing your 6-year-old into a store and having him sit down in an aisle, become hysterical, and refuse to move until you gave in and bought him the latest object of his desire. After burning through over $200 million in real—not Monopoly—money, the company went bankrupt in early 2001 and sold off its $40 million toy inventory to the KB Toys chain for $5.4 million. KB Toys shipped the inventory out to its stores, and if you were a smart shopper you saved a few bucks on your Christmas shopping for the kids if you hit the malls at the right time.

The next group of theories focused on the Internet's direct marketing capabilities. Here the pundits appeared to be a bit more on target. By 1999, it was apparent that e-mail would slowly chew up the U.S. Post Office and replace conventional mail, direct marketing's primary vehicle. Online list brokers such as PostMasterDirect appeared and began doing a lively business creating and renting a wide variety of e-mail databases targeting an increasingly large variety of industries. One writer at *The Industry Standard*, a magazine that lived and died by the dot-com boom, predicted that Web-based infomercials would revolutionize e-tailing.

The pundits, however, had again missed the point. Direct marketing in the United States has traditionally supported conventional retail operations. On average, for every one product sold directly via mail or e-mail, two or more will be sold at a store as a result of a direct offer. Infomercials operate on the same model; most break even on their direct sales of various types of successful infomercials. Profits are made by driving customers to retail stores to buy the latest Ronco breakthrough in better living.

Finally, as all else failed, the theory of *momentum* was introduced to justify the billions being poured down various Internet financial rat holes. The momentum theory boiled down to the belief that if you were losing money at low sales volumes, ramping sales up would demonstrate your business was capable of "scalability" and that this would eventually lead to profitability. It apparently never crossed the minds of many people that the reason dot-com losses grew as sales increased is that many of these businesses were inherently unprofitable. Accelerating sales volumes thus meant you were scaling up to reach insolvency at a greatly increased velocity.

Up, Up and Away

From 1996 to 2000, the dot-com bubble grew with amazing speed as venture capitalists (VCs) and investors poured seemingly endless streams of cash into hundreds of various Internet ventures. The valuation models advanced by Wall Street and the VC community were particularly interesting. Most were based on the concept of *multiples of forward revenues,* an accounting practice that in other times and places might get you sent to jail for fraud.

In this valuation model, if dot-com company A received $100 million in investment capital in year 1, used that cash to generate $200 million in revenues in year 2, and then borrowed another $100 million to generate an additional $200 million in revenue in year 3, the company would be evaluated at $800 million (2 × $400 million) come IPO time. Except no one was actually waiting for year 3 to come around before going public: 8 to 9 months was the usual target. And none of the models seemed to take into account the obscure notion of "profits." All that seemed to matter was "building brands" and generating "momentum" (i.e., serving up millions of profitless page views and selling lots of stuff to lots of people regardless of whether sales of the stuff made any money).

The mania reached its height in 1999 and early 2000, with over $160 billion being pumped into more and more dot-coms of increasingly dubious bona fides. The bubble burst in April 2000 and was followed by 3 years of a declining stock market and hemorrhaging portfolios. The fallout from the crash dragged into 2002 and helped drive the Dow Jones Industrial Average below 8,000 and the NASDAQ to 1,200. When it was all over, the dot-com winners included the following:

> *eBay.* A solid success, eBay was a Web translation of all those local *Bargain News* and *Buy Lines* newspapers we'd all grown up with. Unlike many other Web businesses that tried to make this claim, eBay's model was truly and inherently "inventory-free."

*E*TRADE*. Hmmm. There's a problem here. E*TRADE was only sort of a dot-com. The company had actually been offering online stock trading since 1983, and CompuServe and AOL had carried the service since the early 1990s.

America Online (AOL). Well, sort of. AOL had preceded the Internet boom by many years and made a lot of money as the leading proprietary network before the Internet meltdown. But after the merger with Time Warner, creating a new company, AOL Time Warner, the online giant's advertising model promptly tanked, leaving everyone marveling at AOL founder Steve Case's impeccable timing in buying a larger, more profitable company than his own with inflated stock that begin to deflate almost minutes after the acquisition. The new company managed to lose $50 billion in a single quarter in 2002, leaving everyone longing for the good old pre-Internet days when the company sold you online access by the minute. Case and most of the AOL side of the company were summarily kicked out or "resigned" from the merged mess, while the survivors got to work figuring out how to remove the "AOL" from the company logo. Maybe not such a good example after all.

Yahoo. OK, maybe profits were pretty scarce the last several years and revenue growth was flat, but the company made some money during the dot-com boom. But income went south as Web-based advertising income collapsed. And having a stock that plummeted from a high of $348.00 per share to $8.00 per share made everyone cranky.

eBay. Sorry, I already mentioned them, didn't I?

Amazon.com. You must be joking. The company, founded in 1995, finally turned a net profit of a giant, huge, unbelievable $5 million after losing over $500 million the year before. It then turned around and lost another $23 million in the first quarter of 2002. But, good news—this was down from $234 million in the year-earlier quarter. And sales jumped 21 percent to $847 million! Money managers swooned at genius CEO Jeff Bezos's newly found ability to simply lose money, not lose it hand over fist. As the year 2003 hove into view, the hope of sustained profitability by Amazon warmed the hearts of Internet advocates everywhere. It would have been nice if the company had waited until then to tout the stock.

Priceline.com. OK, it had lost a lot more money than it had ever made, and in 2001 its profits were a paltry few million, but it did seem as if there were some money to be made selling unfilled airline seats and hotel rooms at a discount on the Internet. And one advantage to the collapse was that we didn't have to listen to William Shatner sing anymore. Then he came back. But at least he didn't sing.

The Wall Street Journal (WSJ) Online. Another problem. Most of the people who subscribed to the WSJ online also bought the paper edition. Is this really an example of dot-com success? Oh, what the heck! Let's say yes!

Monster.com, HotJobs.com, etc. Yep, like eBay, a solid success. There's a pattern here. If a dot-com is selling an information commodity that by its nature requires no inventory to be managed, it can sometimes make money.

eBay. Did I mention eBay?

Of course, if you dig hard enough, it's possible to find some small success stories here and there, companies that serve small niche markets and make modest profits. For instance, a new Web site, F*****Company.com, sprang up in 2000 with the mission of documenting the ongoing collapse of the dot-coms. The site offered visitors the opportunity to bet on when the next e-venture would fail, advice on the best time to loot your cubicle before you were thrown out of the building, tips on how to keep hold of your company-issued laptop, and the chance to slander upper management with no fear of reprisal. The brainchild of Philip J. Kaplan, known informally as "Pud," the site soon started to do a nice business in sales of T-shirts, a book bearing the Web site's euphonious name, and subscriptions to the site's inner sanctum of information and tips. In the same vein, several firms found there was money to be made in liquidating the assets of failed dot-coms.

There were also a few dot-coms that crawled out from beneath the rubble of the dot-com collapse, dusted themselves off, and put together sensible business plans that offered some hope of success. Like, for instance, eHobbies. Dedicated to serving the needs of those obsessive-compulsive types driven to re-create the world in miniature, the company had burned through $20 million in venture funds while building up a payroll of over 150 people and had quickly gone insolvent. Two former employees bought what was left from the meltdown and relaunched the site with no venture capital and no payroll (the founders couldn't afford one until they were making some money). A few months after its resurrection, the founders of the new slimmed-down eHobbies were profiled on National Public Radio extolling the virtues of minimal overhead, low payrolls, and real profits.

And that was about . . . it. Depending on your scoring generosity, you could count the number of major dot-com successes on the fingers of one hand. All in all, not much of a return on investment to show for all those billions of dollars spent. Not to mention the trillions of dollars of paper wealth pulled from the portfolios of hapless investors worldwide as the dot-com bubble burst. As the new economy disappeared behind stacks of unsold inventory and piles of bankruptcy applications, the old economy reappeared and promptly fired hundreds of thousands of people from their jobs.

~

The Last Days of Disco: The ASP Craze

By 1998, a gimlet-eyed observer would have noticed that there was something rather . . . well . . . odd about the "high technology" boom sweeping the nation. The problem was that if you looked closely, there was precious little that was high tech about it. What, exactly, was so new millennium about selling books, furniture, food, wine, toys, stamps, and pornography directly to consumers while building warehouses to store the books, furniture, food, wine, toys, and pornography? (No one bought the stamps—people went to the post office instead. Or used e-mail.) Yes, you needed a Web browser to surf the Internet, and this had been very leading-edge stuff in 1994, but by 1998 your kid knew more about how to surf the Internet than you did, just like he was the only person in the house who knew how to program the VCR. And what was so high tech about a VCR?

As the Internet bubble reached the outer limits of its expansion, there was no question that real high tech was feeling left out of all the fun, particularly the software firms. The hardware companies were actually doing OK. Before the dot-coms shut down their warehouses and left piles of pet food and peppers wrapped in plastic baggies rotting on the loading docks, they were buying expensive Sun Microsystems servers by the thousands and truckloads of Cisco routers. The result was that the stock prices of the hardware companies looked pretty good—not inflated-past-the-limits-of-all-human-intelligence-Amazon.com good, mind you, but very respectable nonetheless.

By contrast, the software guys were wondering where **their** Internet riches and glory were. After all, it was software that had made the dot-com phenomenon possible. The whole thing ran on Web browsers, application servers, Internet protocols, and HTML, but look how it had all turned out. Netscape had burned brightly for a while but then was smothered into submission by Microsoft and Internet Explorer. There had been a couple of mildly hot start-ups such as Vermeer Technologies and FrontPage (Microsoft had promptly snapped them up), and Allaire with its ColdFusion products. E.piphany, a publisher of customer relationship management (CRM) software, had enjoyed watching its stock, driven by Internet mania and interest in this new product category, reach heights unjustified by its sales and profitability.

And for a few weeks in 1999, the Linux guys had done OK in the market. Companies such as Red Hat and VA Linux Systems had taken advantage of the dot-com boom to go public and had seen their stock prices driven to very temporary but giddy highs by the Internet mania. But almost as quickly as their stocks rose, they fell as people realized that there were few profits to be made in a market dedicated to selling a free version of UNIX for PCs that anyone could download from a Web site if he were so inclined.

But these minor successes aside, most of the software firms had been relegated to the role of selling the virtual equivalent of pans, picks, and shovels to others mining Internet gold. It was a profitable endeavor, but not a very glamorous one for an industry that since the early 1980s had become accustomed to being fawned over as American business's precious new young thing.

But software was ready with a riposte. If the 1960s could make a comeback in the form of the Internet, was there any reason why the 1970s couldn't do it as well? It was time for the rebirth of . . . time sharing! (Computers, not condos.)

Disco Inferno

Time sharing was the mainframe-based centralized model of computing that dominated the industry to the end of the 1970s.[10] It worked by permitting an individual to access mainframes via terminals and work in virtual sessions that created the illusion that each user had control over the whole machine. Time share software was paid for on a rental basis, and the applications available were limited, expensive, and proprietary to particular companies and/or machines. By the mid-1980s, time sharing was moribund, driven out of most markets by networked PCs running comparatively inexpensive desktop applications, though the technology did hold on in areas such as the airline industry's SABRE flight reservation system.

Software vendors quickly realized this old wine in a new bottle deserved a new appellation and one was promptly coined: application service providers (ASPs). Advocates explained that the ASP schema would replace PCs, or *fat clients,* running desktop applications such as Microsoft Office or Macromedia Dreamweaver with *thin clients* called *network computers* (NCs) running software programs being dished up by banks of remote servers. As with time sharing, applications would be rented or used on an as-needed basis, and boxed/licensed software would soon be a thing of the past.

The NC was the brainchild of Larry Ellison, founder of database powerhouse Oracle who, like many high-tech CEOs, has a deep and abiding fear of Bill Gates. An NC was basically a PC with its floppy and hard disk stripped out and was, as conceived of by Ellison, designed to make Windows and Windows-based desktop applications obsolete. Instead of relying on a desktop OS, users would employ Web browsers as their interface to an array of applications stored on the aforementioned banks of servers and fed to users via the Internet. Files and projects would likewise be stored remotely but could be accessed 24/7 via any computer or NC that had Web access.

---

[10] My first experience with time sharing was with a financial modeling package called "Finar" used by my father to perform simulations of intermediate stock market swings. The cost to rent usage of the package was in the thousands of dollars. Finar was later purchased by MicroPro and in 1983 became a PC-based product called "PlanStar," which was available for a few hundred dollars. A better known exemplar of this type of software was introduced a few years later under the name of Javelin. These data modeling packages take a "top-down" approach to spreadsheet creation. Though powerful, these products have never been widely accepted by the market.

The benefits that were supposed to accrue to both companies and their IT departments from this new/old approach were many. NCs were going to be much cheaper than PCs and corporate accountants could look forward to saving lots of money on a key capital expense. IT loved the idea that it was going be able to "lock down" applications and desktops and return to those halcyon days when MIS gods strode through the corridors of power and told employees that what was good for them was good for the company (digitally speaking).

Users were also going to benefit from being liberated from the necessity to learn how to turn their computers on and off and understand such esoteric concepts as "floppies" and "hard disks." Productivity would also rise as clandestine sessions of Solitaire and stolen moments with Minesweeper came to an end. Everyone could finally forget about all this "knowledge worker" nonsense as employees resumed their proper roles as corporate drones working maniacally on single tasks administered from a central source.

And for the software companies the ASP model promised a revenue nirvana. In ASP World there would be no more expensive upgrade programs with their direct marketing overhead and wads of CDs being tossed around the landscape. Instead, software use and updates would be managed and policed via electronic distribution over the Internet. Even better, in much the same way that renting a home is ultimately more expensive than buying one, software publishers would be able to develop consistent revenue streams from renting their applications and charging more to use them. After all, the ASP model was relieving a corporation's IT department of the burden of having to test and deploy new programs and upgrades, and that was certainly worth a premium!

There was also the delightful prospect of breaking into lucrative markets the "old-line" software firms seemed to have locked up. Microsoft Office has 90+ percent market share in business applications? No problem. Just load that ASP-based office suite into a browser and start making money. And no need to worry about recouping hosting and development costs—you would be able to offer free applications via the Web and have the cost of deploying and maintaining them borne by advertisers! Just look at the response to that Zima banner on the HotWired Web site! Heck, if an ASP generated half that response rate, it was still found money. And once customers were hooked, you'd upgrade them to a premium service that charged real money on a subscription basis. You just couldn't miss with this ASP model.

In a hurry not to let the moment pass it by, the industry leaped enthusiastically into the golden ether. From the late 1990s to 2001, more than 500 companies received over $10 billion in venture capital. The industry went furiously to work building the infrastructure and software required to retrieve time sharing from the Lost World of Polyester and transport it forward into the Age of the Internet.

The efforts quickly bore fruit. Soon there was an ASP solution for every market and taste. For those who wanted Web-based business applications, there was HotOffice.com. The basic service was free and paid for by banner advertising. Those in need of enterprise resource planning (ERP) and e-commerce for their Web sites could turn to Pandesic, a joint venture between software giant SAP and hardware colossus Intel. If you were intrigued by Web-based time tracking and invoicing, there was RedGorilla.com. And for those concerned about storage costs, sites such as iDrive.com, which allowed you to save your files on Web servers, were built to help. Providing the hardware infrastructure needed to support this new world of time shar– . . . er . . . Web-based software were firms such as Exodus and USI, both of which were spending billions to cover the American landscape with buildings stuffed with servers and bristling with wires.

Nor was that all. Several trade shows dedicated to the ASP market promptly sprung into being. A new ASP industry consortium was formed. New publications with names like *ASP World* were in the planning stages. ASP stock prices promptly headed into overvalued dot-com territory and thousands of paper millionaires began planning their early retirements. The ASP market was ready for launch!

And then the rocket blew up on the pad.

The Last Dance

There were many reasons for the ASP implosion. One was that people who actually used Web-based applications discovered that in terms of usability and power, the applications, well, sucked. The Web in the late 1990s and early 2000s wasn't designed to act as an application interface, but to allow you to jump around from file to file quickly. It did this well enough if you had a reasonably fast connection to the Internet, but it didn't do much else very well. People accustomed to responsive application interfaces, spreadsheets that raced through huge wads of numbers, and word processors that cut and pasted big blocks of text with alacrity rebelled as they fumbled with slow, clunky, Web-based products that felt as if they were being run on a TRS-80 circa 1978. Only slower.

Another problem for ASP World was that the NC was dying, strangled in its cradle by Moore's Law as it wound its coils of relentless price erosion around Ellison's fair-haired silicon progeny. Initially designed to be sold at the "bargain" price of about $1,000.00 per unit, the NC soon found itself competing against nicely loaded desktops for around the same price. (And unlike the PC, NCs offered computer resellers no good opportunities for upselling accessories and extra goodies, making them extremely unappealing to the distribution channel.)

Also, as the Internet grew, the desirability of the thin-client model underwent a reexamination. A thin-client computing environment meant fat servers, huge storage centers, and big thick digital "pipes" to provide, store, and transmit applications and data. Such an environment may have been an IT manager's dream, but corporate CFOs blanched when presented with the bills. Maybe it made sense to offload some of these computing expenses onto increasingly dirt-cheap PCs, after all. And heck, even CFOs like to play a quick game of Minesweeper every once in a while.

The Napster tune-swapping service's mass popularization of peer-to-peer computing also led to a reconsideration of the thin client versus fat client debate. Although Napster's approach of using the Internet to allow people to transfer music directly from one PC to another was a smash success (at least in terms of usage; Napster had a hard time demonstrating how you make money from the concept), the system suffered from a fatal flaw. Unfortunately for fans of 24/7 mass violation of copyrights on a global scale, Napster's system used servers to create centralized directories of all those purloined files residing on everyone's hard disk. This weakness allowed the recording industry to convince the U.S. legal system to shut the network down until it had mended its ways. (Napster could never figure out how to profit from its "mass theft" business model and went out of business.)

But new peer-to-peer technology didn't suffer from this weakness. Networks such as Gnutella and FastTrack required no centralized servers, but relied on individual PCs to store information about file requests, manage transfers, and create virtual directories to speed up performance. The more fat powerful clients out there, the better, as far as these networks were concerned.

Then there was the issue of information control. Many companies, after taking a look at the hosted model, decided there was no way they were going to entrust mission-critical data to unknown third parties. In fact, they weren't going to entrust it to known third parties either. Ditto for anything that involved critical real-time transactions, such as credit card processing. Many companies insisted that ASPs offer their products for sale the old-fashioned way, via the purchase of a license that enabled them to maintain control over both the software and their data.

And on closer examination, although automatic software upgrades sounded great in theory, in reality they introduced a whole new set of headaches. The possibility of incompatible file formats corrupting data and the chance that an automatic upgrade could break macros, scripts, and applications that currently worked fine made many IT professionals nervous. As a result, many companies decided they preferred to continue to manage their upgrades internally, a choice that gave them more control over the process of testing the impact of new software on existing systems.

It also became clear that charging more for rented applications wouldn't be as easy as once thought. When a company was presented with a prospective tab for a software rental, nothing prevented anyone from doing some simple math that totaled up the yearly cost of renting software and comparing it to the cost of licensing the same product. At this point, software companies relearned the lesson that once markets have become used to existing price points and schedules, they're very resistant to attempts to change them. Arguments about IT savings were countered by rejoinders that the software company was saving money by not having to run an upgrade program.

Exacerbating the problem was the fact that many of the proponents of hosted applications were companies in the CRM and ERP markets. Ostensibly designed to offer business executives top-down views and management of every aspect of their company's operations, purchasers of these software products soon began to derisively refer to them as "shelfware." This unflattering designation arose from the fact that once a company bought one of these mega-sized, multimodule pieces of code and attempted to implement part of it, the expense, difficulty, and cost of doing so often led to the rest of the product being shoved on a shelf and buried.

ASPs also discovered that many segments of corporate America were reluctant to give up the "piracy" discount inherent in conventional software purchases.[11] Software companies are fond of bemoaning the fact that in many markets as much as 50 percent of the software used by companies is illegally copied. And the companies are upset by it too! Very, very upset, and they're going to get on top of the problem and take care of it. Someday. Maybe next year. Or decade. Or whenever.

The upshot of it all is that by 2001, the ASP market bore a grim resemblance to the rest of the dot-com morass. HotOffice found out that banner advertising hardly paid for a single server and cooled into Chapter 11. Intel and SAP pulled the plug on Pandesic. RedGorilla.com turned out to be one sick chimp and died. Exodus and USI went bankrupt. People discovered that hard disk storage cost about $1.00 per gigabyte, so what was the point of renting Internet storage space? The trade shows folded. The ASP consortium closed up shop when most of its membership went out of business or decided that old-fashioned software licensing was still the way to go. In a desperate attempt to distance itself from the unrelenting stream of failures, the industry frog marched the ASP label up against a wall and summarily executed the unfortunate acronym. Taking its place were a plethora of new alphabetical appellations—MRPs, HSPs, HRPs, XSPs, etc.—intended to take everyone's mind off the current depressing state of affairs. Most were immediately hunted down and dispatched. The ASP designation crawled back from the grave and resumed its official role as the standard designation for hosted applications, but it was now in official disgrace and no one talked to it.

---

[11] In early 1999, I was invited to give a presentation at a Software & Information Industry Association (SIIA) seminar on the ASP market and its prospects for success. The SIIA is the latest incarnation of the old Software Publishers Association. One of the reasons consultants and analysts attend these events is to present themselves as experts on a topic and attract future consulting gigs. The hope is that after a stirring presentation, members of the audience will rush up with their business cards outstretched to hire you to put their myriad sales and marketing problems straight. Unfortunately for my plans, I decided to give a straightforward analysis of the ASP market that concluded that most of the current business models and approaches were horsesh– . . . not feasible. I was later informed by the SIIA that many in the audience had found my negative attitude discouraging and I collected very few business cards (well, none, actually). This experience drove home to me the realization that a herd of lemmings in the act of flinging themselves over a cliff are primed to discuss the importance of teamwork, the need to stay focused on the task at hand, and the necessity of maintaining a positive attitude.

To be fair, the news wasn't all bad. There were a few modest successes in certain markets, such as human resources. Although a company's resume database is important, the inability to access it for a few hours or even a day or so isn't critical. In markets with similar characteristics, such as scheduling, project management, and sales force and marketing automation, ASP firms made some headway, especially if their goals were modest and their prices low. By the end of 2001, the ASP market was determined to have generated about $600 million in revenue and very little in the way of profits. And even these figures were somewhat deceptive as many of the surviving ASPs were now also selling their software the old-fashioned way, via licensing. As with the dotcoms, not much of a ROI on a $10 billion investment.

But, good news! By 2002, industry gurus were proclaiming that, yes, there was **indeed** a fortune to be made by hosting applications. It was going to be done via a brand-new technology: Web services, new Internet-based protocols, products, and services that would allow all those desktop applications to communicate and collaborate in new and wonderful ways. And who was going to make all this money? Well, as the June 25, 2002, issue of *Interactive Week* (a publication that soon after folded, itself a victim of the Internet implosion) told us

> *"The key to the paradox is that growth will be driven not by start up ASPs—which have gained mind share but not market share— but by the folks that already sell software by the ton."*[12]

And how were the folks already selling tons of software going to create ASP World? Well, later in the same article, Microsoft theorized that

> *"It's a misconception that people will get Office off a Web site. What is Office in a software-as-a-service world? A client, a way for people to access some services."*[13]

Oh. In other words, get ready to pay for access to an updated spelling corrector for your word processor. Well, it was good to know what the future held. At least we weren't all going to end up having to wear love beads, acetate shirts with floral designs, and ultrawide ties. That was something.

---

[12] "Changing the economics of software business," *Interactive Week*, June 25, 2002.
[13] Ibid.

AFTERWORD:
Stupid Development Tricks

THE COMPLETE TITLE of *In Search of Stupidity* includes the phrase "High-Tech Marketing Disasters," and from these words you might conclude that it's a firm's marketers who usually bear the chief responsibility for major corporate catastrophes. This isn't true. To be worthy of mention in this book, it took the combined efforts of personnel in upper management, development, sales, and marketing, all fiercely dedicated to ignoring common sense, the blatantly obvious, and the lessons of the past. Major failure doesn't just happen: To achieve it, everyone must pull together as a team.

Chapter 4 of *In Search of Stupidity* helps drive this point home. For MicroPro to plummet from the software industry's pinnacle to permanent oblivion took a) upper management's mishandling of development and market timing, b) the marketing department's idiotic decision to create a fatal product-positioning conflict, and c) the development team's dimwitted decision to rewrite perfectly good code at a critical time because it wanted to write even better code that no one really needed. A magnificent example of different groups within a company all cooperating to ensure disaster.

In this spirit, I've decided to include selected portions of an interview with Joel Spolsky that ran on SoftwareMarketSolution (http://www.softwaremarketsolution.com), a Web site sponsored by the author of this book that provides resources and information on products and services of interest to high-tech marketers. (By the way, this interview was "picked up" by Slashdot [http://www.slashdot.org], a Web site dedicated to technology, coding, open source, and all things nerd. It generated a considerable amount of comment and controversy. You can search the Slashdot archives to read what other people thought and gain further insight into Joel's opinions.)

I regard Joel Spolsky, president and one of the founders of Fog Creek Software (http://www.fogcreek.com), as one of the industry's most fascinating personalities. He worked at Microsoft from 1991 to 1994 and has over 10 years of experience managing the software development process. As a program manager on the Microsoft Excel team, Joel designed Excel Basic and drove Microsoft's Visual Basic for Applications (VBA) strategy. His Web site, Joel on Software (http://www.JoelonSoftware.com), is visited by thousands of developers worldwide every day. His first book, *User Interface Design for Programmers*, was reviewed on SoftwareMarketSolution, and I regard it as a must-have for anyone involved in developing and marketing software.

Why this interview? If you've ever worked on the software side of high technology you've probably experienced the following. After a careful analysis of your product's capabilities, the competition, and the current state of the market, a development and marketing plan is created. Release time frames are discussed and agreed upon. Elaborate project management templates are built and milestones are set. You post the ship date up on a wall where everyone in your group can see it, and your team begins to work like crazed beavers to meet your target.

Then, as the magic day looms nearer, ominous sounds emit from development. Whispers of "crufty code" and "bad architecture" are overheard. Talk of "hard decisions" that "need to be made" starts to wend its way through the company grapevine. People, especially the programmers, walk by the wall on which you've mounted the ship date, pause, shake their heads, and keep walking.

Finally, the grim truth is disgorged. At a solemn meeting, development tells everyone the bad news. The code base of the current product is a mess. Despite the best and heroic efforts of the programmers, they've been unable to fix the ancient, bug-ridden, fly-bespeckled piece of trash foisted on them by an unfeeling management. No other option remains. The bullet must be bitten. The gut must be sucked up. The Rubicon must be crossed. And as that sinking feeling gathers in your stomach and gains momentum as it plunges toward your bowels, you realize that you already know what you're about to hear. And you already know that, after hearing it, you'll be groping blindly back to your cubicle, your vision impeded by the flow of tears coursing down your face, your eyes reddened by the sharp sting of saline. And you've already accepted it's time to get your resume out and polished, because the next few financial quarters are going to be very, very ugly.

And then they say it. The product requires a ground-up rewrite. No other option exists.

Oh, you **haven't** been through this yet? Well, just wait. You will. However, as you'll learn, what you're going to be told may very well not be true. After reading this interview, you'll be in a better position to protect your vision and your career in the wonderful world of high tech.

And now . . .

~

An Interview with Joel Spolsky

SoftwareMarketSolution: Joel, what, in your opinion, is the single greatest development sin a software company can commit?

Joel Spolsky: Deciding to completely rewrite your product from scratch, on the theory that all your code is messy and bug-prone and is bloated and needs to be completely rethought and rebuilt from ground zero.

SMS: Uh, what's wrong with that?

JS: Because it's almost never true. It's not like code rusts if it's not used. The idea that new code is better than old is patently absurd. Old code has been used. It has been tested. Lots of bugs have been found, and they've been fixed. There's nothing wrong with it.

SMS: Well, why do programmers constantly go charging into management's offices claiming the existing code base is junk and has to be replaced?

JS: My theory is that this happens because it's harder to read code than to write it. A programmer will whine about a function that he thinks is messy. It's supposed to be a simple function to display a window or something, but for some reason it takes up two pages and has all these ugly little hairs and stuff on it and nobody knows why. OK. I'll tell you why. Those are bug fixes. One of them fixes that bug that Jill had when she tried to install the thing on a computer that didn't have Internet Explorer. Another one fixes a bug that occurs in low-memory conditions. Another one fixes some bug that occurred when the file is on a floppy disk and the user yanks out the diskette in the middle. That LoadLibrary call is sure ugly but it makes the code work on old versions of Windows 95.

When you throw that function away and start from scratch, you are throwing away all that knowledge. All those collected bug fixes. Years of programming work.

SMS: Well, let's assume some of your top programmers walked in the door and said, "We absolutely have to rewrite this thing from scratch, top to bottom." What's the right response?

JS: What I learned from Charles Ferguson's great book (*High St@kes, No Prisoners*) is that you need to hire programmers who can understand the business goals. People who can answer questions like "What does it really cost the company if we rewrite?" "How many months will it delay shipping the product?" "Will we sell enough marginal copies to justify the lost time and market share?" If your programmers insist on a rewrite, they probably don't understand the financials of the company, or the competitive situation. Explain this to them. Then get an honest estimate for the rewrite effort and insist on a financial spreadsheet showing a detailed cost/benefit analysis for the rewrite.

SMS: Yeah, great, but, believe it or not, programmers have been known to, uh, "shave the truth" when it comes to such matters.

JS: What you're seeing is the famous programmer tactic: All features that I want take 1 hour, all features that I don't want take 99 years. If you suspect you are being lied to, just drill down. Get a schedule with granularity measured in hours, not months. Insist that each task have an estimate that is 2 days or less. If it's longer than that, you need to break it down into subtasks or the schedule can't be realistic.

SMS: Are there any circumstances where a complete code rewrite is justified?

JS: Probably not. The most extreme circumstance I can think of would be if you are simultaneously moving to a new platform and changing the architecture of the code dramatically. Even in this case you are probably better off looking at the old code as you develop the new code.

SMS: Hmm. Let's take a look at your theory and compare it to some real-world software meltdowns. For instance, what happened at Netscape?

JS: Way back in April 2000, I wrote on my Web site that Netscape made the single worst strategic mistake that any software company can make by deciding to rewrite their code from scratch. Lou Montulli, one of the five programming superstars who did the original version of Navigator, e-mailed me to say, "I agree completely, it's one of the major reasons I resigned from Netscape." This one decision cost Netscape 4 years. That's 3 years they spent with their prize aircraft carrier in 200,000 pieces in dry dock. They couldn't add new features, couldn't respond to the competitive threats from IE, and had to sit on their hands while Microsoft completely ate their lunch.

SMS: OK, how about Borland? Another famous meltdown. Any ideas?

JS: Borland also got into the habit of throwing away perfectly good code and starting from scratch. Even after the purchase of Ashton-Tate, Borland bought Arago and tried to make that into dBASE for Windows, a doomed project that took so long that Microsoft Access ate their lunch. With Paradox, they jumped into a huge rewrite effort with C++ and took forever to release the Windows version of the product. And it was buggy and slow where Paradox for DOS was solid and fast. Then they did it all over again with Quattro Pro, rewriting it from scratch and astonishing the world with how little new functionality it had.

SMS: Yeah, and their pricing strategy didn't help.

JS: While I was on the Excel team, Borland cut the MSRP on Quattro Pro from around $500.00 to around $100.00. Clueless newbie that I was, I thought this was the beginning of a bloody price war. Lewis Levin,[1] Excel BUM (business unit manager) was ecstatic. "Don't you see, Joel, once they have to cut prices, they've lost." He had no plan to respond to the lower price. And he didn't need to.

SMS: Having worked at Ashton-Tate, I have to tell you the dBASE IV code base was no thing of beauty. But, I take your point. Actually, I saw this syndrome at work in Ashton-Tate's word-processing division. After they bought MultiMate, they spent about 2 years planning a complete rewrite of the product and wasted months evaluating new "engines" for the next version. Nothing ever happened. When a

---

[1] Lewis Levin got his start in the industry as the product manager for MicroPro's PlanStar.

new version of the product **was** released, it was based on the same "clunky" engine everyone had been moaning about. Of course, in those 2 years WordPerfect and Microsoft ate Ashton-Tate's word-processing lunch.

JS: Ashton-Tate had a word processor?

SMS: Yes, but nothing as good as WordStar, mind you!

JS: Hmm. That reminds me that Microsoft learned the "no rewrite" lesson the hard way. They tried to rewrite Word for Windows from scratch in a doomed project called "Pyramid," which was shut down, thrown away, and swept under the rug. Fortunately for Microsoft, they did this with parallel teams and had never stopped working on the old code base, so they had something to ship, making it merely a financial disaster, not a strategic one.

SMS: OK, Lotus?

JS: Too many MBAs at all levels and not enough people with a technical understanding of what could and needed to be built.

SMS: And I suppose building a brand-new product called "Jazz"[2] instead of getting 1-2-3 over to the Mac as quickly as possible, thus staking Microsoft to a 2-year lead with Excel, is an example of the same thing?

JS: Actually, they made a worse mistake: They spent something like 18 months trying to squeeze 1-2-3/3.0 into 640KB. By the time the 18 months were up, they hadn't succeeded, and in the meantime, everybody bought 386s with 4 megs of ram. Microsoft always figured that it's better to let the hardware catch up with the software rather than spending time writing code for old computers owned by people who aren't buying much software any more.

SMS: WordPerfect?

JS: That's an interesting case and leads to another development sin software companies often make: using the wrong level tools for the job. At WordPerfect, everything, including everything, had to be written in assembler. Company policy. If a programmer needed a little one-off utility, it had to be hand-coded and hand-optimized in assembler. They were the only people on earth writing all-assembler

---

[2] Jazz was intended to be the Macintosh equivalent of Symphony for the PC. Like most of the integrated products, it managed to do too much while not doing anything particularly well.

apps for Windows. Insane. It's like making your ballerinas wear balls and chains and taping their arms to their sides.

SMS: What should they have been coding in?

JS: In those days? C. Or maybe Pascal. Programmers should only use lower level tools for those parts of the product where they are adding the most value. For example, if you're writing a game where the 3D effects are your major selling point, you can't use an off-the-shelf 3D engine; you have to roll your own. But if the major selling point of your game is the story, don't waste time getting great 3D graphics—just use a library. But WordPerfect was writing UI code that operates in "user time," and doesn't need to be particularly fast. Hand-coded assembler is insane and adds no value.

SMS: Yes, but isn't such code tight and small? Don't products built this way avoid the dreaded "bloatware" label?

JS: Don't get me started! If you're a software company, there are lots of great business reasons to love bloatware. For one, if programmers don't have to worry about how large their code is, they can ship it sooner. And that means you get more features, and features make users' lives better (if they use them) and don't usually hurt (if they don't). As a user, if your software vendor stops, before shipping, and spends 2 months squeezing the code down to make it 50 percent smaller, the net benefit to you is going to be imperceptible, but you went for 2 months without new features that you needed, and **that** hurt.

SMS: Could this possibly account for the fact that no one uses WordStar version 3.3 anymore despite the fact it can fit on one 1.4 meg floppy?

JS: That and Control-K. But seriously, Moore's Law makes much of the whining about bloatware ridiculous. In 1993, Microsoft Excel 5.0 took up about $36.00 worth of hard drive space. In 2000, Microsoft Excel 2000 takes up about $1.03 in hard drive space. All adjusted for inflation. So stop whining about how bloated it is.

SMS: Well, we've had much personal experience with the press slamming a product we were managing. For example, for years reviewers gave MicroPro hell over the fact it didn't support columns and tables. Somehow the fact that the product would fit on a 360KB floppy just didn't seem to mean as much as the idea that the reviewer couldn't use our product to write his or her resume.

JS: There's a famous fallacy that people learn in business school called the 80/20 rule. It's false, but it seduces a lot of dumb software start-ups. It seems to make sense. Eighty percent of the people use 20 percent of the features. So you convince yourself that you only need to implement 20 percent of the features, and you can still sell 80 percent as many copies. The trouble here, of course, is that it's never the same 20 percent. Everybody uses a different set of features. When you start marketing your "lite" product and you tell people, "Hey, it's lite, only 1MB," they tend to be very happy, then they ask you if it has word counts, or spell checking, or little rubber feet, or whatever obscure thing they can't live without, and it doesn't, so they don't buy your product.

SMS: Let's talk about product marketing and development at Microsoft. How did these two groups work together?

JS: Well, in theory, the marketing group (called "product management") was supposed to give the development team feedback on what customers wanted. Features requests from the field. That kind of stuff. In reality, they never did.

SMS: Really?

JS: Really. Yes, we listened to customers, but not through product management—they were never very good at channeling this information. So the program management (design) teams just went out and talked to customers ourselves. One thing I noticed pretty quickly is that you don't actually learn all that much from asking customers what features they want. Sure, they'll tell you, but it's all stuff you knew anyway.

SMS: You paint a picture of the programmer almost as a semideity. But in my experience, I've seen powerful technical personalities take down major companies. For instance, in *The Product Marketing Handbook for Software*, I describe how the MicroPro development staff's refusal to add the aforementioned columns and table features to WordStar badly hurt the product's sales.[3] How do you manage situations like these?

---

[3] Over time, the programming staff noted that requests for this feature from users were dropping. This was absolutely true, as people who wanted this capability in a word processor bought other products.

JS: This is a hard problem. I've seen plenty of companies with prima donna programmers who literally drive their companies into the ground. If the management of the company is technical (think Bill Gates), management isn't afraid to argue with them and win—or fire the programmer and get someone new in. If the management of the company is not technical enough (think John Sculley), they act like scared rabbits, strangely believing that this **one** person is the only person on the planet who can write code, and it's not a long way from there to the failure of the company.

If you're a nontechnical CEO with programmers who aren't getting with the program, you have to bite the bullet and fire them. This is your only hope. And it means you're going to have to find new technical talent, so your chances aren't great. That's why I don't think technology companies that don't have engineers at the very top have much of a chance.

SMS: Joel, thank you very much.

GLOSSARY OF TERMS

ARPANET

The immediate precursor to the Internet created by the Advanced Research Projects Agency (ARPA). No one lost any money on the ARPANET, a fact that leads many people to remember it fondly.

ASP

Acronym for *application service provider*. Software usage and distribution systems in which programs are hosted on servers, not installed on separate desktops. In the late 1990s, the perceived advantages of this approach included providing a steady revenue stream for software companies, less software piracy, and easier management of upgrades. The disadvantage to these systems was that nobody bought them.

banner ad

A type of Web-based advertisement. The standard banner size is 468×60 pixels (about 5 square inches). Nobody watches them.

beta

A prerelease software product sent to end users for testing and evaluation. Right.

branding

A marketing process that attempts to attach desirable intangible qualities to products and services. The process reached its apotheosis during the dot-com boom, a time when sock puppets and incredibly expensive Super Bowl ads featuring things like computer-generated herds of cats wasted amazing amounts of money with no discernible ROI.

channel

An industry term for the high-tech distribution system. The term is used somewhat loosely and often refers to a channel segment, as in "the reseller channel." The channel is sometimes also referred to by hardware and software vendors as "bloodsuckers," "vampires," "weasels," and "those thieves." The channel has its own special vocabulary for the vendors.

channel stuffing

A sales tactic where product is sold into a distributor's or reseller's inventory despite a lack of end-user demand for the product. Channel stuffing can take many inventive forms, such as selling product to a distributor just before the end of a fiscal quarter and then taking the product back immediately after the quarter ends, shipping bricks to a distributor instead of actual products (a hard drive manufacturer once pulled this stunt), etc.

chiclet keyboard

Used on the PC Junior. A membrane-based keyboard technology that companies insist on periodically trying to sell to people even though past experience has taught them no one wants it.

click-through

An Internet ad model that measures response by the number of users who click an ad that links to the advertiser's site. Most response figures use numbers that hover close to the value "zero."

collateral

All material created to support a product, including brochures, posters, sample product, demonstration disks, mobiles, and T-shirts. Frequently referred to as "junk" by members of the press, who often seem to prize obtaining the stuff nonetheless.

competitive upgrade

A software promotion designed to drain sales away from a competitor's installed base. Usually the product is sold at a price close to or below the upgrade price of a competing product. At Borland, these programs are sometimes referred to as "hoist by your own petard."

CRM

Acronym for *customer relationship management*. This category of software is descended from the various sales contact management software packages that became popular with businesses beginning in the late 1980s through the early 1990s. Many of the CRM systems installed in the late 1990s and early 2000s were derisively referred to as "shelfware" because many of the packages didn't work, hurt relations with customers, and were eventually "installed" on shelves across corporate America.

demo dolly

An individual assigned to demonstrate a product, often to a member of the press or an industry analyst. Demo dollies can be of either sex. The most important personal characteristic of a successful demo dolly is the ability to nod wisely even when a member of senior management says something inane.

DOJ

Acronym for *Department of Justice*. This part of the U.S. government occasionally sues large companies who violate U.S. antitrust laws. It's believed by some in the high-tech industry that the DOJ only does this after inspecting the entrails of a chicken and deciding that the omens are right.

ERP

Acronym for *enterprise resource planning*. A class of software designed to integrate every aspect of a company's operations, from customer service to warehouse management. Frequently, use of these products requires a business to "reengineer" its business processes, which in turn often leads to the need to placate angry customers who are receiving multiple bills for items they didn't order. This helps drive purchases of CRM software.

gray market

A system designed to sell products outside of normal "authorized" reseller channels. Gray markets usually spring up when large companies buy more products than they can sell in order to achieve bigger discounts, and then turn around and sell their excess inventory "out the back door" to smaller resellers. These resellers in turn sell the product to customers (sometimes without warranties or service agreements). Everyone in high tech is constantly bemoaning the existence of gray markets, but they never seem to go away. Participants in these markets can be distinguished by their nervous tics, an unfortunate byproduct of their constant winking.

GUI

Acronym for *graphical user interface*. A software operating environment that provides users with a visual desktop metaphor. The modern GUI avoids the trash-can icon because its use usually leads to a lawsuit by Apple.

HTML

Acronym for *Hypertext Markup Language*. A formatting language designed for viewing documents posted on the World Wide Web. Also known as "Greek" to people not familiar with the 1970s concept of editor/formatter text processing.

IDE

Acronym for *integrated development environment*. A software development tool used by programmers to write programs. A good-quality IDE is often named as a respondent in the divorce proceedings between a programmer and his or her spouse.

infomercial

A form of television advertising designed to elicit a direct response to an offer via a phone call or visit to a Web site. Cher can often be seen on these programs, if you're a fan.

Internet

A worldwide system of interconnected computer networks. Because it's supposed to make information free, everyone wants to control it.

IPO

Initial public offering (of stock). During the dot-com boom, IPOs were often used to legally defraud millions of people who should have known better.

ISP

Acronym for *Internet service provider*. A company that provides access to the Internet.

ISV

Acronym for *independent software vendor*. A developer or publisher of software products.

Java

A programming language designed to compile and run under a virtual microprocessor or "machine."

LAN

Acronym for *local area network*. A group of PCs linked to run in a cooperative fashion.

marcom

Short for *marketing communications*. The department in a business responsible for creating and administering collateral development, PR, and advertising, along with the scheduling of trade show participation.

MDF

Acronym for *marketing development funds*. Refers to a type of promotional program widely used in high-tech marketing. MDF programs usually involve a vendor paying funds to a distribution partner in return for access to a sales channel or to a manufacturer to obtain discounts on purchases. In some industries this process is called "bribery," "extortion," or "payola."

Moore's Law

Not actually a law, but an observation. Moore's "law" states that the number of transistors contained in a microdevice doubles every 18 months. Moore's Law accounts for the fact that the new computer you just bought will be worth the price of a boat anchor 6 months after purchase. Actually, the boat anchor will be worth more.

NIC

Acronym for *network interface computer*. A PC without a disk drive designed by Larry Ellison that no one buys.

NOS

Acronym for *network operating system*. An operating system designed to run a network of desktop computers.

OOP

Acronym for *object-oriented programming*. A programming methodology that combines code and data in "packages." The technology is incomprehensible to most users of software.

open source

Both a movement and a process of creating software that believes that the underlying source code of products should be freely accessible to users. Many open source programmers believe Bill Gates is Satan. Bill Gates believes many open source programmers are communists.

OS

Acronym for *operating system*. A program that allows a computer system to operate its internal hardware, manage its memory, communicate with application programs, and make Bill Gates richer than God.

peer-to-peer

A networking technology that allows computers to communicate and exchange information directly instead of through a server. Peer-to-peer networks are most frequently used to defraud record companies, whom no one likes anyway.

positioning

A marketing process that attempts to "place" a product in a desirable "location" in a prospective buyer's mind. The most successful positioning strategies in high-tech consist of first telling people what the heck it is you want them to buy.

p-System

A 1980s "Write Once, Run Anywhere" precursor to Java. The performance of p-System programs tended to be poor, and figuring out how to properly capitalize the name of the OS drove everyone crazy.

RDBMS

Acronym for *relational database management system*. A methodology for storing and retrieving data from computer systems that relies heavily on tables. Periodically, database programming specialists engage in abstruse arguments about which database system is more or less relational than another. These arguments can sometimes reach levels of ferocity equivalent to those seen during the Thirty Years War, but because programmers are poor fighters, no one is usually hurt.

ROI

Acronym for *return on investment*. The amount of money earned on investing in a particular program or business. The concept wasn't in use during the dot-com boom.

search engine

A program designed to search and index information on the Internet.

server

A computer running a NOS or a Web-based application such as e-mail.

shelfware

Unused software. *See also* CRM.

SIG

Acronym for *special interest group*. A subdivision of a user group, dedicated to examining one particular application category or product. For example, a user group may have a word-processing SIG, which might, in turn, be divided into smaller SIGs dedicated to specific word-processing products.

SOHO

Acronym for *small office/home office*. A class of products aimed at small, independent businesses and entrepreneurs.

SRP

Acronym for *suggested retail price*. The price no one actually pays for a product, except in the case of Microsoft Windows.

subtractive marketing

A marketing process that strips desirable features out of a successful product and then attempts to position the pathetic, leftover hulk as a good "value." Marketers who rely on subtractive marketing must hope that their customers are idiots. Usually, this hope is disappointed.

URL

Acronym for *uniform resource locator*. A "virtual" address for a Web site. Used by Web browsers to locate things to buy, communities to argue in, and pornography to view. Fortunately, no one ever goes to the porn sites.

SELECTED BIBLIOGRAPHY

Auletta, Ken. *World War 3.0: Microsoft and Its Enemies*. New York, NY: Random House, 2001.

Bank, David. *Breaking Windows: How Bill Gates Fumbled the Future of Microsoft*. New York, NY: The Free Press, 2001.

Carlton, Jim. *Apple: The Inside Story of Intrigue, Egomania, and Business Blunders*. New York, NY: HarperBusiness, 1998.

Cassidy, John. *Dot.Con: The Greatest Story Ever Sold*. New York, NY: HarperCollins Publishers, 2002.

Chapman, Merrill R. *The Product Marketing Handbook for Software, Third Edition*. Killingworth, CT: Aegis Resources, 2000.

Cringely, Robert X. *Accidental Empires: How the Boys of Silicon Valley Make Their Millions, Battle Foreign Competition, and Still Can't Get a Date*. Reading, MA: Addison-Wesley, 1992.

Kindleberger, Charles P. *Manias, Panics, and Crashes: A History of Financial Crises, Fourth Edition*. New York, NY: John Wiley & Sons, 2000.

Davidow, William H. *Marketing High Technology: An Insider's View*. New York, NY: The Free Press, 1986.

Dvorak, John and Adam Osborne. *Hypergrowth: The Rise and Fall of Osborne Computer Corporation*. New York, NY: Avon, 1984.

Ferguson, Charles. *High Stakes, No Prisoners: A Winners Tale of Greed and Glory in the Internet Wars*. New York, NY: Times Books/Random House, 1999.

Kaplan, Philip J. *F'd Companies: Spectacular Dot-Com Flameouts*. New York, NY: Simon & Schuster, 2002.

Kuo, J. David. *dot.bomb: My Days and Nights at an Internet Goliath*. New York, NY: Little, Brown and Company, 2001.

MacKay, Charles. *Memoirs of Extraordinary Popular Delusions and the Madness of Crowds*. New York, NY: Farrar, Strauss and Giroux, originally published in 1841 with some additions in 1852.

Manes, Stephen and Paul Andrews. *Gates: How Microsoft's Mogul Reinvented an Industry—and Made Himself the Richest Man in America*. New York, NY: Simon & Schuster, 1994.

Peters, Thomas J. and Robert H. Waterman, Jr. *In Search of Excellence: Lessons from America's Best-Run Companies*. New York, NY: Harper & Row, 1982.

Peterson, W. E. Pete. *Almost Perfect*. Roseville, CA: Prima Publishing, 1994.

Rivlin, Gary. *The Plot to Get Bill Gates: An Irreverent Investigation of the World's Richest Man . . . and the People Who Hate Him*. New York, NY: Times Books/Random House, 1999.

Rosenberg, Donald. *Open Source: The Unauthorized White Papers*. Foster City, CA: IDG Books Worldwide, 2000.

Segaller, Stephen. *Nerds 2.0.1: A Brief History of the Internet*. New York, NY: TV Books, 1998.

INDEX